TIME PASSAGES

Determined To Escape Poverty, A Former Small-Town Orphan Sets Out on A Journey of Self-Discovery and Growth

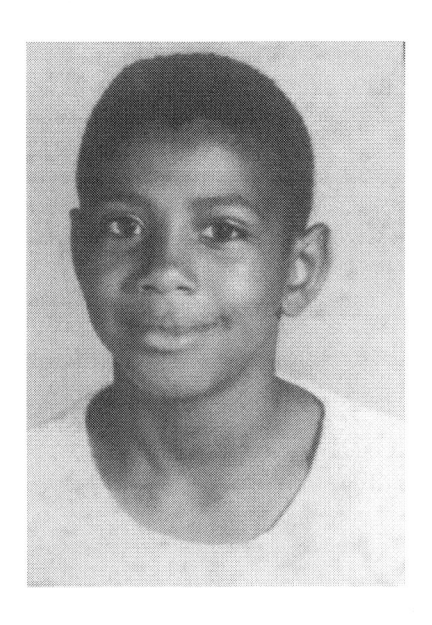

The Life and Adventures of Percy L. Freeman

AUTHOR'S NOTE

This book is a nonfiction account of my life, offering a unique perspective on each person and event that has shaped me. These experiences unfolded at the specific locations and times listed. In a few instances, I've altered names to safeguard the privacy of individuals and sources. Some events are recounted based on information gleaned from interviews, military, police, and court records. Most of the information is a recollection of my life's journey, acknowledging the inherent imperfections of human memory and official documents.

When I set out to author this book, my primary goal was to share the story of my life experiences with my family. I wanted to convey how these experiences have shaped me and how I've used the lessons learned to make decisions and influence others, particularly during my time in leadership roles.

During my extensive research into family history, I was struck by the scarcity of information about how my ancestors lived and survived during challenging times in America. The few obituaries I found often revealed only a brief life history. This book, in part, is a history of my life, intricately intertwined with our family's past. We owe future generations a duty to ensure our history is preserved and passed down, available in archives and libraries for all to learn from.

Today, there are forces at work that seek to erase African American History by banning books, closing libraries, and replacing historical truths with 'alternative facts.' We must stand up and fight to preserve our history, ensuring that the rich tapestry of our past is not lost.

"Do not get lost in a sea of despair. Be hopeful, be optimistic. Our struggle is not the struggle of the day, a week, a month, or a year, it is the struggle of a lifetime. Never, ever be afraid to make some noise and get in good trouble, necessary trouble."

John Robert Lewis, Civil Rights Leader, Congressman

FOREWORD BY PETER WHITE

International prolific acoustic guitarist, songwriter, and producer

I had the pleasure of meeting Percy on the Smooth Jazz Cruise in early 2024, and he told me about the book he was writing. It was to be named after a song I wrote with singer Al Stewart in 1978: *Time Passages*. This naturally piqued my interest.

Like Percy, I was born in the 1950s but our lives could not have been more different. Growing up in the small town of Letchworth Garden City in England, I had quite an uneventful childhood. Everyone in the town looked like me. I didn't even meet a Black person until I was sixteen. Strangely, in high school, my class received an assignment to author an essay about growing up as a poor Black child in the American South. Living in that small town in England, I had no idea how to complete this assignment. I'm sure that the point was for us to use our imagination, but we had no starting point, no idea what life was like in, say, Juliette, Georgia in the 1960s. Thanks to Percy Freeman's wonderfully engaging book - now I do!

Reading Percy's first-hand account of growing up in the South during the Civil Rights era makes me realize how different his life was from my own - and we are the same age. Living in rural England, I was interested in the music coming from my radio, not world news - I was barely aware that there was a war in Vietnam for instance. What Percy has written has filled in a lot of space for me, and it perfectly encapsulates life in an era of great change, a fascinating read for someone who grew up on another continent entirely. Following him as he traces his roots back to Africa is gripping and his account of reconnecting with Joan, his childhood sweetheart after almost 50 years apart is very endearing.

This book will absorb you as you follow Percy's journey through his various life adventures - serving in the US Air Force, playing football in Italy, private investigator back home in Georgia, working for the Fulton County District Attorney's office, and many more. Bravo Percy - you did it. I'm proud to count you as a friend!

ABOUT THE AUTHOR

Percy Freeman was born in a house on a dirt road in Juliette, Georgia. His mother was sixteen at his birth. Three years and ten months later, she would depart from this earth due to burns from a house fire. Percy did not identify his father until October 2022 and learned his father died eighteen days before his mother. His father, Percy Heulett, was murdered in Chattanooga, TN in 1960.

His grandmother and step-grandfather raised Percy until he ran away from home at age sixteen. He succeeded despite living in poverty and not having educated grandparents or anyone to assist or support him with schoolwork at home. After leaving his grandparents' house, he lived with friends and relatives until he graduated from high school in 1974. During his first sixteen years, he lived in homes without indoor plumbing. Fireplaces, and wood-burning stoves heated the rented family home up to age 16. After high school graduation, he joined the United States Air Force and served as a Missile Systems Specialist and Technician for five years. He played semi-professional football for two years in the Northern Italian Football League (NIFL). After leaving active duty, Percy joined the Georgia Air National Guard (GA ANG) and served for another 27 years. During his journey, he earned a bachelor's and two associate degrees. He was self-employed as a Private Investigator, and served at local, county and federal agencies as a Police Officer/Investigator, District Attorney Investigator, and Special Agent/Federal Aviation Administration (FAA). He retired from the GA ANG as a Chief Master Sergeant, previously serving as First Sergeant, Munitions Inspector, Human Resources Advisor, and Mentor. He received numerous awards from the FAA, Air Force (Air Guard), Dekalb County Police as a Neighborhood Watch Coordinator, and Letters of Appreciation from Judges and Police Administrators. He was nationally recognized by the National Guard Bureau and the State of Georgia for his contributions in Diversity Education, Recruiting, Retention, and Mentoring military personnel.

He is and has been a caretaker for a relative with health challenges for over twenty-eight years while at the same time raising his own family and assisting other relatives and friends.

Percy has researched family history for over thirty years and has connected families, specifically DNA-connected families seeking to find their father. In 2003, he created a PowerPoint presentation named *Finding Your Roots* to teach others how to find their roots. Since then, he has completed three extensive family history books.

Despite his numerous challenges, barriers, and discrimination, Percy always maintained a cheerful outlook on life. His resilience and determination to continuously improve his life are truly inspiring. His bright outlook is evident in his love for travel, having visited all 50 states and 45 countries. His story is a reminder that a positive outlook can help overcome even the most daunting obstacles.

TABLE OF CONTENTS

Title Page — I

Author's Notes — II

Foreword by Peter White — III

About the Author — IV

PART ONE: Growing Up in A Small Southern Community During the Civil Rights Movement

CHAPTER 1 CHILDHOOD MEMORIES — 11

CHAPTER 2 MOVE TO BOWDOIN ROAD — 47

PART TWO: Adventures During My Professional Assignments

CHAPTER 3 ACTIVE-DUTY MILITARY ADVENTURES — 71

CHAPTER 4 AIR FORCE DISCHARGE AND RETURN TO ATLANTA — 95

CHAPTER 5 LAW AND ORDER, TO PROTECT AND SERVE — 121

CHAPTER 6 DISTRICT ATTORNEY, 1987-1996 — 143

CHAPTER 7 DISTRICT ATTORNEY, 1996-1998 — 169

CHAPTER 8 FAA INTERNAL AFFAIRS INVESTIGATIONS — 175

PART THREE: Finding My Roots, Community Service & Helping Family

CHAPTER 9 VOICES OF MY ANCESTORS — 197

CHAPTER 10 THE VIRGIN ISLANDS AND METRO ATLANTA — 229

CHAPTER 11 TAKING CARE OF FAMILY — 261

CHAPTER 12 RETIREMENT AND RETURN TO JULIETTE   *269*

PART FOUR: Meeting People, Loving Smooth Jazz, And A New Beginning

CHAPTER 13 UNEXPECTED ENCOUNTERS   *287*

CHAPTER 14 INTRODUCTION TO SMOOTH JAZZ   *301*

CHAPTER 15 FIFTY YEARS LATER   *311*

PART ONE PHOTOs   *351*

PART TWO PHOTOs   *357*

PART THREE PHOTOs   *363*

PART FOUR PHOTOs   *371*

ACKNOWLEDGEMENTS   *379*

PART ONE

Juliette River Rats Baseball Team
"Popcorn Speir and Marvin Bowdoin, Coaches

Marvin Bowdoin, Sr and Tony
Photo courtesy of Monroe County Reporter

CHAPTER 1

CHILDHOOD MEMORIES

I was born in a small-town community called Juliette, Georgia, and am a member of the Baby Boomers generation. During my early years, I experienced Jim Crow laws and segregation. I witnessed protests and demonstrations for equal justice and equality for all Americans. I soon realized that America did not adhere to the beloved Constitution, for which it waved the flag and sang the Star-Spangled Banner. Sometimes, cultural changes are needed in America from its archaic ways of thinking. The importance of equality should be our guiding principle, driving us to envision changing our culture, moving away from old business practices, and taking urgent action to effect the changes. I lived in poverty as an orphan but took advantage of the opportunities presented to succeed in life. Finding my roots became a passion as I researched for myself and others to learn about their unknown family trees. I have encountered barriers, and challenges, and learned lessons throughout life. I discovered love through family, relationships, friends, and, most recently, a wife of less than two years, my former high school sweetheart.

My life began in April 1956 in a house on a dirt road. According to several family members, I was born in a three-room house on what is now Bowdoin Road. I entered this world with the assistance of a midwife, Mrs. Georgia Redding. My earliest memory is from around age three when the flames burned my mother in a house fire. The house burned on Groundhog Day, February 2, 1960. I was three years and nine months old when I walked with my older half-uncle, Johnny Boozer Jr., to my 2nd great-grandmother's house on McCrackin Street. We affectionately called her Grandma Hop. Her name was Carrie (Swan) Dillard. She married Dan Dillard, and after his death, she lived in a three-room house across from Juliette

United Methodist Church, a scene in the movie Fried Green Tomatoes. Little did I know, my life would forever change after that short walk, approximately 350 yards from our house on Old Juliette Road near Georgia Highway 87, United States (U.S.) Highway 23 to Grandma Hop's house.

My mother returned home after visiting her Grand Aunt Laura (Dillard) Jackson's house on McCrackin Street. According to my Aunt Johnnie Mae Boozer, she went there to write a letter on behalf of Aunt Laura, her mother's aunt. When my mother arrived at our uninsulated wooden home, Aunt Johnnie Mae and her younger brother, Kenny, were there. Aunt Johnnie Mae was about 13 years old, and Kenny was less than a year old. Johnnie Mae remembers my mother asking why the house was so cold. It was a cold place to live during that Middle Georgia winter in February 1960. Typical temperatures were in the 40s daily.

To warm up the house, my mother poured kerosene to light a fire in the wood-burning fireplace, which accidentally ignited her clothing. Immediately, everyone ran outside. My mother saw a puddle of water and immersed herself in it to extinguish her burning clothing. What she did not know was that the water would cause more harm to her burns. In the meantime, a truck driver, who was quite fond of my mother, according to Aunt Johnnie Mae, drove by and saw the house was on fire. He parked his truck along Georgia Highway 87 and ran to the scene. He saw my mother injured and retrieved a blue quilt, which he had used to protect furniture while moving it in the truck. He wrapped her in the quilt and stayed with her until help arrived. An ambulance transported my mother to Atlanta, where she died of third-degree burns and pneumonia at the early age of nineteen on March 3, 1960.

My uncle and I rushed back to our house from Grandma Hop's house when we saw the smoke in the distance, but the memories of that day have faded into the past. I can only recall seeing a tractor-trailer parked on the side of the highway. The fire and smoke were visible as we approached the scene.

On the day my mother was burned, I did not know or remember that I had a sister because she was not living with us at the time. Later, I learned about my half-sister, Carolyn, who was about twenty-two months old, living with relatives in Gladesville, a community southwest of Monticello in Jasper County, Georgia, about 13 miles from Juliette.

This tragic event not only took my mother's life but also separated our family. My grandfather's sister, Hattie Sands Gordon, and her husband, Willie Gordon, owned a 150-acre farm that included several cows, goats, chickens, mules, and other farm animals. My grandmother shared that because Carolyn was lactose intolerant and could only drink goat's milk, they had goats, so she lived with them. Years later, however, I learned we are not blood-related to Jessie and Hattie Sands.

After my mother passed away at age 19, my grandparents, Mary (Freeman) Boozer and Johnny Boozer (step-grandfather), along with their children, my aunts and uncles, and I moved to downtown Juliette on McCrackin Street. Three-row houses existed next to the Homer Chambliss Community Store. Juliette Road still needed to be constructed from Highway 87 to Jones County. McCrackin Street was the only way to drive to that location. We lived in a middle three-room house until the early 1960's. John and Laura (Dillard) Jackson lived in a home on the right-hand side, and Ms. Elmira Myrick lived in the house on the left. The Monroe County Volunteer Firehouse and Middlebrooks District voting precinct sits on that site today. I don't recall many events while living there, except we did not have indoor plumbing or electric lights. We used kerosene lamps. The only heat source was a fireplace and a wood-burning stove for preparing meals. We owned an icebox to store blocks of ice to keep food from spoiling. Yes, we were poor, but we were content with the situation we could not change, finding peace in our circumstances. My grandparents cared for our basic needs, and we always had the essentials, such as food on the table and clean clothes. I remember Grandma Sue would boil water in a large black cast iron pot to wash our clothes, then hang them out to dry on a clothesline. The clothes would dry from the natural sun and wind.

I recall another incident when my Uncle Johnny and I were walking the 'shortcut' through the woods across a creek to visit Aunt Laura after she moved to the "line" now called Bowdoin Road. After we left our house and crossed the creek, we encountered two young white boys who asked, "What are y'all Niggers doing walking in our woods?" My uncle replied, "You better get your Cracker ass out of our way." They complied, and we never had a problem with them again.

We would pass a former sawmill while walking our regular path through the woods in Juliette. The sawdust was piled high in mounds, and the covered roof was approximately twenty feet high. It often became our natural playground. Sometimes, we would walk down the street to the EL Williams General Merchandise store. Going there was always a treat because Mr. Ed, the store's owner, sometimes gave us "RC" (Royal Crown) Cola and peanuts. Aunt Laura's brother, Robert "Wig" Dillard, worked at the store when we were kids and continued working there until his death. Ed Williams III, grandson of the owner and my high school classmate, mentioned Wig in one of his books about Juliette.

According to the Monroe County Historical Society, Robert M. Williams operated the first Juliette Post Office and was the first Postmaster. When the town was established, the first Juliette public school for white students was built. It burned down and was rebuilt near Bowdoin and East Redding Road. The Blount family—Frank and Ethel—rented the old school from the Williams family and used it as their residence for many years until they died in the mid-1970s.

During the mid-to late-1990s, Charles Card purchased the old school property from Robert Williams. The building is still standing today but is deteriorating quickly. Before significant wood rot and deterioration happened, I walked inside to check it out. No "no trespassing" signs were visible, so I took my time to mentally document my observations. Paper, trash, and assorted debris were in and around the interior. Surprisingly, I spotted a 1918 World War I, U.S. Army, M1910 mess kit in perfect condition. Now, it is part of my collection. It is the same type of kit my great-grandfather, Willis Freeman, Jr., used during his Army service in 1918.

According to my Grandaunt Carrie, before 1915, African Americans or Blacks in Juliette attended school in a building on the grounds of the Saint Paul African Methodist Episcopal Church (A.M.E.). After the completion of Spring Hill Baptist Church, the year unknown, it was used as a school on weekdays until Monroe County funded and built a school around 1937 on Old Juliette Road. Juliette's first publicly funded school for Black people was a two-room structure. The people in the community pooled their money together to purchase the land for $50.00.

Carrie Freeman Gilmore reported that Monroe County supplied the materials for construction. The educational structure was for grades 1-7. Teachers who taught in Juliette were Mrs. Josephine Clements, Mrs. Mattie Jacobs, Mrs. Virginia Tomlinson, Mrs. Lillie Mae Redding, Mrs. Helen Ponder, Mrs. Eva Ponder, and Mrs. Annie Count.

The Historical Society also reported that during Juliette's early days, several general stores were operated by Robert Williams & Son; E.M. Williams; Dan Driskell; J.M. Byars & Son; Bert Bowdoin, father of Marvin O. Bowdoin, Sr., and E.L. Williams operated a general merchandise store, which was transformed into the Fried Green Tomatoes restaurant in preparation for a movie set during the early 1990s. After the movie, it remains open for service today—Thursday through Saturday. The original depot, once the location to catch the Number five train to Atlanta, was relocated to the north side of the restaurant for tourists to view, preserving the ongoing relevance of Juliette's history. Near the train depot was a road across the tracks that led to the wooden one-way traffic bridge across the Ocmulgee River to Jones County.

Juliette is an unincorporated community in Monroe County, Georgia, formerly known as Brownsville and Iceberg.

For mail delivery and zip code 31046, a small portion of Juliette is considered in Jones County, Georgia. According to the Monroe County Historical Society, Juliette existed around 1882 when the railroad began to run from Atlanta to Macon. Records indicated the town of Juliette received its name from Juliette McCrackin, who was either the wife or daughter of the engineer who supervised the grading and construction of the railroad there. Early census records list the area as the Middlebrooks District, a testament to the significant role of the Middlebrooks family, large landowners during that time, in shaping the community. Today, the voting precinct at the volunteer fire department is named Middlebrooks.

The Juliette community is located approximately 23 miles north of Macon, Georgia. In downtown Juliette, McCrackin Street is where the former train depot is now located on the north side of the Whistle Stop Café. The building for the original post office remains but is now open as a retail shop. Less than 200 yards away is the dam that stretches across the Ocmulgee River from Monroe to Jones County. Juliette has become a recreational area for fishing, swimming, canoeing, boating, jet skiing, and kayaking tours on the Ocmulgee River and Lake Juliette. There is also a campground, operated by High Falls State Park, with approximately 20 sites near the banks of Lake Juliette.

The 1994 flood, caused by Tropical Storm Alberto, created havoc in Juliette and other locations in Georgia, significantly impacting life in middle Georgia. Debris and even a home floated down the Ocmulgee River. The flood, which destroyed bridges and roads throughout Monroe County, was a remarkable sight. The river reached around thirty-five feet, twice the seventeen-foot flood level. Juliette has experienced less severe floods, but in 1994 and 2009, it was different.

After the filming of *Fried Green Tomatoes* in Juliette, the town has been the focal point of three popular southern, humorous books by Juliette native, Ed Williams III. Following the "Fried Green Tomatoes" fame, the scenes used for the town's main street were renovated and have become a tourist district, complete with a fully operational Whistle Stop Café. Other movie productions filmed in Juliette include *Cockfighter* starring Warren Oates; "A Killing Affair" starring Peter Weller; and the documentary, *Fried Green Tomatoes: Juliette, Georgia Lives* starring Danny Vinson. The Juliette Volunteer Fire Department displays a small cafe scene, from the movie, *The War* starring Kevin Costner. The most recent movie scene filmed on the bridge crossing the Ocmulgee River from Juliette to Jones County in 2016 was a movie named *Baby Driver*.

NORTH MCCRACKIN STREET

During the Middle to late 1960s, we moved about two and a half miles north on McCrackin Street and rented a house on land once owned by a Black family, the Waltons. A well-known descendant of the Walton family is Ester James Junior, Jr. (E.J.), a former linebacker for the University of Alabama and former National Football League (NFL). He played with the Saint Louis/Arizona Cardinals and Miami Dolphins. This land is where most of my childhood adventures happened, which I will gladly share.

It was an old house built many moons ago, with no insulation or indoor plumbing—no indoor shower or toilet. Two fireplaces produced heat during cold winters. At some point, we obtained electric lights to illuminate the home. The house was L-shaped and had four rooms, including the kitchen.

Except for the grownups, our family slept in one room with three full-sized beds, three chests of drawers, and our limited wardrobe, including clothes for church, school, work, and play. Walking up the wooden steps, you step onto a board wood floor. There were two doors. The one to the right led to the "guest room" that doubled as the family room. To the left was my Grandparents' bedroom. It was simple: they kept the television in their room once we received electric power service. Walking from their room through a doorway, you entered the kids' room with the three full-sized beds. There was a window centered on both outside walls. Continue through the next doorway straight ahead; you enter the kitchen. To the immediate right was the exit doorway at about the center of the wall facing south. A window was on the left side of the center wall facing north. The exterior of the home, built using wooden planks or siding, appeared grayish weathered. I do not recall seeing anyone paint the house while we lived there. The tin roof showed years of rust in the form of a reddish-brown color. Eventually, we obtained propane gas for the stove and oven.

Our rented home was on fertile land next to a dirt road about eighty yards from McCrackin Street that continued in two directions and intersected at two points with Georgia Highway 87. The road in front of our house turned downhill towards the family of Mr. Lucious "L.W." McDowell and Louise (Walton); they parented four daughters, Mary Alice, Shirley, Katherine Bernice, and Carolyn, and three sons, Marvin, Melvin, and Donald. Louis is also a descendant of the Walton family sometime during the mid-1960s, Mr. L.W. died. A car accident caused his death as he attempted to leave American Legion Post 569. He entered Georgia Highway 83, and a vehicle traveling without lights struck his car. His family moved to Chattanooga, Tennessee, not long after his death. Several McDowell kids later moved to Detroit, Michigan, where they reside today.

After the McDowell family moved away, another family—Mrs. Willie Ann Myrick and her family—moved into the house. They had previously lived in Jones County. We shared water from a well that required a bucket tied to a rope to raise the water from 40 to 50 feet below. The healthy water was about one hundred yards from our house and 50 yards from the McDowell home. The other road continued along the left side of our house into the woods towards the Ocmulgee River. The woods were our playground. There was always natural food available for us to eat as snacks. In our front yard was a pecan tree to the right and a pomegranate tree to the left. On the right side, center, about 35 feet from the house, was a red apple tree and a walnut tree. Near the hog pen, a yellow apple tree was in the rear of the house. Raising hogs was widespread for most

Black families in Juliette during the 1960s. Usually, hog-killing time is late fall when the weather becomes cooler. The temperature worked in favor of preserving meat. On the left side of the house were fig and peach trees. Across the dirt road and in a southwestern direction was a pear tree, mostly hidden from view by brush and pine trees. We found plum trees, strawberry patches, blackberries, blueberries, muscadines, scuppernongs, and persimmons around the property. We were happy kids in our environment and took advantage of the treats our creator provided naturally.

Our vegetable garden was about 75 to 100 yards from the house's northwest corner. We grew cabbage, collard greens, peas, beans, sweet potatoes, white potatoes, peppers, peanuts, watermelons, cantaloupes, corn, and more. Another customary practice during this period was "canning" food in mason jars to preserve it for future use. Today, we buy the same type of canned products in grocery stores.

I will never forget placing a chicken's neck on the wood chopping block to chop its head off and then watching the headless chicken dance around until the motion stopped. Next, after removing the internal organs, my grandmother would place the chicken in hot water to make it easier to remove the feathers or to "pluck the chicken." That freshly killed chicken was some of the best-fried chicken I have ever eaten. We raised our chickens in a chicken coop, which was also the source of fresh eggs each day.

While growing up in rural Middle Georgia, we learned to survive off the land. My step-grandfather hunted squirrels, rabbits, and deer, which often became a part of our meals. I recall eating a hot, freshly made biscuit with squirrel and gravy. We ground deer meat to make burgers and spaghetti, which is how people use ground beef today. It was a great substitute. We became proficient hunters, especially rabbits and squirrels. When we saw a squirrel's nest in a tree, we would shake the tree or vine attached and shoot the squirrel as it exited the nest. For rabbits, we would watch for rabbit poop on the ground and follow it to areas on the ground near covered brush or fallen trees.

The 410-shotgun helped to secure the meal quickly! Every year on New Year's Eve, my step-grandfather would shoot his 3030 Winchester rifle into the woods behind the house, our celebration to bring in the new year. Since there were no streetlights, the moon and stars served as a tremendous personal planetarium.

Grandma treated us with special attention when she could afford it. But she was not employed anywhere where she could make good money. Her sole source of income was cleaning the homes of white families in Juliette. The pay was minimal, but she used it wisely. I recall her working for the Cochran Family on McCrackin Street. One member of the Cochran family, Denise, was my age, and we eventually graduated the same year from Mary Persons HS. This family was not considered middle class by "white" or any standards.

Every Saturday, the "Vegetable Man "would visit, and during the summer, the "Ice Cream" truck arrived in front of the house. It was a joyous time; we would save money for our special treats, such as candy and cookies. I recall hearing someone yell several times, "The Ice cream man is here," or I would listen to the music announcing the truck's arrival. Ice cream introduced more sugar to our systems, more than we were accustomed to eating, except for cane syrup over pancakes! The other truck that visited brought a different treat and no music. However, I cannot forget the cakes and sweet potato pies Grandma made regularly, but especially for church meals.

No one in our house ever owned a car, so we depended on others for transportation. We would get dressed in our suits and walk almost two miles to Saint Paul A.M.E. Church twice monthly on the first and third Sundays. Attending church was not a choice for us. My grandmother required it, except on rainy days. Sometimes, someone would give us a ride. Saint Paul was also the location of the annual Camp Meeting or Homecoming. The road to the church, now East Redding Road, was lined with vendors and booths selling food, nonalcoholic beverages, candy apples, cakes, pastries, fish sandwiches, and Bar-B-Q. Behind the scenes, vendors sold alcoholic drinks including moonshine. Since the church could only hold a few people, most of the kids stayed outside and considered the event a neighborhood reunion. People who had moved away to states in the north and other locations would often return for this annual event. Like everything else, when people move away, their kids do not experience the community's accepted culture, so the customs and norms often change over time. While the Camp Meetings continued, unfortunately, the vendors on the street and the reunion of former residents of Juliette stopped. The membership at Saint Paul Church, formerly Ishee Chapel, included less than 20 regularly tithing members when it closed in 2024, primarily due to a lack of membership. Surviving Finney, Freeman, Gilmore, and Boozer family members supported Saint Paul. The church reopened in August 2024 as Saint Paul Christian Community Church and Joseph A Finney, Sr. Community Center.

The other two churches in Juliette are Spring Hill Baptist, primarily supported by the Brown family, and Saint Peter Rock Missionary Baptist, which receives significant support from the Johnson and Slaughter families.

African American families living within a four-mile radius of Juliette and East Juliette today include Appling, Benjamin, Blalock, Brown, Finney, Goolsby, Jackson, Jarrell, Johnson, Lowe, Middlebrooks, Moore, Myrick, Ponder, Toles, Redding, Ridley, Sands, Slaughter, Ussery, Watkins, Willis and the newly arrived McDew family.

Life in rural Juliette in the 1960s was different, but fun. I recall each Christmas when my grandmother prepared for us a substitute for the "stockings that hung by the chimney with care." She used brown paper bags filled with candy, nuts (almonds, Brazil nuts, pecans, walnuts), apples, oranges, tangerines, peppermints, pencils, and writing paper for schoolwork. The smell of the nuts and the oranges, the candy taste, the sound of the crackling fireplace, and the sight of the brown paper bags filled with goodies are some of the memories I cherish.

One year, though, 1966 or 67, thanks to my grandmother, I found my surprise gift hidden in the attic before

Christmas. Next to the fireplace in my grandparents' room was a closet on the right side of the fireplace. Inside the closet was a built-in ladder to the attic. I could not hold back my joy at receiving my first bicycle, but the anticipation of Christmas day made the wait even more exciting. After Christmas, I rode and rode that bike until the bearings wore out, and I fell from the bike due to a locked wheel. That is when I learned about bicycle maintenance.

Living in "the country" provided a different lifestyle during the 1960s. While kids today spend more time inside the house watching television, playing video games, and using social media, we lived during a time when we relied on Mother Nature and the outdoors for fun and entertainment. We went fishing and swimming in the Towaliga and Ocmulgee Rivers, the two significant water bodies in our area. Wikipedia notes the Towaliga River, which starts in a small lake in Henry County near Georgia Highway 81, is a 52.3-mile-long tributary of the Ocmulgee River in central Georgia that passes through High Falls State Park, a popular spot for outdoor activities. The Yellow, South, and Alcovy Rivers feed into Lake Jackson in Butts County, a beautiful and serene location. The Ocmulgee River's life begins at the south end of Jackson Lake and ends when it joins the Oconee River northeast of Hazlehurst. At that point, the convergence of those two rivers forms the Altamaha River, which flows over 150 miles to the Atlantic Ocean, a journey of breathtaking beauty and tranquility. Ocmulgee River scenes are featured in the movie, "Murder in Coweta County."

CHANGING TIMES IN JULIETTE

Before entering my teenage years, I started to develop a work history due to the need for money. That is when I began working at Bowdoin's Grocery store years before the movie was filmed and I continued working there part-time for about a year, pumping gas, cleaning, mopping, stocking, and bagging groceries. After turning 14, I found employment elsewhere during the football off-season.

In 1968, after Dr. Martin Luther King's murder, people started to demand change. Marvin O. Bowdoin, Sr. operated a general merchandise store like Ed Williams, with one major exception. He owned a segregated restaurant on a major thoroughfare, Highway 87, United States Highway (U.S.) 23. While working at the store, African Americans, including employees, were required to eat in a makeshift eating area that also served as the restaurant's storage room. There were three tables covered with a red checkered tablecloth. Whites ate their meals in the nice diner with a soda fountain, jukebox, and booths. The restrooms were also segregated and labeled for all to see. The restroom for Black people was dirty, smelly, and inoperable. During my employment there, some Black folks came to the diner and were refused service because of their race. In Juliette, the word on the street was that Marvin O. Bowdoin, Sr. told them he would close the restaurant before he served them. Later, the protesters filed a civil rights case against Bowdoin, resulting in the restaurant's permanent closure. The Juliette Road and Georgia Highway 87 intersection is now named the Marvin O. Bowdoin Intersection. What happened will always be part of Juliette's history and culture during the Civil Rights Movement.

Artis Lee Holder is the author of *Whites Only in America*. He was born in Indian Springs, Georgia. As a young boy, he worked as a pin boy at the local bowling alley and skating rink. A pin boy is a person stationed in the sunken area of a bowling alley behind the pins who places them in the proper positions, removes pins that have been knocked down, and returns balls to the bowlers. In his book, he writes about witnessing the horrible treatment of an elderly Black couple. Prentice Henderson (Army veteran) retired Attorney is now deceased; Grover Holder (Marine Veteran) became an Electrical Engineer; Artis Holder also worked in the field of Nuclear Engineering; William Tanner (Marine Veteran) retired from Snapper Lawn Mowers, McDonough, Georgia, and unfortunately, Kenny Green (Marine) took his own life in Jenkinsburg, Georgia on June 2, 1987. According to Artis, he grew tired of fighting against evil in the world. Like so many veterans, he did not receive the help he needed to save his life.

In 2023, I spoke with Artis Lee Holder, one of the persons who protested and participated in the civil rights case involving Bowdoin's restaurant in Juliette. He was sixteen years old at the time and was traveling through Juliette, headed back to Butts County after a visit to Robins Air Force Base with friends and relatives who had just left active-military duty. They were seeking employment at Robins. Artis Holder described the incident: "As best I remember, it was early one Saturday morning, and my brother, Grover Holder, had just returned from Vietnam. I was the sixteen-year-old driver," Artis reported. They decided to eat breakfast during the return trip. There were three other occupants. Henderson, Tanner, and Green. They arrived at Bowdoin's restaurant around 9:00 a.m., walked in, and sat at the counter. "When my brother Grover placed his order, they told him, "We don't serve 'em here." His brother responded, "We don't eat 'em," Artis said. Then, things got noticeably quiet as the patrons suspected trouble. Grover said, "I just got back from Vietnam fighting for and serving a country that doesn't want to serve me breakfast?" Artis said the silence was more than his weary soul could bear as Grover jumped over the lunch counter and asked, "Where is the frying pan?" According to Artis, that's when Prentice, a law student, interrupted and said, "Let's go, we'll be back."

According to Artis, they drove home, changed into their Sunday Best suits, and drove to Atlanta, where they met two African American Federal Bureau of Investigation (FBI) Agents assigned to the Civil Rights Task Force. After hearing their story, they followed them back to Bowdoin's in Juliette. Artis said they walked in and politely sat at the lunch counter. Once again, they refused to serve Black people. At that time, FBI Agents intervened, showed their credentials, and cleared the restaurant. Some patrons got "to go" plates, and others were so scared they left their food on the table. Within fifteen minutes, the padlock was on the door, and the local Sheriff's deputies were all over the lot. Artis remembered some Black employees at Bowdoin's seemed relieved that someone had finally broken the racial barrier years after the Civil Rights Act was signed on July 2, 1964. Artis said the case went to court, and Bowdoin lost. After losing, Marvin Sr closed the restaurant and expanded his store. The segregated laundry mat behind the store remained unchanged for years, with exceptions. Black people started using the white side, but whites would not use the formerly designated black side.

Marvin Bowdoin, Sr., and Marvin Jr. lived in brick houses a few feet apart, about two hundred yards west of their store on Juliette Road. The general merchandise store and restaurant were on the northwest corner at Juliette Road and Georgia Highway 87. Between their homes and the store was a large pond, fully stocked with fish. Marvin Bowdoin, Jr. fathered two girls and a son, Tony, six years my junior, Mary Persons High School graduate and co-owner of Bowdoin's Grocery, passed away peacefully in his home at age 58. As a young boy, Tony played baseball on the local little league team, the Juliette River Rats.

Marvin Sr. has three sisters, Gladys, Faye, and Lois (Paulson) Bowdoin. Lois and Gladys lived on McCrackin Street, and Faye lived on what was once a dirt road, now Bowdoin Road. Gladys and Lois were our customers. They purchased blackberries, blueberries, and strawberries from us to make cakes and desserts. Sometimes, as we walked McCrackin Street towards Juliette Centro, we saw Ms. Gladys sitting on her porch. "Hey boys, how are y'all doing today?" She said, "Y'all want some coconut cake." She asked. "Yes, Ma'am," we replied. "Well, come over here; plenty leftover; we've eaten our share." Her generosity was always evident. "Thank you, Ms. Gladys." She always asked, "How is Mae Sue doing?" "She is good," we would always reply. We soon realized Ms. Gladys would only give away cake after it had been sitting in her kitchen for days. Most of the time, the cake was good, but sometimes, it was stale.

Ms. Lois lived further south on McCrackin in a lovely home with a detached garage. She would also sit on her porch occasionally. Her husband, Frank Paulson, was a truck driver and was often away working. "Hey, boys, I need some fresh blackberries," she yelled. "Yes, Ma'am, I'll get you some tomorrow," I said. "Good, I need to make two blackberry pies," she announced. This was a common request from Ms. Lois, who was known for her delicious pies. "Yes, Ma'am," was my response. My aunt Carrie told me my sister received her middle name from Ms. Lois Bowdoin. This was a testament to the close relationship our family had with Ms. Lois.

Within five years after the closure of the restaurant, the Bowdoin family built a baseball field where integrated teams played baseball within the shadows of Marvin's home and the former segregated restaurant. The baseball field reminded you of the movie, "Field of Dreams." They installed lights for night games. As you drive west on Juliette Road, you can still see the utility poles with lights stretching towards the sky, slightly above the growth of young pine trees. Tony did not have far to travel for practice or to play games. The field of dreams was built within two hundred yards of his home. The games were not just about baseball; they were about breaking down barriers and fostering a sense of community. After each game, the Black and White players would swim together in the private fishing pond that was halfway between their house and Bowdoin Grocery store. A symbol of unity was slowly but surely growing in the community.

According to Robert Williams, Juliette Cattle Farmer, former County Commissioner, UGA Physical Education Instructor, and owner of the building that houses the Whistle Stop Café, the Juliette River Rats adult and youth teams integrated during the 1970s. This was a significant event in the history of the team and the local community, as it marked a step towards racial equality and the breaking down of segregation barriers in sports. Marvin Jr. personally recruited black ball players Clyde and Alvin Benjamin. According to Clyde, when Marvin Jr. came to their home, they thought he would ask them to work at the store. Once Marvin mentioned a baseball team, his parents approved. They climbed in the back of Marvin Jr.'s pickup truck, and he took them to Bowdoin Field, where they started practicing.

Clyde was twelve and became a star player for the River Rats. He credits Benjamin "Popcorn" Spear for teaching him how to pitch. Most River Rat games were played in Forsyth because the city teams would not travel to Juliette, which was only nine miles East Northeast of the city. One year, the River Rats won the Championship game. Clyde pitched a great game and hit two home runs for the win. He had pitched several no-hitters during the season. After the championship game, fans gave Clyde praise and cash. Today, Clyde works as a crane operator and lives in Juliette, Georgia. His brother Alvin is a truck driver and is Clyde's neighbor. Along with the Benjamins, other Black players from Juliette included Larry, Freddie, Kenny Watkins, Robert Brown, Eugene and Tannis Appling. Clyde and Tannis played for the Juliette Bombers and the Berner and Juliette (B.J.) Express. Todd Wilson, a long-time friend of the Bowdoin family, said he was one of the best players on the team. Although he hit several home runs himself, Todd credits Clyde for his performance in helping Juliette win a championship game.

Robert Williams also shared some unexpected and delightful moments from the River Rats' history. He fondly remembers his brother, Jerry Williams, playing the National Anthem on his harmonica. Larry Watkins also recalls a particularly memorable occasion when Cher Bono, who was dating Greg Allman at the time, surprised everyone by showing up and singing after one of the games, adding a touch of entertainment and amusement to the team's history.

Larry Watkins said they went to Covington, Georgia, to play an all-white team. The Black players did not play in the game due to concerns about their safety. This was a stark reminder of the racial tensions that still existed in the 1970s, even after the integration of the River Rats. They also traveled to and played in Barnesville, Georgia.

Robert Williams stated they held a Juliette Street Dance one weekend. They hired the Fox City Band to perform. Suddenly, Dickey Betts appeared from the crowd with his guitar and started playing with the band. He played so well with them that it seemed to the crowd he had played with them for years. The Juliette crowd had a wonderful time.

Robert, who earned a bachelor's degree and a master's degree from the University of Georgia (UGA), invited football players to play games for charity on Bowdoin Field in1977. He donated proceeds to Juliette Churches, a local charity that has been instrumental in providing food, and assistance to underprivileged families in Juliette, Georgia. The other funds raised were for the baseball teams. The impact of this charity event was profound, as it not only raised significant funds but also brought the community together for a common cause. After the game, he would host a barbeque for the players at his home on Juliette Road. The UGA players enjoyed the event and would also swim in the fishing pond. One of the players was Benjamin Zambiasi, a former linebacker from Valdosta, Georgia, and Mount De Sales Academy, Macon, Georgia, drafted by the Chicago Bears in 1978. He played professionally with the Hamilton Tiger-Cats and Toronto Argonauts for eleven years in the Canadian Football League (CFL).

Another player Robert remembers is offensive lineman Mack H. Guest, III, owner of LAD Truck Lines, Inc., Watkinsville, Georgia. Guest, a Macon, Georgia native, graduated from Central High School in 1975 and played as an offensive lineman under Vince Dooley from 1976-78, earning All-SEC honors in 1978. In a heartwarming interview, Guest reminisced about the time after spring practice when he and his fellow players were invited to a charity event sponsored by Coach Williams. They proudly donned their UGA Jerseys for the event, joining other University of Georgia Football players like Willie McClendon, Ulysses Norris, Michael Johnson, Frank Ross, Johnny Henderson (deceased), Steve Dennis, Mark Farriba, Mark Hodge, Charlie Fales, Pat Collins, and Jim Milo.

Even baseball Coach Earl Fales joined in the game. The cookout at Coach Williams' home was a memorable event, with people from Forsyth, including Billy Shivers, owner of the Exxon Station.

Willie Edward McClendon, a Brunswick, Georgia native, played running back at UGA alongside Mack Guest. His talent was recognized when he was drafted by the Chicago Bears in 1979, where he played until 1982. His exceptional career led to his election to the Georgia Sports Hall of Fame, a proud moment for UGA and all his fans, culminating in his induction in 2015.

Johnny Henderson, a versatile athlete, graduated from Mount de Sales Academy in Macon, Georgia. His time at UGA was marked by his participation in both baseball and football. After UGA, Henderson enjoyed a brief professional career, highlighting his skills with the Chicago Cubs, Kansas City Chiefs, and Baltimore Colts.

Ulysses Norris, Jr., a junior tight end for the Hurricanes in 1973, made a successful transition to professional football after his time at the University of Georgia. He played seven seasons combined with the New England Patriots and Buffalo Bills, a testament to his skills and dedication to the sport.

After the game at Bowdoin Field, they participated in a cookout at Robert Williams's house, and all the players swam in the pond behind his house. "It was a hell of a good time," said Guest. As a side note, Guest and Jep Castleberry, my former quarterback at Mary Persons High School in 1973, were born on the same day in the same hospital in Macon, Georgia. Guest also recalls meeting Jep in the 1975 High School All-Star game. "Jep attended Auburn University, and I attended the University of Georgia," said Guest. Another all-star team member was future Atlanta Falcons running back (1979-1989), William Andrews, from Thomasville High School.

ALLMAN BROTHERS ENTERTAIN JULIETTE RESIDENTS

Marvin Jr. said to the best of his memory around 1977, Black drummer Jaimoe, who played with the Allman Brothers Band, requested that the band perform on Bowdoin Field to help raise money for the River Rats, a beloved local sports team. One weekend, they set up a stage on a flatbed trailer and entertained the crowd. People came from several counties and donated money. Brack Goolsby, another Juliette River Rats fan, held a bucket at the gate and collected thousands of dollars. As the band performed, one of the fans became slightly intoxicated and decided to go streaking around the field. Dickey Betts tried to hit the streaker with his guitar when he ran up on the stage.

According to Larry Watkins, during one game, a fan who had been drinking heavily during the game became a little rowdy. Someone called the Sheriff to address the issue. When they arrested the guy, Marvin Sr., the father of Marvin Jr., pulled out his pocket knife and said, "Let me poke him on the ass one time." Marvin stuck his knife on the man's "butt." Todd Wilson's version was a little different. He said after the streaker ran across the stage, Dickey Betts hit him with his guitar and broke it. The streaker continued to attempt his escape from capture, but he failed. Marvin Sr. pulled out his knife but did not use it. Instead, he kicked the streaker on the butt.

As the Allman Brothers became popular, several stars visited their East Juliette (Jones County) farm. When visiting "The Farm" leaving Bowdoin's store, drive east on Juliette Road, cross the Ocmulgee Bridge, immediately turn left on River Road, and drive down the dirt road for several miles. The road is isolated, with only three or four homes, and it ends at Georgia Highway 83 in Jasper County as it passes through the Piedmont National Forest.

Marvin Jr. said Dickey Betts began wearing "Indian" Native American clothing because Sandy, his wife or girlfriend, was of Canadian Indian heritage. When I visited Juliette in 1976, I recall seeing a woman with long dark hair before I departed for England. She drove a green Mercedes Benz. One could easily mistake her for Cher. Wayne Spear said he went to

"The Farm" several times to drink beer with the band. Sandy, who was Canadian, said, "This Budweiser beer ain't worth shit. You all need some Canadian beer." Wayne said entertainers and celebrities always stopped at Bowdoin's store on the way to "The Farm." Wayne shared that during another visit to "The Farm" a person whose name he preferred not to mention, was sitting on the deck rolling his Prince Albert Cigarettes, preparing to smoke one. Betts walked outside with a Cigar box loaded with marijuana and asked the Prince Albert guy to roll some sticks. Each time he finished rolling one, someone would grab it. At the end of the evening, the cigar box was empty. He also recalls seeing Don Johnson, Paul and Linda McCartney, Waylon Jennings, Charlie Daniels, Nick Nolte, and James Arness, also known as Matt Dillon from Gunsmoke. James was there looking for his daughter, who had lived on "The Farm" for a while. Other celebrities seen in Juliette include Jason Aldean.

Tony Bowdoin's Facebook messages from February 2010 read as follows: "Does anyone remember the streaker? The Allman Brothers did a concert at the Bowdoin Ballfield to raise money for our River Rats baseball team. Well, someone had a little too much to drink." and
"Can anyone name all the celebrities that have visited Bowdoin's…To name a few: Cher, Don Johnson, Paul, and Linda McCartney, and many more."

CONCERNS ABOUT ALLEGED WATER CONTAMINATION

The Robert W. Scherer Power Plant is a coal-fired power plant that opened in 1982. Marvin Sr. encouraged the building of the plant, stating that it would bring jobs, benefits, and pensions to local workers and others from miles away. After opening, the plant added seven million dollars to the Monroe County economy. Tony Bowdoin (1962-2021) was one of the first residents whose water was tested, and the results showed potentially unsafe levels of hexavalent chromium linked to liver and kidney failures, cancer, and ulcers.

Many people in Juliette will remember Tony's fight with colon cancer. Tony was one of several residents in Juliette living near America's fourth largest coal-fired electric generating plant. In a lawsuit, Juliette residents claim the plant unlawfully released and deposited coal into the community's underground aquifer well and drinking water system. The suit was filed in Fulton County, Georgia, home of the power plant's corporate office. The lawsuit alleges that coal ash was stored in an unlined basin that contaminated the groundwater surrounding the plant. Some residents suffered from health problems such as cancer, thyroid damage, and cardiovascular problems. In an interview, Tony said, "I hadn't told anybody, but something wasn't right with me. I've quit drinking the water."

In February 2023, the original lawsuit against Georgia Power in Fulton County was transferred to Monroe County. The pending suit claims Plant Scherer had knowingly allowed the coal-fired plant to harm adjacent properties, causing severe health problems. The Monroe County Superior Court Judge, Tommy Wilson, requested a trial in 2024. Thanks to Tony and other Juliette residents for the fight that resulted in Monroe County's installation and connection of Juliette to the City of Forsyth's water source. The contractor installed the last water line pipes on Hilltop Street and East Redding Road in 2023 After installation, residents would pay a $500 fee for water meter installation and be financially responsible for connecting the water to their homes, and a $22.00 monthly operating fee. In 2024 the case was settled in Monroe County Superior Court. Juliette residents involved in the suit conceded that Plant Scherer didn't hard local wells, according to an article posted in a local paper dated December 4, 2024.

In the settlement agreement, the state Department of Public Health concluded in 2013, that uranium and radon found in private wells in Juliette around Plant Scherer were naturally occurring. As a result, plaintiffs' attorneys dropped their 11-year lawsuit.

When I visited Juliette during my adult years, I saw Tony Bowdoin as a representative of the new generation working at the family store. We would talk about everyday things, such as our love of snow skiing and traveling. His personality did not reflect his grandfather's past deeds. Everyone must change in life. Some people change faster than others. Tony was a new generation of the Juliette Bowdoin family, and his presence was a testament to the enduring spirit of our community. Years later, in 2017, Tony and Marvin Bowdoin, Jr. sold the store to an East Indian businessperson. We would then learn the creek running behind our former row house on McCrackin Street was contaminated for years, dating back to the 1950s. The Bowdoin family had previously sold the building north of the store, formerly rented by the Juliette Post Office, to someone who now sells fishing gear, bait and tackle ammunition, and other items related to fishing and hunting. The store owner once played baseball with the Juliette River Rats. When a dispute arose over bait shop customers creating parking problems for the convenience store, the new Indian owner installed a concrete barrier to prevent parking on his property. The bait shop owner allegedly reported to the county that the convenience store had no septic tank and was illegally dumping sewage in the creek. As a result, the store owner had to spend thousands to fix the problem. After decades of sewage in the creek, our former playground is again flowing with uncontaminated water from Highway 87 runoffs to the Ocmulgee River.

Calvin Stewart was one of my childhood friends in Juliette. Although separated by one year at birth, we occasionally engaged in mischief, such as throwing rotten eggs at cars on Halloween. Although I was not in Juliette at the time of the incident, Glenda Lowe stated that Calvin stopped at Bowdoin's store to purchase some oil for his car. One of the employees, Willie "Judge" Brown, poured the oil into the engine and spilled some on top of the engine. When Calvin drove the car from the parking lot and started north on Highway 87, smoke started billowing from under the hood. He raised the hood, and the engine was on fire. He returned to the store and asked the cashier to call the fire department. The cashier allegedly refused. Calvin slapped him and ran out of the store, over the hills, and through the woods. When the Sheriff arrived at Bowdoin's to address the issue, the cashier told him the "Lowe Boy" hit him. Calvin had lived with his relatives in Juliette, the Lowe family, but his legal name was Calvin Stewart. However, according to his cousin Glenda Lowe, he was never arrested for the incident. Calvin is now deceased.

Marvin Bowdoin, Jr. always treated me with dignity and respect when I worked at the store and later when I visited Juliette. He always mentioned the days I played football at Mary Persons High School. When I worked at Bowdoin's store from around 1968 to 1970, he would provide transportation for me to and from work. His father, Marvin O. Bowdoin, Sr. died at age 89 in 2002.

JOE THE ALLIGATOR NO LONGER WELCOMED

Later in life, I heard stories about alligators in the Bowdoin Pond, which is located about 100 yards west of the store. During an interview with Marvin Jr in 2024, he said some guys stopped by the store after returning from Florida and asked if he wanted a couple of gators for his pond. He accepted them and fed them for years. One died, and the other continued to survive. He would feed meat to the lone gator at the same spot near the pond. He named the gator Joe and continued to feed Joe for years. Joe grew to about six feet long and decided to eat Marvin Jr's dog. Afterward, Marvin Jr. planned to get rid of Joe, and someone wanted to accept it for one reason or another. However, when the Georgia Department of Natural Resources learned about the possible gator exchange, they threatened to jail Marvin Jr., so he gladly encouraged them to capture it. They placed a trap for the gator with a chicken inside the cage but failed to capture Joe. Marvin Jr. said, "You guys are doing it wrong; I know how to catch Joe." Marvin Jr. instructed them to place the trap at the exact location where he would routinely feed Joe. Finally, Joe was captured and received a ticket straight out of Juliette

WHO KILLED ALBERT THE MYNA BIRD?

The black myna bird lived in a Bowdoin store cage for many years. His name was Albert. According to Marvin Jr., he was intelligent and clever. Mynas communicate with other birds using sounds such as chirps, clicks, whistles, or growls. They became popular during the 1980s. Their life span is between 12 and 25 years. Albert lived at Bowdoin's Grocery Store before the 80's. Albert was a different bird. He whistled at women. Customers visiting Bowdoin's would often engage in conversation with Albert. As a result, his command of the English language increased, according to Marvin Jr. "He built up a large vocabulary." Albert would ask, "What is your name?" "My name is Albert," he would answer. I recall seeing Albert while working at the store, but I did not converse with him. My Uncle Kenny, who also worked at Bowdoin's Grocery, told me the story of when Albert met his sudden death. Bowdoin's Grocery usually closes around 8:00 p.m. each day. One night after closing, someone illegally forced entry into the business. According to Kenny, who heard about the incident from some guys at Mary Persons High School, as the thieves were busy at work, unexpectedly, they listened to Albert's words, "Nigger stealing, Nigger stealing." Marvin Jr. received an intruder alarm notification at home. He immediately drove to the store. When he arrived, all was quiet, except he found Albert murdered. Over the many years, Albert met numerous customers, some of whom would hang around the store socializing daily and speaking with Albert. Albert would remember words, especially when someone repeated those words to him. According to Marvin Jr., we will never know who taught Albert the word "Nigger" because Albert can't tell us. That will remain one of Juliette's secrets.

ROBERT WILLIAMS UNINTENTIONALLY AIDED THIEVES

Robert said he was leaving Macon, Georgia, and returning to the University of Georgia in Athens after a stop in Juliette. In Macon, near Riverside Drive, he spotted a couple of young white male hitchhikers. Robert stopped and gave them a ride. He drove north on Georgia Highway 87 and stopped at Bowdoin's Grocery Store. It was after 8:00 p.m., and the store was closed. He told the guys, "This is as far as I can take you." They exited his vehicle, and he proceeded west on Juliette Road to his home, leaving them in the parking lot. Marvin's alarm was activated a few minutes later, notifying him that someone had entered the store. He responded and caught the two young boys inside the store. He held them until the sheriff's deputy arrived to arrest them. The following morning, Robert stopped at the store to purchase coffee and learned the two boys he delivered to the parking lot after store hours were the culprits of the burglary. Marvin Jr. stated that Bowdoin's Grocery was the victim of more than 123 burglaries and robberies during their 61 years in the business.

BEST STEAKS AND PORK CHOPS

Between 2007 and 2017, Larry Canto Lovell, AKA "Meat Cutter," worked at Bowdoin's Grocery as a Butcher. Terry Jackson gave him the name Meat Cutter. Before becoming a meat cutter, Lovell worked in the deer processing and storage building behind the store. Other Butchers who worked for Bowdoin's Grocery were Mike Melvin, Roger Blount, Willie Brown, Joe Sands, Marvin Sr., Marvin Jr., and Tony Bowdoin. Lovell said, "Marvin showed me how to crack ribs and cut chicken and steaks according to order." In the rear of the grocery store was a large cooler and the meat storage department. Bowdoin's purchased its meat from Colorado Beef Company, Atlanta, Georgia. Lovell said they sold steaks, chicken, pork chops, souse meat, bologna, soy meat, sliced ham, and other meats. One of my favorite snacks as a teen and into adulthood was four slices of spiced ham and a honey bun.

Lovell said there were times when they were overwhelmed with orders, such as when Georgia Power ordered 350 steaks for a company event. Marvin Jr. said Georgia Power once purchased 50 hams. Bowdoin's busiest time was during deer hunting season when hunters would buy several steaks to grill at their campsites. Many of them hunted in the Piedmont and Oconee National Forests. Lovell said a Florida lawyer named Howard Watkins would visit Juliette, live in his cabin, and purchase "a lot of steaks." People would come from Butts, Jasper, Jones, Bibb, Monroe, Lamar, and other surrounding Counties to buy the great steaks from Bowdoin's Grocery. The Mary Persons High School Booster Club loved their steaks. Lovell said Marvin Jr.'s wife, Mrs. Linda, was like his mother.

Marvin said he never thought someone would invade his house while he was home. One night in 2011, Marvin and Mrs. Linda went out the back door after closing. Lovell was with them. He followed them to their home and made sure all was safe. Little did he know a potential robber was watching them. After Marvin and Mrs. Linda Bowdoin entered their home and secured the front door, Marvin Jr. took the dog to the back patio. They sat relaxing in the living room watching American Idol for about 25 to 30 minutes. Mrs. Linda said her leg was hurting, so she did not go to the kitchen to cook as usual. After Marvin had finished watching TV, he walked down the hallway to his office. Minutes after entering his office, he heard someone kick open the front door. He had laid his double barrel shotgun on the table when he entered the house and placed his 45 caliber on top of the refrigerator. Immediately after hearing the break-in, he yelled, "Linda!" She did not respond, so he started walking down the hallway with his only remaining gun, a 22-caliber pistol. Suddenly, he saw the masked man holding a shotgun, and Marvin fired off two rounds. The guy fell, but Marvin either missed him or he did not bleed. The person got up and ran out of the house. Again, Marvin yelled to Linda, "They are trying to kill us!" "You got the phone, Call 911." Mrs. Linda called the Monroe County Sheriff's Office and then called their son Tony, who lived about two miles from the store on Bowdoin Road.

Tony said he received the call and drove there as fast as possible. Upon arrival, he considered going to the back door but thought his father might mistake him for the intruder. He ran back around to the front door and met his parents. Shortly after that, the sheriff's deputies arrived. There was no blood on the floor or ground. However, they found footprints on the door and matching prints on the ground. No one was arrested for the attempted robbery.

WILLIAM HUBBARD ELEMENTARY SCHOOL

My attendance at Hubbard Elementary School in Forsyth began at age six in 1962 and ended with a transfer to Mary Persons in the fall of 1970. I do not remember details from those years, but it was a wonderful and dissimilar experience from my everyday life in Juliette.

In 1963, I was in the second grade at Hubbard Elementary School when the assassination of President John F. Kennedy happened. After getting off the school bus near McDowell's house, we walked to their house to watch the black-and-white television news coverage of the assassination. Since this was during the civil rights movement, we were concerned about America's direction afterward. How would we be treated, or how would our world change? Why did they kill the President? Over the years, changes were made through laws to improve life for Black people and minorities, and 2024 will be a year of changes no one expected.

Field trips are an excellent way to expose kids to places beyond their local geography. During the 1969-70 school year, we were fortunate to travel by bus to Silver Springs, Saint Augustine, and Cape Canaveral (Cape Kennedy), Florida. After we visited Cape Kennedy and saw Apollo 13 in its hangar, NASA launched the capsule into space on April 11, 1970. Once in space, Apollo 13 developed some problems. Remember the famous phrase, "Houston, we've had a problem here." Other trips included The Little White House at Warm Springs, Georgia, Lookout Mountain, and Chattanooga, Tennessee. A field trip from Mary Persons included a tour of the General Motors plant in Atlanta. I don't recall participating in other trips sponsored by Mary Person High School.

I participated in at least two fights during my eight years at Hubbard, including one with William Buckner and Arthur Lee Myrick. The fight with Arthur Lee is the most memorable because it happened on a school bus in Berner, Georgia. He started the fight, and I refused to submit to any punishment for my participation while defending myself. As the bus approached the convenience store in Berner, the bus driver, Mr. R.L. Watkins decided to kick us off the bus and allow us to walk it off while he parked at the store with other students still on board. We started walking south on both sides of Highway 87; I walked on the right side and Arthur Lee on the other side. After walking about 50 yards, Mr. Watkins drove up and asked us to get on the bus. I refused because I felt punished for no reason. Arthur Lee got on the bus. Mr. Watkins drove slowly alongside me as I continued to walk southbound, and he continued trying to persuade me to get on the bus. Finally, he went away and left me walking alone. I arrived home later after walking about three miles. When I arrived, my grandmother told me I was "stubborn." I had to walk outside and pull a branch, a "switch," she called it, from a tree so she could "beat my ass." My step-grandfather worked for Southern Railroad and was out of town and came home mostly during weekends.

The fight with Buckner was a result of playing the dozens. If you are unfamiliar with this game, it involves a verbal exchange of insults between two people in front of an audience. The game aims to provoke the other player to cry or fight you. The words can sometimes become profane and nasty. I started getting warm while William and I exchanged blows for a few seconds. As I started to pull off my pullover sweater, William began to strike me on the head while my shirt covered my head.

I was helpless for seconds while the use of my arms was restricted. The fight was not intended to hurt each other physically but taught me never to let my guard down.

Hubbard offered a program allowing poverty-level students like me to receive lunches during the school day. While it was sometimes embarrassing, it did not deter me from accepting a free meal. So, after I selected my tray with food, I would tell the Cashier, "NP," which meant "No Pay." It created a situation where other kids sometimes made fun of me, but it was a way to survive, and we did not have a wide variety of food at home. I did not know how to order a steak. If I had gone to a restaurant and been asked, "How would you like your steak cooked?" I would not have known to say, "Well done, medium, or rare." We only ate country-fried steak or steak and gravy.. Limited exposure to life experiences hinders personal growth, maturity, and overall life experience.

The early years gave us some fun times at school. During recess, we would play marbles. It was a simple game that held a special place in my heart. I remember drawing a circle in the dirt, scattering the marbles within the circle, and aiming to score points by knocking marbles outside the ring using my shooter marble, a beautiful cat eye marble. Once you hit a marble out of the circle or ring, you continued shooting until you missed it. If your shooter marble remained in the ring, you had to shoot from that position. The game was over when all the marbles were out of the ring. You would keep all the marbles you knocked out of the ring. Game over! But not really. Playing marbles was more than just a game. It was a learning experience that helped us develop various skills, including space and dimensions. Marbles taught engineering skills when children learned about cause and effect as they experimented and learned to keep the marble rolling due to the amount of force applied. Children learned to think logically and sequentially as they anticipated the path of the marbles after contact. Playing marbles helped improve our hand-eye coordination and muscle memory through repeated motions and activity. We learned creativity and patience, social skills, math skills, and geometry, and increased our cognitive development.

When we began the school year at Mary Persons in the fall of 1970, we faced new challenges as first-year students, experienced a new culture, and attended a new school with mostly White administrators and teachers. No one knew what was ahead of us, but it was a change in a positive direction.

My journey at Hubbard was significantly shaped by the typing class taught by Mrs. Lula Dillard. The fact that Hubbard offered this class to eighth graders was a stroke of luck. Little did I know then, the importance of typing skills in my professional journey. This experience underscored the pivotal role of education in shaping our career paths. The training I received at Hubbard was truly invaluable. It prepared me to type reports as an investigator throughout my career. I used shorthand writing for notes during interviews and later typed the reports. The evolution from ribbon typewriters to electric typewriters and finally, computers, was a testament to the progress I made, all thanks to Hubbard and Mrs. Lula Dillard.

My academic journey at Atlanta Junior College in 1981 was marked by a significant event. I remember vividly the research I did on the Love Canal, a neighborhood in Niagara Falls that became an infamous landfill and environmental disaster in America. The problem, which first became public knowledge in 1977, was when people in the community started to develop health problems, including leukemia, serving as a stark reminder of the enduring impact of environmental issues. Today, we are dealing with contaminated water in Juliette, in my hometown, allegedly created by the power company's ash pond. This matter is currently pending in the Superior Court of Monroe County, Georgia. This was a stark reminder that there are Love Canals all over America!

LOCAL DEATHS CREATE UNEASINESS

As a young child, I saw and heard things of no genuine interest at the time, but now, I have questions! Our neighbor, Oscar Myrick, brother of Willie Ann Myrick, was killed late one evening during a "hit and run" as he walked from his house toward Bowdoin's grocery store on Highway 87, US 23. He was less than one-half mile from home when he met his death. After the incident, we continued to walk past where it happened. His shoes were resting in the right of way, southbound nearby where there was once blood on the ground to identify the exact spot where his body last contacted the soil. As we saw the tire tracks, it was clear that the vehicle left the roadway to strike him. It taught us to walk away from the road to stay safe as kids. We decided to take extra measures. During the 1960s, the Department of Transportation cut and controlled grass growth by about 50 feet on the right of way on both sides of the main highway. We started walking along the right of way instead of close to the road. This change benefited us because it allowed us to find strawberry patches, blackberry patches, and plum trees not seen from the path close to the highway.

Mr. Myrick's death was not the first unsolved case in Juliette. Another incident happened near Highway 87, US 23, near our home on North McCrackin Street near what is now named Harvest Drive. Lucious "L.W." McDowell had abandoned a non-working vehicle on the unnamed road leading to his house from the main highway. When you turned onto the dirt road, it proceeded directly eastward and crossed over what is now Harvest Drive, then up a hill to the McDowell house on the left, facing west. Before Harvest Drive, the right of way on the left and right side ended before approaching the tree line on both sides. The abandoned vehicle sat next to the side of the road close to the tree line. One day, we learned Mr. El "Buddy" Jarrell had been killed and burned in the car. When we arrived at the scene the following day, we could see the sheriff's office had cordoned off the area to secure the crime scene. We were not allowed to get too close, but the odor and the entire scene created a situation where we needed to exercise caution. We did not know what happened, except someone had burned in an abandoned car. Mr. Jarrell lived approximately four miles away on Byars Road. Rumors circulated that certain people were responsible for the murder. However, we never learned if anyone was ever arrested for the murder. One of his daughters informed me that he was a very vocal man, and many people, black and white, did not find his personality favorable.

I recall walking the dirt road from Aunt Laura's house to our house on North McCrackin Street after becoming aware of the two unsolved cases. By the time I started walking the route home, darkness had fallen. There were no streetlights, only pastures, and forests on both sides of the road. After passing the paved section of the road that ended near the senior Williams' home, I had walked about three hundred yards when I heard a vehicle and saw headlights moving toward my direction of travel. At that moment, I thought about the Black men who had been killed. In a split second, I ran about ten feet into the woods and hid until the car passed. As I watched the brake lights get brighter, I realized it was probably Mr. Ed Williams II heading home for the evening. However, I could not take the chance to find out whether the person in the car was friendly. After the car turned into the driveway, I continued walking home. At age 12, I had to make split-second decisions for my safety. Years later, I would do the same as a Law Enforcement officer, deciding to shoot or not shoot in a matter of seconds.

FINDING TOYS IN THE WOODS

While living on McCrackin Street, we sometimes walked from one place to another through the woods in a parallel direction of the street to avoid being seen on isolated sections of the long, unpopulated dirt road. One day, while walking that path, we came upon a trash pile used by the Ed Williams II family. It was about thirty yards in the woods across the street from his house. As someone once said, "One man's trash is another man's treasure." We found discarded and broken toys, such as cars and trucks, in the trash pile. Some of them had missing wheels and broken parts. We collected them and took them back to our home, where we would spend hours repairing them, using whatever materials we could find. This process of rebuilding and repurposing these toys for our personal use and enjoyment was a testament to our resourcefulness. I'm sure the Williams family figured out someone was rummaging through their trash pile. They may have decided to leave specific items for us because we continued visiting the pile and collecting broken toys. Our homes were a half mile apart, but our worlds differed in how we lived daily. As we grew older, we became less interested in toys. Our bicycles provided quick transportation around Juliette to visit our friends about one to two miles away.

PICKING GEORGIA PEACHES

Around the age of eleven or twelve, while living near North McCrackin Street, I took advantage of every opportunity to earn money. Georgia is known throughout the world for its peaches. Summertime in Georgia means one thing: peach season. Farmers sell Georgia-grown peaches by the crate from May to September, and restaurants feature them on their menus. Georgia is also well known for Peach cobbler and pies.

A White farmer in the Cork Community, a figure of respect and admiration, owned a peach orchard located just south of Flovilla, Georgia, near Highway 87 in Butts County, approximately two miles north of the Monroe County line. Each year during harvest time, he would drive to local communities, including Juliette, to pick up kids and adults who sought to earn money and take them to his farm to pick peaches. In preparation for the day's work, we wore long-sleeved shirts to avoid the itchy peach fuzz and hats to avoid the intense heat of a summer day in Georgia. They gave us a tin bucket, and once we filled it with peaches, they paid ten cents per bucket. Naturally, we would eat some peaches while working. They were delicious and a great nutritious snack. The farmer drove us back home at the end of the day with a few coins in our pockets.

Within a few hundred yards of where the peach orchard once produced beautiful peaches, there is a little history that many people do not know. Today, a historical marker posted there by the Georgia Historical Commission displays the following:

KILPATRICK AT CORK

On Nov. 17, 1864, Kilpatrick's cavalry division, which was covering the right flank of General Sherman's army on its March to the Sea, moved from Bear Creek Station (Hampton), 30 miles, NW, down the north bank of Towaliga River to threaten Griffin and Forsyth. This threat caused the Towaliga bridges to be burned by Wheeler's cavalry to protect those towns and the large Confederate hospital centers there.

On the 18th, Kilpatrick's division reassembled here at Cork. The next day, it crossed the Ocmulgee River at Planters' Factory (4 miles E) and moved South to cover the front and flanks of the infantry columns and faint at Macon.

CHAPTER 2

MOVE TO BOWDOIN ROAD

In the summer of 1969, after the school year ended, we moved into a smaller house on Bowdoin Road, next door to Mr. Will and Mrs. Clara (Barrow) Moore. Joe Willie and Lula Mae (Lowe) Jarrell previously occupied the house. Coincidentally, the house where I was born was on the right side, north of the Moore's home. Since we did not have water in the house or a well, we obtained water from Moore's outside water faucet. We were happy paupers and survived in the best way available. Once again, we lived in an old house with fireplaces and three rooms, two bedrooms, and a kitchen, which provided shelter for my Aunt Jean, Uncle Johnny, Uncle Kenny, myself, and my grandparents, Johnny Boozer, Sr., and Mary Sue (Freeman) Boozer. Later, I learned from Ancestry DNA that Will Moore's son-in-law, Cullen Walton, Sr., is my maternal grandfather. He left Juliette in 1942 and moved to South Bend, Indiana. My mother was born in 1940.

Shortly after we moved, Mrs. Willie Ann Myrick and her family also moved to Bowdoin Road. Now, I realize what was happening. The families were forced to move due to gentrification and changing times. In 1970, the year of forced integration, about the same time Bowdoin's restaurant closed, and after we moved, the Juliette Baptist Church relocated from Hilltop Street to Highway 87, near McCrackin Street, across the highway from where Willie Ann Myrick lived. The church sold its Hilltop Street property to R.L. Watkins, whose home was directly across the Street. To the north of the church, John, and Laura (Dillard) Jackson purchased three adjoining acres from the Dorsett family, and at the end of Hilltop Street, Gladys Brown purchased a home. Juliette Baptist Church was located on the Street with all Black families, and the church decided to move north, resulting in the relocation of the only two Black families living on North McCrackin Street. Today, Juliette

Baptist Church and The Sanctuary Church are located within one hundred yards of each other on Highway 87 near north McCrackin Street. Ironically, in April 2022, I purchased five-and-one-half acres across the Street from The Sanctuary on the south side of North McCrackin. It was the same place where I would wait for our school bus each day before we moved in 1969.

TRAVEL TO MIAMI

One of my favorite Grandaunts, Dorothy, lived in Atlanta, Georgia, Chattanooga, Tennessee, and Miami, Florida. Her niece and my aunt, Johnnie Mae, moved to Miami to live with her in 1965 or 1966. Johnnie Mae, the oldest living sibling, is my oldest aunt, but more like an older sister to me. When she moved to Miami, I knew I would visit her one day because she rarely returned to visit her parents. Years later, in 1969, I visited her and Aunt Dorothy at their home near 13th Avenue and 60th Street in Liberty City.

Following the 1968-69 school year, I traveled alone from Juliette to Miami, Florida, on a Greyhound bus. While there, I witnessed a riot for the first time. There was much tension in America then, and it did not pass me without influence. While standing in Aunt Dorothy's yard, I saw burning tires piled on 13th Avenue to prevent police vehicles from traveling through the area. Their efforts were temporary and did not have a tangible impact on the situation. Later during the day, I witnessed the looting and burning of businesses on 62nd Street. I followed my aunt to the corner of 62nd Street and 13th Avenue and saw people looting at the fish market. After the break-in, the live chickens escaped from the market and crossed the Street into the housing project. I'm sure someone had a great fried chicken meal that day. Someone knew how to properly prepare a live chicken for cooking. I also visited Virginia Key Beach; a beach frequented by Black Miamians. It was my second visit to a beach; the first was in St. Augustine, Florida, during a field trip sponsored by Hubbard Elementary School.

In Miami, I was involved in my first car accident. My Aunt Johnnie Mae was driving a Volkswagen Beetle when she turned left in front of another vehicle. I was in the back seat, behind the front passenger, when the collision occurred, causing my nose to bleed. My head hit the back of the passenger seat and little did I know, this might have been my first concussion. It also led to a separated septum, which I discovered years later. This was just the beginning of my adventurous spirit, as I would go on to experience at least two more concussions while serving in the Air Force and playing semi-professional football in Italy between the ages of 21 and 22.

My first experience with "puppy love" was in Miami with a girl I met at the Magnolia Park swimming pool in Liberty City. After the first meeting, I attempted to go swimming each day. We were the same age, and hormones began to rage. Since I was thirteen, I soon realized that our fun at the pool would be temporary, so I tried to enjoy as much time with her as possible. I discovered there were physical reactions when I was attracted to a pretty girl. As a teen, I was also a little adventurous. My puppy love challenge was to climb a coconut tree and retrieve a coconut. Well, my thirteen-year-old maturity kicked in, and I climbed the tree. After a few seconds, I was back on the ground in pain after being stung several times by yellow wasps or hornets. My first attempt to impress a girl could have been more impressive. My face was swollen, and I was embarrassed.

As always, every good thing must end, and so did this great trip from rural Georgia to the big city of Miami. But it was now time to return home to Georgia. I had a fun time but thought it would have gone better. My family took me to the Miami bus station, where I prepared for the trip home alone at thirteen. After leaving Miami, the bus stopped in Jacksonville for a bus change. At some point, before arriving in Jacksonville, I secured my ticket. As I attempted to enter the bus for the next leg of the trip home, the driver stopped me at the door and asked for my ticket, but I could not find it. He politely told me to get off the bus before he departed the station. I was a thirteen-year-old in Jacksonville, Florida, without money or a bus ticket.

We did not have a home phone. I started to consider my options. Cell phones did not exist in 1969. I soon realized I held a valuable new portable AM/FM 45 record player. I quickly located the nearest pawn shop around the corner from the bus station. After walking into the business, I told the owner I wanted to sell my portable record player to get money for a ticket. He asked to see it. I saw my ticket at the bottom when I pulled it out of the box. At that point, I thanked him and returned to the bus station to catch the next bus home. Upon returning to Juliette, I learned about the restaurant closing. I returned to work at Bowdoin's Store until the winter of 1969. I began practicing organized football at Mary Persons High School in the spring of 1970.

I recall one incident at Mary Persons High School, my first year interacting with White students. We rode the school bus together for the first time. As I stated, we survived chilly weather by burning wood in the fireplace to keep warm during winter.

During cold mornings, we would light the fire to prepare for school. There were two fireplaces, one in our room and the other in my grandparents' room. Since the house was not insulated, air would flow through the house, and most of the smoke would exit through the brick chimney. While riding the school bus, a student, Cheryl, said, "You stink like smoke." Since I was accustomed to living with smoke from fireplaces all my life, at age 14, I never thought about how I smelled to others. It was because many Black people residing in Monroe County's rural areas smelled like me. After Cheryl's remark, I became more aware of how differently we lived from others in the community, including some Black people. The Benjamin family lived in a nice concrete block and brick home on what is now East Redding Road. Mr. Clyde Benjamin, Sr., worked for Snelling and Snelling. They built bridges throughout the south. Snelling paid higher wages than the local jobs so that Mr. Clyde could afford nice toys for his kids, such as motorbikes and go-carts. Clyde and Alvin Benjamin were the envy of all the Black kids in Juliette. They used propane gas for heating their home.

A HISTORY OF ABUSE

Johnny Boozer, Sr. was born in Greenwood, South Carolina, and ended up in Georgia while working for Southern Railway. Several men in the surrounding counties were also employed with Southern Railway, now Norfolk Southern. During much of my childhood, Johnny Sr would work for a week at a time out of town. When he returned home on Friday with money in his pocket, he would often spend the weekend consuming moonshine and getting intoxicated. There were several places to choose from, each with its unique charm. Irene (Moore) Watkins operated a Juke Joint on the hill, now Hilltop Street, a lively spot where locals gathered to enjoy music and drinks. Mr. Thunt had one arm and sold moonshine from his house near the old bridge on the Jones County side of the Ocmulgee River, a place with its own stories and legends. Another juke joint was operated by a lady named Farris in Jones County, which was also the scene of the murder of Glen Blalock. These juke joints, along with the absence of liquor stores, were integral parts of the local culture, and the men of Juliette frequented them within a two to three-mile radius. Johnny Sr became abusive to his children and grandchildren after consuming moonshine. The alcohol caused his behavior to change drastically. His speech became slurred, and since he worked on the railroad, performing physical work, he was a physically strong man. When not drinking moonshine, he was a nice, humble person. After consuming alcoholic beverages, locals would say he spoke Gullah Geechee because they could barely understand his speech.

In 2024, during a conversation with my half-aunt, Johnnie Mae Boozer, she revealed why she left home at such a youthful age. She recounted a disturbing incident that led to her decision. "It was almost dark that evening when Daddy asked me to go with him to get some water from the well down the hill from the house. We were living in the house on the old

Walton place. As we approached the well, Daddy tried to touch me, so I ran towards the McDowell house and continued running to the dirt road leading to Highway 87 until I reached my granddaddy's house on what is now Newton Road. I told Granddaddy what happened." Her grandfather, Willis Freeman, Jr., played a crucial role in this challenging time. He reassured her, saying, "Baby, you can stay here, and I promise he won't bother you here." This unwavering support from her grandfather was a comfort in such a tough time.

Johnnie Mae did not return to live with her father and mother from that day forward. She would only visit her mother while her father worked out of town. Willis Freeman, Jr., had remarried Lettie Myrick after his first wife, Mattie Grier Freeman, died in 1963. Lettie Myrick's niece, Gaynelle Myrick, the first child of Gladys Myrick Brown, also lived with them. Sometime around 1965, Willis Freeman, Jr., and his family, including Johnnie Mae, moved to Berner, Georgia, about three miles north on Highway 87, to a house on a dirt road near Dorothy Shannon Myrick. Johnnie Mae lived there until her Aunt Dorothy sent her a bus ticket to move to Miami, Florida. She became pregnant with Michael before deciding to move to Florida.

Life at Box 106 Bowdoin Road was not easy. Despite the below-poverty-level conditions we lived in, we had to deal with physical abuse. There was no taking away your phone, no limits on watching television, and no restrictions like those imposed on children today, such as "time out." We were physically beaten to the point where we looked like we had just received a beating from an enslaver.

In 1980, after Johnny Mae (Boozer) Rodriguez's son, Michael Boozer, moved from Miami to live with his grandparents in Juliette, Mary (Freeman) Boozer had had enough of abuse and alcoholism. In June, she left the house and moved in with her daughter, Jean (Boozer) Brown, because her husband had beaten her grandson. According to Kenneth Boozer, he and his girlfriend visited Juliette on the day of the beating. He had left his girlfriend at Jean's house about 30 yards behind Johnny

Senior's house while he went to a Juke Joint. When he returned, his girlfriend reported she heard Johnny Sr. beating Michael, who was 15 years old. Upon hearing about the abuse, Kenneth called the Sheriff's Office and reported the incident. When they arrived, Johnny Sr. had left the scene. Kenneth does not recall what happened afterward, but Johnny Sr. did not go to jail. It would be the last time Johnny Sr would physically abuse anyone. Six months later, on Christmas Eve, while living alone at Box 106 Bowdoin Road, he died. On Christmas Eve, he walked about one mile to Bowdoin's Grocery to enjoy the annual event, during which Marvin O. Bowdoin, Sr., served moonshine to patrons. On Christmas day in 1980, Johnny Boozer Sr. was found dead in his home at age 58, a result of drinking too much moonshine.

FIRST TIME PLAYING ORGANIZED SPORTS

During the fall season of 1970, the elementary and high schools in Monroe County integrated for the first time in their history. I played B-team football at Mary Persons as a defensive back/safety and running back. We started practice in the spring and the summer before classes began in the fall.

In 1972, a significant year in my life and in the history of our team, I reported to the field house after our team meal. The usual routine is for all the receivers, quarterbacks, and running backs to get their ankles taped before the game. We were partially dressed in our uniform, usually wearing an undershirt and our football pants; we would sit on a table with our feet extended out so the assigned coach could perform the taping. Coach Gases was assigned to tape my ankles that day. As soon as he started taping, he said, "Damn, Percy." I knew what he was smelling. It was my feet from wearing old shoes. When you are poor, and your wardrobe, including shoes, is limited to one or two pairs, constantly exposed to the elements, it might create a little odor.

Sometime after the incident, I was spending time together with four players on the MPHS football team. Two white and two Black. One of the White players suggested we go shopping in Macon, Georgia. I decided to go along, even though I had no money. It turns out none of us had money. It was my first time stealing something valued at ten dollars or more. First, we drove to a store on Riverside Drive, walked inside, and started shopping separately. I don't know what the other guys did, but I took a pair of shoes from the rack, carried them to the dressing room, changed to the new shoes, and placed the old shoes in the trash. I walked out of the store wearing a pair of beige and blue suede shoes. Edward Williams' Elvis song must have been on my mind. It's amazing how a new pair of shoes can boost your confidence. I left the store and waited for the other guys near the car. As far as I was concerned, my shopping had ended for the day. Someone in the group suggested we go to another store on Gray Highway. Well, since I was a passenger, I had no choice. However, when we arrived at the next store, I decided to stay in the car; another player stayed in the car with me, and the other three went inside to do more shopping. After 15 to 20 minutes passed, two players returned to the car. As we waited for the fifth player, watching the exit door and hoping he would appear soon, suddenly as he started to exit, a security officer grabbed him and took him back inside. Immediately, we drove from the parking lot and proceeded east on Gray Highway. After spotting an isolated spot on the highway, we discarded all the loot from shopping, including my new shoes, in a ditch on the side of the highway. Luckily, the detained player left his zip up boots in the car. After discarding my new shoes, I slipped into his boots, which fit perfectly. We returned to the parking lot to find out what happened to our friend. After parking for about two minutes, the police arrived and took us to the station for questioning. As I sat at the investigator's desk during questioning, he leaned over to look at my shoes. He suspected I was wearing new shoes. Whew! After about 30 minutes, four of us were released. The player caught by security had to remain there until his parents picked him up from temporary detention. We returned to Gray Highway to retrieve our loot from the ditch. People must have assumed the items were trash on the side of the road because it was all there just as we had left it.

The only reason I stole a pair of shoes is simple, I was in need. As I think about it now, it reminds me of the scene in the movie 'Glory' when Private Silas Trip, played by Denzel Washington, received a beating for stealing shoes he needed. I had no money and was barely surviving. I only stole what I needed to save embarrassment from smelly feet. I couldn't work a part-time job while playing football, and I didn't want to stop playing. Football was my lifeline during those challenging times. When I watched the security officer detain one of my friends, it was a lesson I would never forget. Although I walked away with a pair of new shoes valued at around ten dollars, I knew I had done something wrong, and I knew I had been influenced by group behavior. There was no peer pressure, but the guilt was heavy on my shoulders. None of my friends from Juliette were in the group of five. This experience made me question my morality and self-identity, and it's a lesson that has stayed with me to this day. It's a stark reminder of the weight of personal responsibility and the impact of individual actions on our moral compass.

Organized football was a new experience and an outlet to escape from my home environment. Camaraderie and team building were something I needed in my life at the time. Since we did not have a car, I depended on Ed Williams II and Edgar Slaughter Sr. for rides from football practice. While playing on the football team, I gained new friends but continued to live below the poverty level. I enjoyed taking a long shower at the school gym because I did not have a working shower at home.

I played varsity football at Mary Persons from 1971 to 1973 and lettered for three years. While a team member, we lost only four regular season games and tied one in three years. I played in two of the three losses and missed the last two games of the 1973 season due to an injured wrist. During my first year on the varsity team as a Sophomore, I started as Safety on defense and rotated in and out of the tailback and fullback positions as needed.

The local newspaper, The Monroe Advertiser, and the Monroe Reporter highlighted my playing time in at least three games.

In the September 1973 Monticello Hurricanes vs. Mary Persons football game, on the first series of downs in the second half, Mary Persons took the ball to the Monticello seven-yard line, where Percy Freeman drove to the one. Two plays later, he ran up the middle across the striped line for the Bulldog's fourth TD.

The Monroe Reporter's article highlighted the Bulldogs' unwavering determination to win.
After two consecutive years of losses in a home game against Manchester, the Bulldogs, led by Ricky Colbert, Percy Freeman, and Wadey Clements, launched a fierce backfield attack on the Blue Devils. They advanced from their own forty-one to the twenty-six-yard line, with Freeman ultimately scoring a touchdown on the first down.

In an away game, Mary Persons defeated Telfair County 48-7. Percy Freeman intercepted a Trojan pass on their forty-two-yard line, and in four plays, the Bulldogs were within smelling distance of a TD on the nineteen-yard line.

The Bulldogs finished the season with a record of 9-1, but we did not enter the playoffs due to a Region game loss to Peach County.

In 2023, I was inducted into the Forsyth Monroe County Hall of Fame. It was a proud moment for my family and friends. Because of their love and caring for me when I needed it, I invited Edgar and Henry Slaughter, my teammates. Their parents were the primary reason I remained in Monroe County and graduated from Mary Persons High School. I regret that I never got a chance, as an adult, to fully express what they had done for me and their impact on my future.

FORSYTH MONROE COUNTY HALL OF FAME INDUCTION CEREMONY 2023

Good evening, everyone,

I am truly honored to be Inducted into the Forsyth-Monroe County Sports Hall of Fame. Thanks to the Board Members for selecting me.

This evening, I would like to recognize my family, friends, and Bulldog teammates. I am eternally grateful for your support and friendship!!!!

Thanks to the late Coach Dan Pitts, Coaches Dumas, Love, Cook, Gasses, and other coaches for their skills and contributions to our winning seasons and personal growth as young men. Thanks to my former Aviano Eagles Coaches, John Droke, and Randal Bertrand, all NIFL teams, including the Eagles, for great memories and the adventures of a lifetime.

To Mr. Edward Williams II and Mr. Edgar Slaughter, Sr., thank you for giving me a ride to and from football practice during my four years at MPHS. Without their support, I would not have played football with the Bulldogs.

To Jean Boozer and the Slaughter Family, Edgar Jr, Henry, and Kenneth, thank you for allowing me to stay in your home and share your space during a challenging time.

Tony Robbins, American author, speaker, and coach, said, "Your current situation does not determine your future. Your future is determined by your decision to succeed."

After my 14th birthday and mandatory integration of the Monroe County School system, I attended football summer camp at Mary Persons High School under Coach Pitts. My first participation in organized football began in 1970. We shared communal showers, ate meals, and slept on military folding cots in the gymnasium. I slept on a cot near Edward "Elvis'

Williams, III, who entertained us nightly before "lights out" while singing Elvis Presley's songs such as *Blue Suede Shoes*. Some team members developed friendships that continue today. One year earlier, we lived in a culture that enforced segregated schools, pools, restaurants, diners, laundromats, and restrooms.

I recall the hard work, summer heat, wind sprints, and more wind sprints during camp. I enjoyed the competition, team meetings, discussions, diversity, and friendship. We worked well together because we shared a common goal: to win games. Yes, we are members of the teams that contributed to Coach Pitts' history-making winning record and his 100th victory! As a member of the 1970 B-Team, we ended the season with a 10-0 record, including defeat of Pike County's Varsity team during their inaugural season.

In the words of Michael Jordan, "Talent wins games, but teamwork and intelligence win championships."

In 1971, I started playing football as a Defensive Safety on the varsity team and as a substitute running back. We won twenty-six games in three years, lost four, and tied one. Three of my favorite memories are intercepting a game-changing pass against Telfair County and scoring touchdowns against Manchester and Monticello. One of my worst memories is sitting on the sideline with an injured wrist in 1973 while Paul Ross, a 200-pound fullback from Peach County, enjoyed his best game and destroyed our hopes of playing in the playoffs that year when he scored four touchdowns and ran for 240 yards in an important Region game, resulting in a nine and one record, and the end of our season! Paul Ross went on to play for Woody Hayes at Ohio State University.

Several citizens in Monroe County suggested the Mary Persons Football Team was one of the greatest contributors to the successful integration of the school system. Friday night lights created an atmosphere of unity and support. In other words, The Bulldogs became the glue that held the community together.

Henry Ford once said, "Coming together is a beginning. Keeping together is progress. Working together is a success."

After graduating in 1974, I joined the United States Air Force and was assigned tours of duty in Denver, CO, Panama City, FL, and England. I transferred to Aviano, Italy, in May 1977. Upon arrival, I learned about the new semi-professional North Italian Football League, a league that included Army and Air Force teams, which later became part of the United States Air Forces in Europe or USAFE Football League, with 32 teams primarily competing in England, Germany, Spain, and Italy. USAFE was established after World War II in 1946 and operated until 1993 as entertainment for military personnel and their dependents stationed in Europe. The league included former NFL, college, and high school players who joined the military.

In the spring of 1977, at age 21, I tried out and was selected to play football for the Aviano Eagles in the NIFL as running back/receiver, kick returner, and Safety. I also served as one of four Team Captains for two seasons. In the NIFL, I quickly realized I was playing football with men who had several years of experience and good insurance. After the commander of the 509th Airborne Rangers parachuted out of a helicopter and landed dead center on the 50-yard line with the game ball, I thought, "I am in a different league now." If you were chased by 11 members of the 509th Airborne Rangers or Camp Darby Rangers, who are trained killers that remind you of Paul Ross clones, you, too, would run for your life. There was no concussion protocol. So, you may ask, what are the signs of a concussion? Does "He just got his bell rung" or "Why am I seeing stars sound familiar?"

I recall one game in Pisa, Italy (the city of the Leaning Tower), televised with 13,500 fans in attendance. It was an awesome, unforgettable experience. I kept copies of the Stars and Stripes newspaper articles from my "glory days" and periodically reviewed and shared them for nostalgia's sake.

After attending the 2022 Forsyth Monroe County Sports Hall of Fame Banquet with my fiancée, Joan Whitehead, she said, "Seven touchdowns in one game, that's amazing," so she nominated me for the 2023 Hall of Fame based on my contributions to winning seasons at MPHS and record-setting performances in Italy.

I am proud to say my 1977 record as the leading rusher in USAFE/NIFL with 1089 yards and as the leading Eagles receiver with 502 yards, 16 touchdowns, and several interceptions will never be broken by anyone because the USAFE League ended in 1993. The Aviano Eagles joined USAFE's Mediterranean Sports Conference after two seasons there.

In closing, Helen Keller reminded us, *"Alone we can do so little: together we can do so much."*

Today, more than ever, if we want to remain a team, the United States of America needs togetherness! Again, thank you for your attendance and this honor!

In 2024, I contacted Chuck Hall, Class of 1975, who became the starting fullback for MPHS during the 1974 season. He stated that after I graduated, Coach Pitts would show game film of my blocking techniques when I rotated in and out as running back. Hall became the first 1000-yard rusher (including playoff game) for Mary Persons and earned a scholarship to the University of Louisville. Duke Watson of Forsyth, Georgia is carrying on the Bulldog's legacy and setting records as a freshman running back at the University of Louisville.

My grandparents never attended one football game, track and field event, or boxing match during my four years at MPHS. As a teen, I learned my grandmother received a $40 monthly welfare check from the government to assist with my well-being. Yes, I was a welfare recipient. The environment I lived in was different from one where education was encouraged. There were no books in the house except for an occasional Reader's Digest. Neither my grandmother nor step-grandfather graduated from high school. The expectation was, however, for me to graduate and get a job. No role models were around to encourage me to seek higher education or other opportunities. College was not on my radar. Depending on the subject matter or interest, I performed as an A, B, and C student. Math was not my favorite subject!

As I reflect on my teenage years, I realize something was missing. First, I never felt a close connection to Johnny Boozer. He was not related to me by blood and did not exhibit the behavior of a father-son relationship. I did not feel any love. My life was task oriented. I was expected to do what I needed to do to survive. However, he did the best he could, given his life was shaped by his experiences, which included a lack of education, discrimination, and other factors such as alcoholism. Even with limited education, he would provide for his family. He cultivated his garden, raised his animals, and provided food and shelter for us.

My maternal grandmother also lacked a formal education. She was fifteen years old when my mother was born. As a result, she had to become a woman, and school was no longer nan option for her. She would spend the rest of her life cleaning homes for low wages. Similarly, she did not exhibit love and affection towards her kids. I don't recall receiving hugs from my grandparents. I received more affection from my grandaunts Alice and Dorothy. "Come here, boy, and hug me," I remember Aunt Dorothy always greeting me with a smile each time she visited from Miami. Aunt Alice was the first person to tell me, "Look me in the eye when you are talking; it shows your strength," she said.

During my senior year at MPHS, I attempted to participate in the Track and Field Team and ran the 400-yard race, now 400-meter. I ran terribly and was breathing heavily as I watched the other runners leave me in their dust. Coach Pitts was disgusted with my performance. I was embarrassed and did not run that race again. Training was necessary, but I was not dedicated to that task then; I was more concerned about day-to-day survival in Juliette, Georgia. The coaches were unaware of my situation and did not ask about my struggles.

In the spring of 1973, my junior year in high school, MacArthur Freeman, no relation, a boxer and senior at Mary Persons High School, was invited to the National Golden Gloves Championship in Lowell, Massachusetts. The school hosted a fundraiser at the gymnasium to help raise money for MacArthur's travel expenses. The Athletic Department requested volunteers to box in exhibition matches as space fillers. Other trained boxers were on the schedule, but they wanted to increase student participation. Clarence Walker and William Buckner approached me to fight in the exhibition, but I declined. I was smart enough to know both guys had a more extended reach than me. I had watched boxing matches with great fighters such as Muhammad Ali, Sonny Liston, and Joe Frazier, so I fought Eddie Walton. His body build resembled Joe Frazier's, so I decided to fight against him. The fight would last for three three-minute rounds.

In 1973, I participated in my first boxing match in front of a large crowd. I decided I would emulate Ali. I shuffled my feet, danced around, and threw several punches. Little did I know I was tiring myself unnecessarily. But it was a show. After about the middle of the second round, I felt like my arms weighed 150 pounds each, and my legs weighed 200 pounds each. However, I remembered to keep my arms up for protection. I was tired and hoping the match would end soon when I received a blow to my head that sent me spinning and seeing stars. This event was no longer a show; it was survival. I know now that Eddie's blow to my head was a concussion. When Eddie struck me, I could only think about how embarrassing it would be if I got knocked out. I quickly thought of getting away from him by dancing away Ali style and covering until the bell rang. Once I recovered, I continued to throw punches and protect my head, and when the bell rang, I had won my first amateur fight by scoring points after almost becoming a knockout victim. Coach Dan Pitts was impressed. MacArthur Freeman moved on to the Nationals, where he lost to Marvelous Marvin Hagler, who later became a world champion in the 1980s.

SAVED A LIFE

I was a teenager visiting High Falls State Park in Monroe County, Georgia, with friends and family to swim at High Falls Lake. My younger uncle, Kenneth 'Kenny' Boozer, was in the group. It was a typical balmy day in Georgia during the summer. I don't recall everyone present, but I recall swimming with Bobby Johnson as we saw Uncle Kenny floating on a tire tube toward the dock about twelve to fifteen feet from the shore. The dock served as a diving platform. After we dove repeatedly into the water from the dock, Uncle Kenny decided to join the fun. Once he reached the dock by tube, he dove toward the tube. It was not a smart thing to do. He bounced off when he contacted the tube and went directly into the water. No one was paying attention to him then because we were aware he could not swim well and did not think he would enter the deeper water without holding on to the tube. When we heard the splash and saw the tube floating with no Kenny on it, we knew what happened. Immediately, we looked around the tube and saw air bubbles on the water's surface. Bobby and I went into action by diving near the area of the bubbles. At the time, we were about ten to twelve feet from the shore. Suddenly, we saw Kenny on the bottom, fighting for his life. Bobby grabbed his shoulder, and I grabbed his waist as we pulled him towards the shoreline. Once we reached the five-foot water level, he stood, and we pulled him out of the lake. A life saved.

"He or she has a hard head," A phrase often used to describe someone stubborn. Well, on one occasion, my uncle Johnny Jr and I were walking down the dirt road now named McCrackin Street, walking to my great-grandfather's house or to fish or swim in the Towaliga River. As we started our walk approaching what is now Harvest Drive, we noticed Johnny's younger brother Kenny following us. He may have been eight or nine years old. Johnny Jr. told him to "Go home." When we stopped, he stopped, but he continued following. After we walked another twenty to thirty yards, Johnny Jr. picked up a rock and threw it directly at his brother Kenny. The rock landed dead center on Kenny's nose. Kenny started crying and changed his direction to go back home. Johnny Jr., who was about fourteen at the time, said, "Kenny has a hard head." This story, while it may seem like a simple childhood memory, holds a valuable lesson for all of us about the consequences of stubbornness. It's up to us to learn from it. I learned Johnny Jr. had an anger management problem on that day!

The Juliette Dam is now considered a recreation area for swimming, fishing, jet skiing, water skiing, and kayaking. As a teenager, we used the area around the dam for fishing and swimming. The area called "The Head Gates" had a large wheel used to open the gates and allow water to be released from the west side of the dam. If you have seen the movie Fried Green Tomatoes, this is where Frank's car was retrieved from the river—the areas at the back of the dam range from ten to thirty feet. Once again, Bobby and Clarence Johnson, Sammy and Eddie Walton, Randy Jones, Calvin Stewart, and I swam near the head gate on a summer's day. I heard yelling, and at first, I thought someone had seen a water moccasin. Bobby Johnson, Sammy Walton, and Randy Jones were caught by the suction from the head gate being partially open. It created a suck-hole effect, pulling them down under the water. Immediately, Bobby and Randy went underwater briefly, then reappeared after bouncing off a large pipe beneath the water. Sammy was still caught in the current. Next, I heard Eddie yell, "Somebody save my brother." We could see Sammy fighting to keep from going under. Immediately, I ran to the tree line and found a long tree branch. We extended it out to Sammy; he grabbed it, and we pulled him out of the water.

SUMMER JOBS TO EARN A LIVING

After spring football camp, and before returning to school in the fall, I worked different jobs, such as Bibb Manufacturing Company in Juliette, where I operated a sheet printing machine at age sixteen. The plant produced name-brand sheets called Percale sheets. I also worked at Bibb Manufacturing Company in Forsyth in the yarn department and at Shane's restaurant, cleaning tables and washing dishes. During the summer of 1972, I worked with Pete (Redding) Myrick as an apprentice carpenter. We built Jim Walter homes throughout Middle Georgia. In 2023, after my sister Carolyn took an Ancestry DNA test, we learned that Pete (Redding) Myrick was her father. Ancestry DNA also identified Carolyn as having two other half-brothers. Later, she learned Pete (Redding) Myrick fathered ten children.

On one job, I helped Pete complete work on Dicky Bett's (Allman Brothers) home, near the Ocmulgee River, East Juliette, Jones County. Betts played guitar for the Allman Brothers Band. They purchased 432 acres of land in Juliette and nicknamed it "The Farm." It soon became a "group hangout." There were several nights in Juliette when residents could hear them playing music. The sound traveled through the woods and across the river as they practiced their craft. After Duane Allman died in 1971, the Allman Brothers Band released an album called Eat a Peach. It became their most significant release and peaked at number four on the Billboard Charts. Afterward, the band performed several dozen shows. Employees at Bowdoin's Store reported that Cher visited Juliette riding a motorcycle with Gregg Allman in 1975, wearing leather chaps. Macon Telegraph Newspaper articles confirm Cher was in Macon in February and married Gregg Allman in June 1975.

Before the fall of 1972, my step-grandfather requested money from me after I had worked a summer job. I refused to give it to him, so I decided it was time for me to leave home and become a man. I refused to give him money while he was giving his money to others, getting drunk, and exhibiting behaviors I did not like. Previously, he attempted to beat me with a small tree branch for not cutting firewood as he had requested. I was ready for a change and did not want to live in a home where I had to chop wood to heat the home. Change was not coming fast enough for me, and I was embarrassed to bring someone to my house. I decided to leave home and moved two houses down the same dirt road to live with my Aunt Jean and her husband, Charlie. They used propane gas for heat. Hallelujah! The former dirt road was paved in 1973 and is now named Bowdoin Road.

  I was not the first in the family to "run away" from Box 106, Bowdoin Road, Juliette, Georgia. When Johnny Jr. turned 16 he left home and lived in the woods for a week before Mrs. Gladys Myrick Brown learned of his situation. Since he had started working, she asked him to pay $10.00 per week to live with her family on Hilltop Street. He lived there until 1971 before moving to Atlanta, Georgia at age 17. His brother Kenneth also left home at age 16 to escape child abuse, poverty, and undesirable living conditions. No more cutting firewood for Kenneth or Johnny Jr.

  My stay with Jean and Charlie did not last long because I got into an argument with Charlie after he hit Aunt Jean, who was pregnant with her son David. I left on the same day of the argument and did not know what to expect in the future. Meanwhile, Aunt Jean gave birth to a son, David Brown. Unfortunately, David died on February 29, 2024, at the youthful age of 51. He drove an eighteen-wheeler and made local trips. On this day, David knew he was having problems and pulled into a parking lot at a gas station in Griffin, Georgia. He suffered a heart attack and died in the driver's seat.

  In the summer of 1972, after leaving Aunt Jean's house, I planned to move to Atlanta to live with relatives. However, the Slaughter family graciously asked me to live with them. It was a great arrangement because their sons Edgar Jr. and Henry played football with me at MPHS. While living in their home, I had no disciplinary problems and completed all my required school assignments. They treated me as family, and I will always be grateful for their wonderful caring when I needed it the most. They also used propane gas for heating. No cutting firewood for heating the home. Hallelujah!

At age 17, after receiving a $600 loan from Aunt Jean. I purchased my second car, a 1967 Plymouth Fury III, which I drove until 1974. It eventually developed a transmission problem and would not engage in reverse. Since I played football and did not have a job, I could not afford the repairs, so I continued to drive it to various locations, including parties and other activities. The ride was exceptionally smooth and operated nicely, except when parking, I needed to park in a spot where I could drive forward only.

On New Year's Eve, December 31, 1973, I attended a party with Edgar, Henry, and Bobby Johnson at the Turning Point Club in Forsyth. Although, by law, I was not allowed to consume alcoholic beverages, I managed to break that rule easily. However, I soon realized that I drank too much of the spirits, so I decided to lie down in my car and rest. I regurgitated once or twice outside the vehicle before getting some sleep. About two hours later, on New Year's Day, I heard several knocks on the window. The guys were finished partying and were ready to go home. By that time, I felt refreshed enough to drive approximately twelve miles home. While it was around two o'clock in the morning, I could handle it. After I had driven over twelve or more miles, we were within three hundred yards of the Slaughter home, our destination, when my eyes closed momentarily, and I continued driving straight ahead as I approached the curved section of the highway. When I realized what happened, I tried to drive and maintain a straight line while keeping the wheels centered over the ditch to prevent rollover. When the car finally came to a stop, we saw no damage except a flat tire. It was on New Year's Day between two and three in the morning. No one was in the mood to change a tire in the dark. Fortunately, a Jeep driver arrived, attached a cable to my car, and pulled it out of the ditch. I drove my car to the Slaughter's residence and dealt with it the next day. Happy

New Year! The lesson learned here is that drinking and driving can kill or cause serious bodily injury to yourself or someone else.

A brief time later, I moved into a mobile home with my aunt Jean near downtown Juliette, on the street now named Hilltop Street. I moved in a complete circle around Juliette.

After graduation, I moved to Atlanta and made plans to join the United States Air Force.

When a white male Air Force recruiter called me to his desk to discuss information on my application, he said, "You can't join the military because you are a member of the NAACP."

In despair, I dropped my head and thought, why did I spend one dollar to join the NAACP, and now I can't join the military because of it? At that moment, a Black recruiter sitting at a desk nearby said, "Are you kidding me, dude? I am a member of the NAACP. It is not a terrorist organization." I immediately thought to myself, thank God the brother was here. I'm sure the same scene had been played throughout America due to ignorance. Later, I would use this story to support the need for diversity at every level involving decision-making, enforcement, and creation of laws and policies.

AIR FORCE BOUND

While waiting for my enlistment date, I worked at the Varsity restaurant on North Avenue, cooking hamburgers for one day only. I could not adjust to the heat in the kitchen. The Varsity, which opened in 1928, is a long-running drive-in chain serving burgers, hotdogs, fries, shakes, onion rings, and other American classics. When it opened, it primarily catered to the students of nearby Georgia Tech. It was a stone's throw from Interstate 75 and one block from Bobby Dodd Football Stadium, home of the Yellow Jackets. When The Varsity first opened, it was called Yellow Jackets; ninety-five years later, it is still open. Some have called it the "world's largest drive-in." The North Avenue location can accommodate hundreds of cars at once. At least four U.S. Presidents, John Kerry, Elvis Presley, Clark Gable, Muhammad Ali, Jimmy Fallon, and others have visited the Varsity. Most customers recognize the famous words: "What'll you have?"

Thankfully, the Air Force contacted me with a departure date of August 18, 1974. No more flipping burgers and no more Varsity work for me. Years later, I occasionally return for a Coke, burger, fries, and a chili dog.

I took my granddaughter to the Varsity restaurant when she was six. I wanted her to experience history. I wanted her to experience the burgers, onion rings, and slaw dogs. I am incredibly proud that I was employed there for one day. The famous actor Nipsey Russell began his entertainment career at The Varsity in the 1940s as a "carhop."

PART TWO

Courtesy of Stars and Stripes Europe

CHAPTER 3

ACTIVE-DUTY MILITARY ADVENTURES

I left Atlanta airport for San Antonio, Texas, on August 18, 1974. It was my first time flying on an airplane. It was Eastern Airlines. Upon arrival at Lackland Air Force Base (AFB) and after exiting the bus, the Training Instructor (TI) immediately approached me and asked, "WHERE THE HELL ARE YOU FROM BOY, HAWAII?" Curiosity got the best of him since I wore white pants and a black and white magnolia-flowered shirt. I had been forewarned of what to expect, so I was prepared for the mind games.

The heat in Texas was very intense in August, but we survived the seven-and-a-half weeks of training. For the first time, I enjoyed three meals per day and several dessert choices, and I could return for seconds. Life was good. I was not concerned about the food on the table; it was plentiful. In basic training, we learned cleanliness and neatness, punctuality, teamwork, diversity of thoughts, ideas, and differences in athletic abilities. We learned to work together as a team to get the job done. We worked together to line the beds straight using a string for alignment and spacing. If one person screwed up, all of us received punishment. We learned to fold clothing and place them neatly in drawers. Our TI would make surprise visits at 4 a.m. We would stand next to our beds and lockers dressed only in a tee shirt and underwear. We called him "Hurricane Dube." If things had not been in order, it would have been like a hurricane had struck our dorm room when he left. He would flip over beds, toss clothing from lockers, and disrupt the entire dorm by cluttering the floor with sheets, bedspreads, and clothing. Next, he would give us five minutes to prepare for another inspection. The game was on. If you could not adjust, you would be removed from training for failing the initial test. At one point, when selected to serve as a squad leader, I learned how to march airmen and perform minor leadership duties.

Towards the end of training, the Air Force sponsored a trip to a Braves versus Astros game at the Houston Astrodome. The Air Force paid for my first attendance at a professional baseball game. We were more than a thousand strong in attendance as the crowd cheered and clapped for us. I felt proud to be an American! That was my first indication that the Air Force differed from other service branches.

In October 1974, I started six months of Missile Systems Specialist training at Lowry AFB in Aurora near Denver, Colorado. The training included inspecting, repairing, adjusting, and replacing components and subcomponents on air-to-air tactical missiles. They trained us to perform preventive maintenance inspections and electrical tests on missiles, missile components, support vehicles, and hydraulic and pneumatic systems. The most challenging part of the training was learning electronics and electrical theories.

While assigned at Lowry, I met several local people and military members. We attended parties at homes and clubs. Although I was eighteen, I was allowed to consume alcoholic beverages while on Lowry property. During training, I was introduced to several mixed alcoholic drinks for the first time, such as Seven and Seven, Sloe Gin Fizz, Tom Collins, and Screwdriver. State law allowed anyone between eighteen and twenty-one to drink a maximum of 3.2 % alcohol off base. I attended my first concert at the Denver Coliseum, at which Graham Central Station and The Ohio Players performed. I visited Red Rock Park Amphitheater and frequented the city park regularly to play football. Tee Austin, from Douglas High School in Memphis, Tennessee, became my friend. He and I were the only two Black people in the class.

On Halloween night, we went to a club in downtown Denver named Yellow Pages. It was penny pitcher night for 3.2 % beer. I filled my pocket with pennies. Tee and I sat in a nice, comfortable booth and watched the activity around us, especially the ladies. This experience was my first time living in a large city other than Atlanta as an 18-year-old adult. When the server came over to serve us, she caught my eye. I was still shy, so I told Tee I was attracted to her. She dressed as a cheerleader, and that outfit with a short skirt caught my attention. Each time she came to the table, I smiled but did not act further. Moments later, Tee told her about my attraction, and we exchanged phone numbers. We did not have cell phones then, so we used payphones to call outside the base or the dormitory phone in the lobby. She was a beautiful young lady about five feet three inches tall. Her name was Renee. Sometime after that, we started communicating; she invited me to her apartment on the West side of Denver, which she shared with two other young ladies about the same age. The first time I visited her apartment on the west side of Denver, her roommates' boyfriends greeted me. They were huge guys, both linemen, who played football for a university in Colorado. In 1975, I sat in an apartment with two huge guys and three beautiful women. I asked myself what had changed in this situation and why I felt so comfortable in that environment. The answer was clear: I was no longer in the South, and no one taught me to hate anyone based on race or skin color. I met with Renee on weekends a couple of times. One day, while walking back to my dormitory, I saw Renee and a guy riding in her car away from my dormitory. I waved at them; it was the last time I contacted her. The guy sure resembles my friend Tee, oh well, he also used that phone number. Winters in Denver can be frigid and harsh. Sometime in October 1974, there was a big snowstorm. However, it did not stop us from venturing off Lowry AFB. An Airman from Lowry, who gave us a tour downtown, informed us he was experienced at driving in snow; minutes later, he was involved in an accident on Colfax Avenue, a main street in downtown Denver. No matter what your experience, you must drive carefully under certain conditions. Since the damage was minor, we continued to our destination, the Playboy Club. It was a wonderful time away from Georgia.

ADVENTURES AT TYNDALL AIR FORCE BASE

After graduating as a Missile Systems Specialist, I reported to the Missile Shop at Tyndall AFB, Florida, in March 1975. Before reporting to Tyndall, I visited Forsyth and Juliette. I met Joan in Forsyth, a senior in high school, and would not see her again until years later. After a few days home, I departed for Tyndall on a Greyhound bus from Macon, Georgia. It was a long ride with several stops, including Tallahassee, Florida. When we arrived at the bus station in Panama City, I hired a taxi to take me to the base. As the taxi left downtown, traveling eastward, we drove through an industrial area. I began smelling something horrible and assumed the taxi driver had committed the worst sin against a passenger. I thought the man had farted. I immediately rolled down the window, and the smell became more robust. "What the heck is that smell?" I asked as I rolled up the window. He started laughing and said, "That's the paper mill."

My assignment lasted until November 1976. I lived in a one-level building behind a water tower near U.S. Highway 98, in a two-person room with a guy named Reese from Quitman, Georgia, a small town near Valdosta. After a brief period, I requested a room change because of his foot odor. I moved to another room with a senior Airman named Sonatas, a New Yorker with Haitian roots. We became friends and often attended parties and other events together. He allowed me to use his car to go to the credit union one day. While there, I had a small fender bender, causing minor damage to his new Pontiac. If you are from New York and have purchased your first car, you may become upset when someone damages it. I gave him three hundred dollars in cash when I returned his car. He did not cause a scene. He was very calm and taught me a lesson. He said, "It's just a car, man." Considering my monthly pay was only about five hundred dollars, it was a huge sacrifice.

To my surprise, I met two Airmen from Forsyth, Sergeant Ronnie Ogletree, and Airman Melvin Shannon. Ronnie was the brother of my MPHS classmate Robert Ogletree. Melvin was one of my 1974 classmates, and we had attended twelve years of school together. After a few months, I moved off base and shared an apartment with Melvin until my reassignment in November.

One of the highlights of my experiences at Tyndall included meeting John Edwards before he became the lead singer for the Spinners. John performed at a club named the Safari Lounge while serving as a backup singer for the Spinners. He became the full-time lead singer after Philippe Wynn left the group in 1977. His biggest hit with the group was probably "Working My Way Back to You." Years later, I would meet him again after the Spinners performed at the Amphitheater in Peachtree City, Georgia. William Wooten, their keyboard player who had roots in Juliette, Georgia, contacted me and informed me they were in Peachtree City for a one-night show. He offered six tickets, which I gladly accepted. After the show, he called me to meet him near the stage, and that is when he introduced me to John Edwards, who lived in Peachtree City and had retired following a stroke.

While assigned at Tyndall AFB, I experienced my first hurricane, Eloise, when it hit the base on September 23, 1975. Before the hurricane arrived, the Air Force ordered us to evacuate. Later that evening, as the winds began to intensify, several guys and I started to drive off base, but the winds were strong, and traffic was not moving. After watching street signs forced to bend at a 45-degree angle by the hurricane winds, we returned to our housing on base to gather food supplies. One guy brought vodka just in case we needed to relax. Next, we drove to the Missile shop to ride out the storm. While in the facility, we roasted hot dogs by candlelight. As daylight approached, I rode a bicycle to our dormitory to pick up more supplies and did not use the pedal once; instead, I used the available wind power. We survived the minimum damage, and life continued.

Another milestone at Tyndall was when my shop manager, a member of the Aero Club, asked me and two other young Airmen to fly with him in a Cessna 182. We boarded the small plane on a beautiful sunny day after watching Senior Master Sergeant Gigli perform a preflight inspection. It was the first time I had ever been that close to a small plane. After boarding, I sat in the co-pilot's seat on the right. As we ascended, the aircraft experienced a crosswind, which caused the plane to lift with its nose slightly to the left as the crosswind blew from the right. Sergeant Gigli explained his responses to the wind and assured us it was normal. After takeoff, we flew around Panama City and Panama City Beach. The scariest part of the flight was when we did a figure eight in flight, and the g-force pressed me against the thin metal door. Soon, I became comfortable in flight, and Sergeant Gigli asked me if I wanted to fly the plane. Well, this was an offer I could not refuse. He explained that I would control the wheel only while he controlled the rudders. That meant I controlled ascending and descending only. As we flew along Panama City Beach, I looked down to enjoy the view and unknowingly slightly pulled the wheel backward. Sergeant Gigli replied, "Son if you don't want one of those jets to knock your ass out of the sky, you better level this aircraft at 700 feet." I responded, and minutes later, he regained control. It was a wonderful experience.

At Tyndall, I also witnessed Black History when General Daniel James became the first and only Black to ever serve as Commander of the North American Air Defense Command (NORAD) and Air Defense Command. He was also the first

Black Four-Star General. Fortunately for me, I served at Tyndall under his umbrella of command. I served as a technician on Air Intercept Missiles (AIM) and AIM-4G and worked at the missile shop near the flight line, where I witnessed aircraft conduct training missions each day. After General James arrived at the installation, we noticed an aircraft parked on the ramp. Later, he held a Commander's Call near an F-106 Fighter Jet bearing his name on the side. It was a proud moment for me and other Black Americans serving at Tyndall.

Lastly, while at Tyndall, I once dated a young lady named Francis Hays. She was tall and beautiful, and as we say in Georgia, "Light brown and Pecan Tan." As I recall, she was a military dependent whose father had been assigned to Tyndall and decided to settle there after retirement. Francis was now a grown woman, around age twenty, living independently, renting a mobile home, and attending Gulf Coast Community College. After several meetings, she invited me for dinner and drinks one night. During that time, popular drinks were Thunderbird, orange juice, and Boones Farm wine (Ernest and Julio Gallo). It turned out to be a great evening. Later, while we were in bed, a guy opened the bedroom door, looked at me, and said, "Hey, what's up Bruh?" I was speechless! He said, "Fran, I need to talk with you." Fran said, "What the F are you doing in my house, Nigger?" Well, I was asking myself the same question. She got out of bed, yelling at the guy, as she moved from the bedroom towards the trailer's entry door. She told him, "Give me my effin key, and don't ever come into my house like that again." At the time, I started thinking that this guy could have another key, or worse, he was jealous of her and could have returned to kill both of us. Fran assured me he would not be a problem. Against my better judgment, she convinced me to stay the night. My decision was partly based on his demeanor.

In November 1976, before my tour of duty ended, I received orders for a new assignment to Royal Air Force (RAF) Base, Lakenheath, England. I drove home to Juliette, visited friends and family, sold my 1972 Nova to Uncle Kenny, then traveled to Virginia to visit a friend, "Tee" Austin, before continuing to McGuire AFB, New Jersey. After completing missile systems training, Tee received an assignment to Langley Air Force Base, Virginia. I decided to visit him before traveling to England. While serving in the Air Guard, at a conference in Reno, NV, I attempted to visit him once more in Citrus Heights, California, where he currently lives, but we could not coordinate our schedules, or maybe he was not receptive to meeting with me because he was the guy riding in the car with Renee. However, the drive from Reno to Citrus Heights was an adventure that included a tour of the Ponderosa, where the iconic TV show Bonanza was filmed, travel through Donner Pass on Interstate 80, and a visit to Lake Tahoe.

ADVENTURES IN ENGLAND

After arriving at McGuire and spending the night, I caught a military flight to RAF Mildenhall, England. When I stepped onto the ground in England, it was my first time in another country. The weather was cold, with overcast skies. RAF Mildenhall's primary mission was air transport, while RAF Lakenheath's mission involved F-4 fighter aircraft. Lakenheath is approximately six miles north of Mildenhall, near Cambridge, England. Bordering cities include Peterborough, Coventry, Leicester, Bury Saint Edmunds, Brandon, Bedford, and Northampton. London is about eighty miles to the southwest. After arrival, I moved into a room on the first floor of a new three-story dormitory across the street from the football field and Lakenheath High School. Outside on the right side of the building was a patio with a seating area and grill. I spent days there when the weather warmed up and enjoyed hanging out with my new friends. This building became my home and a place to socialize for the next seven months. At some point during my stay there, I went to a party and met Elex. We started dating with approval from her mother, a schoolteacher, and father, a Master Sergeant working in the Social Actions Office.

The relationship lasted briefly because the Air Force had different plans for me. However, we remained friends and are friends today. After three months in the country, I received orders to report to a new assignment to the Munitions depot in Germany. When I accepted the assignment to Lakenheath, I did not know a planned aircraft conversion was happening. The conversion involved changing from an F-4 fighter aircraft to a fighter bomber (FB-111). Since the F-111 did not carry missiles, only bombs, I no longer had a job at Lakenheath. One of the employees in the missile shop asked me to trade for a stint in Korea, but I declined and traded for Aviano, Italy.

During the last three months of duty, my jobs changed regularly because my job preparing missiles for shipment was done. We shipped all the tactical missiles to other installations. I worked sentry duty for about thirty days at the gated entry to the munitions complex. Each day, I held an M-16 assault weapon, adequately trained to defend our stored weapons from any attack. Due to my lack of a higher security clearance and the weapons system with the new aircraft assignment, I was reassigned from the "Bomb dump." My latest assignment was driving a forklift for about thirty days in the commissary warehouse. Most of my coworkers had left for another permanent change of station (PCS). I was dating, so I was not rushing to leave England.

In November 1976, after living in England for only a few days, I attended my first United States Air Forces in Europe (USAFE) Championship football game at RAF Bentwaters. It featured RAF Bentwaters against Bitburg Air Base, Germany. The base was located approximately one hundred miles northeast of London and forty-one miles south of Great Yarmouth by the Sea, a city bordering the English Channel. The overcast skies prevented the sun from being visible when the game started. There was a chill in the air, and fog dominated the area. The ground and playing field were soft from all the previous rains. After living in Georgia and seeing red dirt all my life, I lived in Florida, where there is light brown dirt. The dirt in England was different; it was soft, dark, and almost black. As a result, gaining traction on the playing field was challenging. The long cleats were not working well, which made the running game difficult. The result was a defensive battle and a low-scoring game. Bentwaters won the game! While living in the dorm across the street from the football field, I watched Lakenheath's team practice once or twice. Little did I know then that I would play for another team, the Aviano Eagles, in the North Italian Football League (NIFL) from 1977-78.

As I traveled off base in the local community, I noted the different lifestyles practiced by the English. Since they cooked fresh food daily, their refrigerators were smaller because they bought food from the market each day. When I visited a local market, I noticed chickens hanging on hooks with their heads and feet still attached. I was familiar with killing chickens but seeing them hanging on hooks in the open market was odd.

No matter what country you live in, attending parties at age twenty is a regular activity; it was no different for me. During one party in England, I asked for a rum and coke and noticed no ice when the host handed it to me. "May I have some ice, please?" I spoke. He walked me to the door, opened it, and asked me to step outside. He asked, "Do you feel how cold it is outside, mate? Do you still want ice in your drink?" I said, "No." He opened the door and allowed me to re-enter. I understood and only requested ice in my drink or asked for ice again around March 1977, when the temperature warmed. England was the coldest place I had ever lived in my life. If you have ever heard the phrase, "Colder than a Well Digger's butt," you know what I was experiencing in that foreign land.

One of my Lakenheath friends owned a convertible MGB and allowed me to borrow it one weekend in March or April 1977. I drove through the countryside to Great Yarmouth by the Sea, a seaside resort town in Norfolk near the English Channel. It was just another adventure for me, but my experience was an education in cultural differences. I drove around the beach town looking for a club or party atmosphere. What I found were Pubs with the same activity. The girls danced with each other, and the guys played darts and drank beer. I learned to play 301 and 501 on the dartboard and did not dance with the girls.

Growing up in the South, I witnessed incidents of overt racism and prejudice. I did not expect to experience it on a military installation in England. While playing cards with friends in my dormitory room one evening, we noticed a bright light illuminating the window. We looked outside and saw a cross-burning on the football field. We ran outside to find out what was happening. There, in plain view, near the endzone, someone had erected a cross wrapped in cloth and set it on fire to send a message or attempt to intimidate African American airmen. As we watched, the fire department arrived and extinguished the flame. Later, I learned the base investigated the incident, and the investigation identified the perpetrator as a white male who had issues with British White women dating African American or Black airmen. I did not learn what happened in terms of his punishment.

I would later learn there were also incidents of terrorism in Forsyth and Monroe County, Georgia. A football player in high school dated Black and white girls who were attracted to him as a star athlete, or it was his charm. There were some folks with the same attitude as those American Southerners in England who disapproved of interracial dating. The athlete reported finding black cat heads in front of the door at his family's home. On one occasion, someone poured gasoline or some type of accelerant on the ground in the shape of a cross and lit it to send a message to the young athlete that his interracial dating was not accepted in the county.

Today, some people who oppose interracial marriages and dating are okay with it if you agree with their political views, or if you are a famous athlete. I offer the following examples in politics: Republicans, Former Surgeon General Jerome Adams, Former Kentucky Attorney General Daniel Jay

Cameron, Congressman Tim Scott and Byron Donalds, Herschel Walker, and Supreme Court Justice Clarence Thomas; In sports, there is Tiger Woods, Michael Jordan, Charles Barkley, and others. Is it selective racism? How many of these alleged racists would gladly stand in line to get a picture or autograph with these politicians or professional athletes?

In the 1980s, for a romantic evening, a young couple drove to the Lake Juliette picnic area, now a State Park and camping area. Upon arriving in the park, they immediately noticed what they perceived as a cross-burning. Several people gathered around, dressed in white, with temporary popup tents as if they planned to spend the night. The couple quickly reversed and departed the park. They didn't know what was happening, but they did not believe it was a prayer service or baptism.

After the cross-burning incident at Lakenheath, I was selected by the Munitions Maintenance Squadron to appear before the Squadron Board for a promotion to Senior Airman (E-4). I participated in practice sessions and appeared before the board. After anxiously waiting in the lobby for my turn to sit before the board, they finally called my name. I noticed all white enlisted airmen when I walked through the door and sat at the table. Immediately, I felt intimidated and out of place. I sensed something was wrong with this picture, and it was reflected in my demeanor. I was extremely nervous and uncomfortable. Years later, I would fully understand what happened that day. I missed an early promotion because I sat in a room with an all-white board that would decide on my future. What added to the situation was that no one on the board attempted to make me feel comfortable. They did not know I had witnessed a recent cross-burning. The events in England would impact on me for the rest of my military career. It may not have been the makeup of the board solely responsible for my actions that day. It could have been the fact that I had minimal experience with public speaking and low self-esteem from growing up in poverty. It was time for a change. Afterward, I spoke publicly at every opportunity to improve my skills, including enrolling in public speaking classes.

Although I left England in May 1977 for a new assignment in Italy, I caught a space-available (Space-A) flight back to England in June or July to visit my friends. The journey began at the Aviano Flight Terminal. After paying a ten-dollar fee, I waited until my flight arrived without a guarantee that I would be permitted to get on the flight. That is why it is called space available. Fortunately for me, a medical evacuation McDonnell Douglas DC-9 arrived at Aviano with Frankfurt, Germany, as its destination. After landing there, I had to make plans for the next leg of the flight. Wiesbaden, next to Frankfurt, is a military installation with a hospital. Upon arriving there, I checked in for a flight to England, but no direct flight was available, so I signed up to fly the next day to Ramstein Air Base, where my chances would be better of securing a flight to Mildenhall, England. At Wiesbaden, I checked in at military lodging before walking to the Non-Commissioned Officer's Club, commonly called the NCO Club. There, I consumed my first German beer, Hofbrau. After two beers, I felt a little intoxicated and learned my first lesson about drinking German beer. The alcohol content was higher than in the U.S., 6.3 %.

The next day, I flew on a small seven-seat Cessna from Frankfurt to Ramstein with the pilot and three other passengers. On the same day, I got lucky and caught a flight from there to Mildenhall, England on a Navy C-140. It was odd flying with the seats facing the aircraft's rear, but the flight was smooth to my destination. When I arrived in England, I realized my vacation would be short, so I decided to make the best of it. It was time to party and have fun with friends I met there but had only known them since November 1976. After a week of fun in England, it was time for me to return to Italy. I reported to the terminal; it was another lucky day with Space-Available (Space A). I boarded a Lockheed L-1011 Tristar, a military chartered aircraft, and we departed for Aviano, Italy.

Elex and I formed a lasting friendship and continue to maintain it today. After graduating from Alabama A&M University, she joined the U.S. Army and served for four years. After leaving the Army, she returned to Alabama, where her parents moved after her father retired from the Air Force. Her mother continued teaching, and her father took a post-retirement position at Gunter Annex, a USAF installation in Montgomery, Alabama. She became a schoolteacher in Union Springs, AL, and taught kids until she retired. She was married, had two children, and is now divorced. On occasion, when I traveled to Montgomery for work, we would meet for dinner, and I met with her parents a few times before they both departed this earth. Once her parents passed and her kids moved to Texas, she decided to do the same. Now, we continue to communicate and maintain contact through Facebook. She is a wonderful person and a great friend. Before moving to Texas, she and her daughter Mercedes visited me and my wife during an Atlanta Falcons tailgate party near the Georgia Dome.

ADVENTURES IN ITALY

In May 1977, I arrived at Aviano to start a new adventure. Due to flight operations, the Air Force divided the base into two areas, one for flight operations and the other for living in a typical environment, including services, grocery shopping, clubs, dry cleaners, recreation center, gymnasium, cafeteria, Chapel, etc. According to Aviano's history published in 2005 by the Air Force, airfield operations at Aviano Airfield began on January 1, 1956. The original name was Aeroporto Aviano. USAFE operated the airport starting on February 15, 1955. The city of Aviano is located about two miles north of the airfield. In 1977, most military housing quarters for young Airmen were situated near downtown. Like most military installations, it housed the cafeteria, commissary, base exchange, chapel, schools, recreation center, class six store, officers and non-commissioned officer's club, gymnasium, temporary lodging, visitor's quarters, and more. This section of the base was physically located within a couple of miles from the base of the Dolomite Mountain range and in the Friuli-Venezia Giulia region, Pordenone Province. The Piancavallo Ski Resort is part of that municipality.

After settling down in my dormitory, I quickly made friends both at work in the Missile Shop and off work including Robert Nolan, James "J.C." Riley, Darryl Bowman, Tony Holly, and Charles Gentry, to name a few. I enjoyed seeing the beautiful landscape and farmland in the area. It seemed like a small town, but the larger city, Pordenone, was seven miles away. During my off time, I did what an average 21-year-old would do, attend parties and cookouts, hang out, and enjoy life with my new friends. However, my purpose for serving was to supervise a crew to maintain Air Force air-to-air missile systems during the eight-hour days. We were always off duty during weekends until we participated in Operational Readiness Exercises and Inspections (ORE & ORI), when we sometimes worked twelve-hour shifts. I recall my shop supervisor was named Master Sergeant Yelton. He was one of the nicest people I met in the military.

During my second year at Aviano, my friend J.C. and I moved into an apartment near downtown Pordenone. I purchased an old Fiat 1100 family car. J.C., who had a more extended assignment, bought a beautiful red convertible Alfa Romeo. Our apartment was on the second floor near a main highway, with the rear balcony facing north towards the Dolomite Mountains and Aviano. Across the street, in front of our apartment, was an underground supermarket. While living in Italy, I developed a love for jazz music and Bose speakers. I purchased my first Bob James album.

Participating in athletic activities has always been a part of my life. I spent countless hours playing basketball at the base gym, working on my skills while staying in shape and enjoying the fellowship. Again, it was a place to socialize and meet new friends. One basketball player whom I will never forget is Sergeant Swoopes from Decatur, Alabama. He was a talented ballplayer who played on the competitive base team. Although I loved basketball and had a few great moments, my skills could have been better to rise to the level where I could compete with the best players. Nonetheless, I played four to five times per week.

The United States Air Force in Europe (USAFE) formed an American-style semi-professional football league in 1946 to entertain service members and their dependents throughout Europe, with teams in England, Germany, The Netherlands, Greece, Italy, and Spain. The United Kingdom Sports Conference (UKSC) initially consisted of the Alconbury Spartans, Bentwaters Phantoms, Chicksands Fighting Chicks, Fairford Falcons, Greenham Common Pirates, Lakenheath Eagles, Mildenhall Marauders, Upper Heyford Sky Kings, Weathersfield Raiders, High Wycombe Bucks, and Burtonwood Bullets. The first Continental Sports Conference (CSC) consisted of the Berlin Bears, Bitburg Barons, Camp New Amsterdam, Landsberg Tigers, Rhein-Main Rockets, Sembach Tigers, Ramstein Rams, Spangdahlem Sheiks, Wiesbaden Flyers, Hahn Hawks, and Zweibrucken. Later, the league was divided into eight teams in two divisions, each with its unique structure and organization. The Eiffel Division featured Spangdahlem, Rhein-Main, Wiesbaden, and Bitburg, and the Rhine Division included Ramstein, Sembach, Hahn, and Zweibrucken. Aviano had a unique journey in the world of sports. Initially, they formed two teams, the Eagles, and the Red Machine. However, in the early eighties, the Eagles emerged as the sole representative of Aviano and joined the Mediterranean Sports Conference (MSC). The conference was a melting pot of talent, featuring the Aviano Eagles (Italy), Hellenikon Olympians (Greece), Torrejon (Spain), and San Vito Crusaders (Italy). Although competitive, the USAFE Championship, a dramatic and exciting event, was usually decided between the UKSC and the CSC. The league was disbanded due to base closures and the downsizing of European military operations. When the USAFE league ended in 1993, only eight teams remained. Other teams from United States Army Europe and Africa (USAREUR-AF) were from Vicenza, the Blue Knights and 509th Airborne; Camp Darby, near Pisa and Livorno, the Rangers; Bosco Rocks; San Vito, the Crusaders; and Milan, the Milano Rhinos, a team with a roster of mostly Italians.

Little did I know my life would change when I learned the base established two Aviano teams to play semi-professional football in the new North Italian Football League, the Eagles and Red Machine. This was a turning point that would shape my future in sports. During the late spring, we started practicing each day after work. The football field was near the flight line and fire department, surrounded by Quonset huts and hardened aircraft hangers. Corn fields could also be seen on nearby private property outside the military facility.

After tryouts, I earned a spot on offense as a running back, receiver, safety on defense, and kick returner, and served as one of four captains. The players on each team were from diverse backgrounds and experiences, including college, high school, professional, and semi-professional teams. Many players had years of experience playing in USAFE and other military leagues worldwide. Many talented players were among the grown men who participated in the game. This journey not only honed my football skills but also taught me valuable lessons about teamwork, discipline, and perseverance.

In 1977, three years after graduating from MPHS, I returned to the gridiron at age 21. During its inaugural season, I joined the Aviano Eagles. My first game was against the 1st Infantry, 509th Airborne Geronimos. Their leader was multi-talented quarterback Ken Warren, a former basketball star at Idaho State, who passed for two touchdowns to help the Geronimos win 20-7. Before the game started, in front of a crowd of over 2,000 fans, Lt. Col. Richard Murphy and Master Sergeant Sherman Hawkins, both 509th, performed a free-fall to the football field. Hawkins brought in the game ball and landed dead center on the 50-yard line. On September 12, 1977, I rushed for 77 yards in 21 efforts in my first game as an Eagle.

Since we played each team twice during the season, we beat Geronimos 14-7 at our home field in Aviano.

At the end of my first season, as a running back, receiver, and defensive safety, I rushed for 1089 yards, caught passes for 502 yards, and intercepted several passes on defense. During two seasons with the Eagles, I averaged one hundred rushing yards per game and more than 50 receiving yards. In a game against the Vicenza Blue Knights, I ran for one hundred twenty yards, caught passes for 56 yards, and scored three touchdowns. During a game against the Camp Darby Rangers, I rushed for one hundred twenty yards in twelve attempts and caught passes for another one hundred thirty-five yards. In a 1978 game against the Milano Rhinos, I passed for a two-point conversion, assisting the Eagles in their 62-0 win.

My most memorable game was played against the Bosco Rocks. On November 5, 1977, at the end of the third quarter, I had reached three hundred twenty-four total rushing and receiving yards and scored seven touchdowns. Coach Droke decided to take me out of the game at the end of the third quarter so as not to humiliate the Rocks further. It was the best game of my life. In two seasons, I set records that have not been broken today and served as one of the four Eagles Co-Captains during my two years on the team.

Another memorable game was the Aviano Eagles and Red Machine All-Star match against the San Vito Crusaders. San Vito is in the eastern southern part of Italy. When viewed from above, the country is shaped like a woman's three-inch high-heeled boot. I ran the ball a few times and had fun. I also enjoyed traveling to the very heel of the boot. When my teammates Roosevelt or Charles ran the ball, I usually blocked for the run or ran a fake to distract the defense. I struck a defender and lifted him off his feet during one play as he sailed through the air and hit the ground. He got up quickly and looked at me as if he wanted revenge. A few plays later, I ran a fake handoff, and after Roosevelt broke past the line, I started trotting along, watching him run into the secondary. Suddenly, I received a blindside hit, forcing me to the ground; it felt like the force of a giant hammer hitting me. When my head hit the Italian soil, I immediately knew it was the most brutal hit of my life. When I got up, something was wrong. Plays later, I received a handoff and ran to the right, then down the field for about forty yards. The problem was I did not know why I was running. Well, it happened in one of the games. Players on the sideline yelled, "Keep running, keep running." I continued running until a player hit me from behind. When I walked off the field, the coaches knew something was wrong. "How many fingers do you see?" One coach asked. "My head is hurting, I don't know," I answered.

My friend Darryl Bowman was born and raised in Ohio. He played defensive end on the Eagles team. Standing about six feet five inches tall, Darryl served as one of the Eagle's defensive captains and was a defensive standout. Later, Darryl and another Ohioan, Dennis, asked me to join them on a ski trip to Piancavallo. It was a small ski resort a short distance north of the housing section of the base. We could look out our dorm window and see the snow-capped mountains and the winding road leading to the resort. Since I considered myself an athlete and lover of adventure, I accepted the offer.

I purchased ski bibs, gloves, thick socks, and a warm hat and joined Darryl, Dennis, and Darryl's Italian girlfriend. My ski adventure began after arriving at the resort and getting fitted for rental skis, boots, and poles. They accompanied me to the beginner slopes and gave me a few pointers as I attempted to learn the snowplow technique. After several lessons, they left me to practice while they caught the lift to go to the mountain top. Periodically, after several runs, they would stop to check on me. I told them I was starting to get the hang of it, but it was a slow learning process.

After lunch, I decided I had become a skier and was ready to tackle the big mountain. Minutes later, I realized I needed more time to be ready to ski with the experienced guys. I took the lift to the top of the mountain, and as I exited and my skis touched the ground, I lost control and went headfirst into the snow and up to my chest. The one thing I had yet to practice was exiting the lift. After regaining my composure and skis, I continued skiing the flat surface toward what I thought would be a smooth trail. My trail appeared narrow and led to a broader trail ahead of me. Before I could reach that point, a cloud rolled in, and I could not see more than three to four feet in front of me. After waiting in place for a few minutes, I continued towards the wide trail. When I got there, it turned out to be a mogul field. Fear took over, and I stood on the trail side and watched other people pass until I mustered enough courage to continue. I skied around them rather than ski over the moguls until I cleared the "mound field." When I reached the smooth surface of the trail, I continued to fall periodically but fell downhill closer to my destination. For most skiers, each trip would typically take ten to fifteen minutes to the bottom of the trail. My first trip took about an hour. At one point, I fell, and an Italian kid, "knee-high to a duck," skied near me, turned his skis to the side as he ended, and sprayed my body with snow as I lay there resting. The action inspired me to learn at a much faster pace. I swore I would conquer the mountain one day. On reflection, I should have taken ski lessons. Years later, I returned to Piancavallo and conquered that mountain as a black diamond-level skier.

In early 1978 I was riding in VW with my friend J.C. Riley when we spotted two Italian ladies walking near Aviano Air Base. We stopped and I starting talking with Paola, while JC conversed with Roberta. We invited them to the NCO Club for beverages. That is when I learned more about her that drew my interest. I learned she had recently divorced and returned to Italy from the United States. Spoke English very well, so it was easy for us to communicate. When we stopped them near Area 1, they were headed to the base area to purchase milk for Paola's three-month-old son from her previous marriage. She was also mother of a five-year-old daughter, Jessica. It was the beginning of a relationship that lasted until I left Italy in 1978. Afterwards, we became friends and remain friends today.

While in Italy I grew fonder of Italian culture. Wine (vino) and pasta became part of my regular diet. I met her mother and sisters and found them to be wonderful people.

One of the most romantic evenings with Paola was a drive up the mountain road towards Piancavallo. We stopped at a secluded clearing on the mountain to view the valley below. It was one of the most beautiful sights. The moon was shining brightly, while the lights in the homes and businesses were il-luminated with a 180-degree view of the valley below. Bats were flying around above us, and that only added to what had already been a beautiful night. We also spent time at Lignano Beach, about a one-hour drive from Aviano. We ate at several local restaurants and enjoyed our time in Pordenone. I treated her kids as if they were my own. Today, after forty-four years, Jessica and Lamont are married and became parents. We are all still friends and continue to communi-cate through WhatsApp and Facebook. Paola married a third time to an airman who worked in the Security Forces at Aviano. In the 1990s, she and her husband visited our Stone Mountain, Georgia home.

As my tour of Italy was ending in November 1978, the football season continued. Knowing I would be leaving the country at the end of the season, I continued to participate and enjoy the games. When the last regular season game ended, we had one more game on the schedule, a postseason game against a USAFE team from Germany. Although I wanted to play, Paola convinced me she wanted us to spend our last day at Avi-ano together. Since I was scheduled to fly out the next day, I gave in and missed playing in the last Aviano Eagles game of 1978. However, I convinced her to watch the game with me. The Eagles won the game.

BEMISS TRAILER PARK AND MOODY AFB, GEORGIA

In December 1978, I arrived at Moody Air Force Base in Valdosta, Georgia, where I would spend the next six months of my final days in active-duty Air Force. I was reassigned to work at the Missile Shop on the Southeastern side of the installation, affectionately called "the bomb dump." I quickly made friends, most of whom were white. Only a few Black people worked on bombs and missiles, especially missile systems. We watched episodes of Mork and Mindy with friends. Robin Williams was the lead actor. Later, I became more comfortable with traveling out into the local area, and my life turned in a different direction. I moved off base and rented a mobile home I shared with an airman who worked in the fuel shop. Next door was another Airman from New York, who bought his first car. He acted as if the vehicle was his everything, including his toy. This kid was in love with that car. It was one of the strangest things I had ever seen. He washed and cleaned it each day and waxed it every other day.

Due to the military rotation of assignments, guys received orders regularly. As a result, one could always find items for sale, including cars. I realized I would be leaving the Air Force in June 1979, so I purchased a 1975 Cutlass Supreme from a Sergeant who had received orders. The car was baby blue with a white Landau roof, blue rims, and white-lettered Goodyear tires. It was the newest car I had ever owned, and I enjoyed driving it. Now that I had wheels, it was time for the adventures to begin.

Once I learned about the party spots, it was time to ride. I recall a club called Twin Oaks in the unincorporated area of Valdosta. It was a beautiful place to dance, consume beverages, meet girls, and have fun. However, much of my weekend was spent playing basketball in the gym. That is genuinely what athletes on military installations do to avoid mischief.

There, in 1979, I met a ball player named Gregory. When we played basketball together, we were only regular guys playing a sport we love, and no one knew our rank or military status on the installation. Years later, I would see Greg again at Publix in Stone Mountain, GA, around 1992. That is when I learned he retired as a Chief Master Sergeant. Greg told me his position was Chief of Maintenance in Thailand when a Monsoon rain happened. At the time, there was no warning, and they grounded the entire fleet of aircraft because all the F-4 aircraft canopies were left open, flooding each aircraft on the flight line. As a result of the tremendous pressure and stress on him, he had a heart attack. After thirteen years, it was indeed a surprise to see him again. I was even more surprised when I saw his daughter standing with him. It immediately reminded me that years had passed, and we were getting older. My daughters were aged two and six at the time. Greg and I have met periodically since 2019 after I moved 60 miles south of Metro Atlanta.

Although I knew I would be honorably discharged in June 1979, I received a temporary duty assignment to Howard Air Force Base, Panama, for eight days. I immediately felt the warm climate when we arrived on a C-130 cargo plane. Soon, however, I would enjoy myself more than I could imagine. We stayed at base lodging for the entire eight days of duty. During the first evening at the club, I noticed the number of women lined up for escort onto the installation. Howard AFB had three different clubs, and local women would line up outside the base waiting for an airman or soldier to sign them in to access the clubs. Seeing such beautiful Black and mixed multi-racial Hispanic women was new to me and exciting. Inside the clubs, it was electric. The DJ was pumping up the music, and there was no shortage of women to dance with. I thought, "Damn, maybe I should reenlist. I like it here."

After eight days of fun in Panama, I returned to Valdosta and my rental home at Bemiss Trailer Park. Reality set in, and I soon realized I was about to leave the Air Force. It was a bittersweet moment, filled with excitement for the new chapter in the Georgia Air National Guard (ANG) and nostalgia for my experiences in the United States Air Force (USAF). About one month earlier, I met with an ANG recruiter who suggested I join the ANG. He found a slot for me at Dobbins Air Reserve Base (DARB), Marietta, Georgia. It was a great idea, and I signed up. The USAF honorably discharged me from active duty on June 18, and I reported for duty in the ANG on June 21, 1979.

On my final day of duty at the missile shop, my co-workers organized a special luncheon in my honor. Little did I know they had something else planned, something I needed to prepare for. They explained that as part of the 'Bomb dump tradition,' they were going to throw me into the nearby pond. 'Not today!' I protested. At that moment, my co-workers began to encircle me. My Warthog vision and speed kicked in, and I turned on my Turbo engine V12. I ran so fast that no one could catch me. Eventually, they gave up, realizing it was too much trouble to dunk me in the pond. It was a moment that truly highlighted the camaraderie and sense of belonging we shared at the missile shop.

In 2017, I would meet with Fred McPhee again. He is seated next to me, wearing the hat at the San Vito NCO Club. Fred was a linebacker for the Aviano Red Machine; Fred currently lives in the Boston metropolitan area. When the Patriots played the Falcons, we waged a bet. Whoever team won would have to pay for dinner in either Boston or Atlanta, depending on the winner. Since my team lost, I flew to Boston and met with Fred for a reunion after not seeing him since 1978. We traveled to Paradise Cove, Maine, for Lobster and Lobster Bisque. My debt was paid.

CHAPTER 4

AIR FORCE DISCHARGE AND RETURN TO ATLANTA

On June 18, 1979, I moved to an apartment complex with a relative in Atlanta near Sylvan Road and Lakewood Freeway, close to East Point. I planned to change my life's direction during the next few months. Since I had trained in electronics, that was the direction I would choose, so I used my GI Bill to enroll in Elkins Institute to prepare for a job repairing electrical equipment in hospitals. I was disappointed when Elkins informed me the next class was entirely unavailable. They offered to enroll me in a class to earn my FCC license while waiting for an opening. There was a class to prepare for the exam. I completed the class, qualified for the second-class permit, and failed the test for the First Class. I soon realized my goals had changed, and I no longer wanted to pursue that profession. At that point, I needed a job while awaiting a decision. I started working at Wells Fargo Security Services and was assigned to the National Bank of Georgia (NBG) and Trust Company Bank in downtown Atlanta near Five Points. While working at the NBG, I met Michael Carr, a Private Investigator, and Attorney George Kennedy McLeod, who co-owned the McLeod Corporation. They offered me the opportunity to become a Private Investigator/Subcontractor. I attended and completed a six-week Private Investigator's course at Atlanta Area Technical School. Upon graduation, I continued working both jobs until 1981, when I decided to enroll in the Criminal Justice Associate Degree Program at Atlanta Junior College, now Atlanta Metropolitan College.

SERVING PAPERS FOR COMEDIAN/ACTOR RICHARD PRYOR

One of my contract assignments from the McLeod Corporation was to serve a court document to Don Frank. He lived in a home near Cascade Road, Atlanta, Georgia, considered a Black upper-middle-class section during the 1980s. I had previously served court papers, but these documents were different. As I began to read it, I thought, this is incredible. Could this be the comedian who has entertained me for many years? Could this be the guy who made people laugh while he performed on stage and in movies? Yes, it was Richard Pryor. Don Frank served as Richard Pryor's Agent and Manager for about ten years. According to Fulton County court records, Frank diverted more than $215,000 from Columbia Pictures for the movie "Stir Crazy" and $800,000 from Warner Brothers Records.

I arrived at Frank's home around 7:00 a.m. After knocking on the door, his wife answered and opened the door, wearing a white robe. She appeared to have just gotten out of bed to open the door about three to five inches. I informed her I was there to serve papers to Mr. Frank. She opened the door wider and yelled his name, "Don, someone here with papers for you." Seconds later, Don appeared wearing a dark robe. "Are you Don Frank?' I asked. "Yes, I am," he answered. "Consider yourself officially served in the matter concerning Richard Pryor in Fulton County court." "Thank you and have a good day." Don and Sheryl divorced in 1986.

TRAUMATIZED BY THE TIMING

While attending private investigation school at Atlanta Area Technical School, I met a beautiful young lady about my age. We talked, enjoyed each other's company, and occasionally went out for dinner and beverages. One day, after saving a few dollars, I invited her to Panama City Beach for the weekend. I was familiar with the city and thought she would enjoy time away from the classroom training that would soon end. After picking her up at her place, we departed for the beach in my baby blue Cutlass Supreme with the white Landau roof. When we arrived at Panama City Beach and settled in our hotel room, we headed directly to the beach to enjoy the sun and water. She was about five feet six inches tall and weighed about one hundred twenty-five pounds. Her skin was a light almond color. Whenever I see actor Eva Marcelle, I remember my former friend, a younger woman, and that weekend adventure in Panama City Beach. In preparation for our trip to the beach, she braided her hair, which flowed down her back about five inches past her shoulders. We rented chairs and an umbrella to avoid the sun. However, to my surprise, she pulled her chair from under the umbrella and started applying a mixture of baby oil and suntan lotion. After a couple of hours, her skin looked bronzed and very sexy. I began to think about what would happen later that evening. After leaving the beach, we got dressed for dinner and went out to eat. She wore a beautiful sundress, exposing her bronze skin. We enjoyed the beach and dinner; now it was time for a reward, at least, that is what I had planned.

When we returned to our hotel room, I started to make a move. My weekend date told me the schedule did not work out for the weekend, and we could not become intimate. "What do you mean? I spent all this money for us to enjoy a great weekend in Panama City Beach, and you say it is not working out?" "Sorry, but I had no control over Mother Nature; it just happened," she said. I was so disappointed and had a tough time accepting her answer. "What exactly are you telling me?" I asked. "It's that time of the month," she said. For whatever reason, I needed evidence. "How do I know you are not trying just to use me for a vacation getaway?" I jokingly asked. "Oh, you don't believe me," she said, "I will show you. "No, I trust you, it's just bad timing. I was in my mid-twenties, and on that day, I received an education about the menstrual cycle phases. I remember the "string." She went to the restroom and showed me unused tampons with a string. Then she explained how it works. We remained friends for a while, then went in different directions in life as we communicated less. Cell phones, social media, and cable TV were unavailable in 1980.

In 1980, I moved from Sylvan Road to Stone Hogan Connector near Greenbriar Mall and rented an apartment I shared with Larry Bowden, with whom I attended elementary and high school. Years later, while Larry worked in Centennial Park during the 1996 Olympic Games, he was injured by shrapnel when a bomb exploded. The shrapnel caused permanent facial nerve damage.

Life was busy between school, work, and play. Campbellton Road became my playground. I frequented clubs named Mr. V's, Cisco's, and Marco's. Since I had no income to live a party lifestyle, I stayed home most of the time, except while playing basketball at the local parks and gyms.

While working for Wells Fargo, they assigned me to work security at Ellman's Jewelry Store on Candler Road near Interstate 20. A gorgeous young lady named Eleanor worked there as a sales associate. Soon, we could not stop talking and grew fonder of each other. Finally, we started dating. She moved into a new apartment on Bouldercrest Road after graduating from Georgia State University while pursuing a career in Education. She must have liked me because she took me to meet her father in Walton County, near Monroe, Georgia. Later, I met her brother and sisters. Our relationship did not last long because I was busy trying to find myself in life and increase my paycheck. I had little to offer her, so we severed the relationship. Years later, I contacted her while she lived in Hawaii, and we became friends again. She had divorced and was moving back to Georgia. Eleanor is happily married to a retired NFL player.
Interestingly, I later learned she and Joan Ferguson Whitehead were at Georgia State University and were in the same Delta Sigma Theta initiation line. Joan was #7, and Eleanor was #8 when they crossed over in the spring of 1978. Other sisters included Sheila #1, Vanessa #2, Rosalind #3, Cynthia #4, Joan #5, Shirley #6, and Tyna #9. Later, in 2022, while dating Joan, I would meet Sheila and Tyna with Joan at a restaurant on Main

Street in College Park, Georgia. Joan and I arrived early and stood outside waiting for the others. Sheila arrived first; we exchanged hugs and kisses, then went inside and secured a table while waiting for Tyna. Fraternity and Sorority members often form lifelong bonds and friendships after undergoing rigorous initiations, like military boot camp.

Some of them may experience hazing to some degree. When Tyna arrived, we all hugged again. They chatted about old times and current life. It turned out to be a great lunch. For me, it became a window into the past of who Joan hung out with in college. Tyna's sweatpants fell as we stood and prepared to leave the restaurant. She assumed I was looking, but I was not. She politely said, "Percy got a free peek at the goodies." Truthfully, I was not looking, but I saw the pants fall and watched Sheila and Joan quickly go into action to help pull up her pants. "It was nice lunch, ladies," I said as we departed for our trip back to Forsyth. Joan and I laughed about it later, and Joan felt a little embarrassed for Tyna.

THE TRANSITION: AIR FORCE TO AIR GUARD

In 1979, I left the active-duty military at Moody AFB, Georgia, and reported for duty on June 21, 1979, at the Missile Shop, Munitions Maintenance, 116th Fighter Wing, Dobbins ARB, Marietta, Georgia. When I entered the missile shop as the first Black person to serve there, I thought I was stepping back in time. The aircraft assigned to the 116th was the F-105 Wild Weasel, produced between 1955 and 1964. It could carry up to 14,000 pounds of missiles and bombs. There were none issued to active-duty units. One of the weapon systems for that aircraft included the air-to-ground (AGM)-45 missile. Guard life was quite different from what I had experienced on active duty. Guardsmen were relaxed but accomplished the Mission when evaluated, usually through operational readiness exercises and inspections. Some Airmen wore wigs so as not to cut their hair.

Sometimes, when I reported for work on a Saturday morning, after roll call or formation, guys would perform their work and then enter a laid-back state of mind, listening to NASCAR races on the radio in their vehicles, reading the newspaper, etc. The missile shop was different; we tested inert missile systems to maintain proficiency and studied during our spare time. All shop members always prepared for the next level by completing required courses such as non-commissioned officer training, driver safety, weapons, chemical warfare, professional development, and leadership training. Despite many "old school" behaviors and "good ole boys" in the unit, they always performed well when evaluated or tested.

The Georgia Air National Guard (GA ANG) has a great history of being ready when called for a higher mission. The unit operated as a Fighter Wing from 1979-1982, flying the F105G Wild Weasel; F-4D Phantom from 1982-1986, and F-15A Eagle from 1986-1996. The unit relocated from Dobbins Air Reserve Base (ARB) to Robins AFB and converted to a bomber mission from 1996 to 2002, flying the B-1B Lancer. In 2002, the unit's Mission changed to reconnaissance that flew the E-8C Joint STARS.

The 116th started flying the F-4D in 1983 and continued until 1986. Behaviors and customs often change during each aircraft conversion. When the unit converted to the F-4 Phantom aircraft, I noticed significant changes, and the unit became more professional. In August 1985, the unit participated in Coronet Meteor at Spangdahlem AB, Germany. It was the first time two ANG units from different states became one unit: the 116th and the 187th TFW from Dannelly Field, Montgomery, AL. We were assigned lodging in downtown Trier, in southwestern Germany, in the Moselle Wine Region. The city had evidence of prior Roman occupation, such as Roman Baths, bridges, and a theater. It is also the birthplace of Karl Marx. While there, after attending a Winefest, I became ill with the flu. I woke up one morning drenched in sweat, and my bed sheets were wet. I asked one of my coworkers to notify my leadership team I was sick. Since the room needed cleaning, I got out of bed and walked down to the Moselle River to allow the hotel staff to clean the room. After returning, someone came to my room and told me everyone had been looking for me and that I should report to "Sick Call" immediately. After getting dressed, I caught the next shuttle bus to Spangdahlem. The doctor gave me a couple of red pills, Sudafed. Within hours, I was feeling much better.

After recovery, I started enjoying the wine again. Mosel Rieslings wines are some of the finest whites in the world. Light and low in alcohol, they can be intensely fragrant and have an outstanding balance of sweetness and acidity. The Mosel River has a beautiful valley landscape adorned with steeply sloped grape vineyards on both sides. It was some of the most picturesque scenery I've experienced. I am looking forward to a return trip to another Winefest and Germany's Oktoberfest for some of the best beer in the world.

When the weekend arrived, we were given time off. Several guys from the shop decided to drive to Amsterdam for the weekend. I joined the group and departed in a French Renault rental car. We traveled through Luxemburg, then onto Bastogne, Belgium, where we stopped for lunch, followed by a tour of the local military museum. Luxemburg is a beautiful country with cleared open fields, vineyards, and breathtaking scenery. In Bastogne, we viewed the U.S. army tank on display in the center of town alongside a bust of General McAuliffe, acting Commander of the 101st Airborne Division, who is credited with saving the city. The town features a museum filled with articles about war, including uniforms, weapons, ammunition, supplies, and other equipment—a real treasure of history.

CHANGES IN THE GEORGIA AIR NATIONAL GUARD

I recall when Technical Sergeant Odom became Captain Odom. Before his promotion from Enlisted to Officer rank, Sergeant Odom experienced the same subtle discrimination as other Black people in the unit. In 2023, on the Fourth of July, I met Lieutenant Colonel Odom, Air Force Reserve, Retired, at a party in Macon, Georgia. He revealed to me the institutional and overt racism he experienced in the 116th Fighter Wing. Although a general officer recommended that he apply for Officer Training School, forces were working against him in the unit. The 116th Unit personnel office told him several times there were no slots available. He persisted with the help of that same general officer, who demanded all information about available slots and a follow-up on the status of Odom's application.

In many cases, Black people would not have received promotions if there were not people in positions who sought fairness and equal opportunity for all. Sergeant Odom held a bachelor's degree and was more qualified than others in the unit. Although Captain Odom became the first Black Officer in the unit, he also became the target of conversation among unit members. Some people felt he was promoted because he was a light-skinned Black male.

I worked strictly on Missile systems until 1982 when the missile and bomb fields merged into the Munitions Systems Specialist and Technician. Duties included testing, assembly, and processing non-nuclear munitions for loading on aircraft, checking safe and arming mechanisms, installing warheads, guidance units, fuses, arming wires, explosive bolts, squibs, strakes, wings, fins, control surfaces, and tracking flares. During the 1980s, I became the safety guy, moving to a new position as the Munitions Safety Inspector. My responsibilities included ensuring airmen followed technical orders to conduct day-to-day operations, particularly inspection of stock samples, updating technical data in orders, inspecting transportation equipment and delivery operations safely, and monitoring records. Safety was the number one concern in every operation. This assignment was with the F-4 Mission, and once selected, I moved from the munition storage area to an office in the large hangar. This position allowed me more exposure to all types of operations surrounding the aircraft.

In 1991, twelve F-15s departed Dobbins through Torrejon AB, Spain, for Balikesir, Turkey. As a support team member, I was one of the 260 Airmen who departed Dobbins on a chartered flight to Balikesir with a stopover in Shannon, Ireland. I recall the airport bar had to restock after our departure. For the next fifteen days, we lived in tents on a Turkish Air Base in a makeshift community called "tent city." This deployment differed from the others regarding visiting historical sights and enjoying time in the local community. On one tour over the middle of the weekend, we traveled to the biblical city of Ephesus, which is an ancient city southwest of present-day Selcuk, Izmir Province, Turkey. The sites in Ephesus included the Temple of Artemis, the Library of Celsus, and major bath complexes. Between 53 and 57 AD (Anno Domini), Paul wrote 1 Corinthians from Ephesus, from the "Paul Tower" near the harbor, where they imprisoned him. Later, he wrote the Epistle to the Ephesians while imprisoned in Rome (around 62 AD).

The bathhouse in Ephesus was a remarkable sight, exhibiting the remains of an indoor toilet system. As I examined the structure, I couldn't help but notice the evenly spaced concrete toilet seat holes, each about two feet (.61 meters) apart. Beneath these seats, a trench drain was visible, allowing a continuous water flow to cleanse the toilets. This feature, I realized, was a testament to the sophistication of historical sanitation, far surpassing the outdoor toilet I was familiar with in rural Juliette, Georgia.

While on a walking tour of downtown Balikesir, we decided to go to a bar and drink beer. There were female Airmen in the group. As we walked into the bar, you could hear a pin drop. We did not know it at the time, but women were not allowed in bars. The women left after learning the new rules of the local culture. Before entering the bar, I noticed a young kid between 10 and 12 following us as we walked down the street. I told the guys what was happening: a pickpocket was targeting us. On the count of two, we all turned and reached out to grab and scare the "young thief." He ran for his life.

The Air Force and ANG are much different from other service branches, and I received a lesson while in Turkey. During the 1990s, the Air Force permanently stationed personnel at Balikesir, Turkey. As a result, they enjoyed many of the conveniences, such as a gymnasium with a weight room and basketball court. One day, three Black Airmen, Leo Jackson, Bo, and I, went to the gym for the first time to play basketball and lift weights. We were in the gym for about five minutes before our First Sergeant, Chief Master Sergeant Baylor, arrived and accused us of trashing the place. He ordered us to leave immediately and banned us from using the gym for the remainder of the 15-day assignment. We climbed in the back of the pickup truck before he drove us back to tent city. We were angry and felt the immediate effects of discrimination in the military. Later, we learned that one or more of the white male pilots were the culprits of "trashing" the gym. The young white male Lieutenant blamed us. It was another chapter on white privilege and racism. In 1994, Chief Baylor became State Command Chief for Georgia, and I became the First Sergeant of the Aircraft Maintenance Squadron (AMS). He had served as 116th Wing First Sergeant before his new assignment.

Before my selection as First Sergeant of AMS, the Guard divided the 116th Wing from a 500-member Unit into two groups, the Aircraft Generation Squadron (AGS) and the Aircraft Maintenance Squadron (AMS). Since the number of members decreased, the rank of CMS First Sergeant (E-9) changed to a Master Sergeant First Sergeant position (E-7) for each squadron. I was a technical sergeant and a traditional guardsman, so it was an excellent opportunity to get a promotion and contribute to the unit's Mission. As E-7, I served as First Sergeant of the 116th Tactical Fighter Wing and 116th Bomb Wing; supervised a staff of five one weekend per month (Fri-Sun) during military duty; served as Assistant Military Venue Officer while working at the Georgia Dome during the 1996 Olympics; managed the second shift from 2:00 p.m. to 10:00 p.m. for 45 days, and served as a leader for both Army and Air National Guard personnel from different units throughout the United States. When I accepted the position in November 1994, I attended the USAF First Sergeant's Academy for about thirty days at Maxwell AFB, Montgomery, AL. While there, I met with my former girlfriend, Elex, who was a schoolteacher in Union Springs, AL, her mother, a retired teacher, and her father, who participated in the investigation of the "Crossburning" at RAF Lakenheath, had retired from the Air Force and was working at Gunter military installation as a civilian.

After completing First Sergeant's Academy training, I drove back from Montgomery, Alabama, to Stone Mountain, Georgia. As I recall, the Thanksgiving holiday was just a few days away. I drove from Interstate 85 to Interstate 285. While driving in the center lane on I-285, traveling between 55 and 65 miles per hour, I had just passed underneath the bridge at Candler Road when I saw a fast-moving old model Cadillac traveling southbound in the left northbound lane. I immediately moved over to the far-right lane and continued traveling north toward home, thinking I would hear about a deadly crash on the news when I arrived home. Fortunately, I did not hear of such an incident. It was a miracle no one was hurt or killed that day.

During the next three years, I served as the first Black First Sergeant in the history of the 116th Maintenance Squadron. During my tour of duty, I went on a temporary duty assignment (TDY) for one week to Green Flag exercises at Nellis AFB, Las Vegas, Nevada. While there, I dealt with some of my first challenges as First Sergeant. Nellis has many visitors, including high-ranking General Officers. While the flight line is a no-hat area, one must wear a hat after crossing the designated lines. As I walked around checking on the welfare of my airmen, I noticed one airman from my unit wearing a Braves baseball cap while in uniform. I became infuriated. My first thought was, "That damn guardsman has lost his effin mind." I walked over to him and snatched the cap from his head. I should have maintained my cool, but I felt a personal attack against my position. He complained to his union representative, Phil Holloway, a Senior Master Sergeant. Since the airman was on orders then, union activity was not my concern. I told Holloway he needed to act his part as a military supervisor and not as a union representative.

In 1997, I was appointed Human Resource Advisor (HRA) for the 116th Bomb Wing and became the first person to occupy the position in the unit's history. The position also included a promotion to E-8. In 2000, I was promoted to E-9, becoming the first Black 116th Traditional Guard Chief. I was appointed to the same position at GA ANG State Headquarters and served there until my retirement in 2006. My job involved advising the Commander on issues to enhance the organization's culture while promoting opportunities for all ANG members to maximize their potential for success to meet mission requirements without regard to cultural differences. I also served as GA ANG Mentoring Program Manager, providing guidance and direction to the two Human Resources Advisors at the Wings. Moreover, I was a facilitator in Diversity Education classes for Army and Air National Guard Personnel, served on the Senior NCO Enlisted Promotion Board for five years, and was a member of the State ANG Human Resources Advisory Board.

While assigned as HRA at Robins AFB, I worked directly for Colonel Tom Lynn, Commander of the 116th Fighter/Bomb Wing/Air Control Wing. Lynn was Commander of the 116th Fighter Wing before the transition to bombers in 1996. He led the Wing's move from Dobbins to Robins and was later promoted to Brigadier General.

When the 116th Bomb Wing moved to Robins Air Force Base, we followed the same tradition as all Air Force Bombers. The Wing leadership painted unique nose art on each aircraft to boost morale. Part of my role as HRA was to identify potential barriers that would negatively impact morale. I usually worked one weekend per month, a half day or full day on Friday, and completed my monthly training by Sunday afternoon. On Friday, I attended a meeting with several Black full-time Technicians. It allowed them to discuss any problems or improvements needed for our overall growth and commitment to diversity. Although they wore military uniforms as civilians during the weekdays, they became true Guardsmen Saturday through Sunday. As technicians, they were under the Wage

Grade (WG), Trade Jobs, and Federal Government Jobs for Occupational Groups. Therefore, members were authorized to participate in union activity.

I opened the meeting by introducing myself and the purpose of the meeting. I also noticed the union representative present. Initially, no one would speak up, so I introduced the icebreaker. Before the meeting, several unit members had spoken about their discontent with the Georgia State Flag, which included the Confederate Battle Flag painted as nose art on one of our B-1 Bombers. Some expressed they were offended by it. Little did I know the opening would cause an uproar throughout Georgia. Some employees had no opinion one way or another. However, most agreed that it was improper for the Confederate Flag of a country defeated by the United States to appear on a United States-owned aircraft. Moreover, the sentiment throughout the state supported changing the State Flag. Some perceived the move as a protest to change, thus adding politics to our Air Force Mission. After the initial shocker, when several people spoke on the flag issue, members started sharing various forms of mistreatment and subtle discrimination practices.

The next day, the State Human Resources Advisor, Chief Master Sergeant Watson Fluellen, called and said, "Percy, you set off a storm," as he chuckled. I told him it was just an unintended consequence of people telling others how they felt without filing a formal complaint. Coincidentally, the person who came up with the idea of placing the Georgia flag nose art on the aircraft was the same person who complained because a Black pilot overlooked his own White crew chief and selected a Black Crew Chief to accompany him for a Tuskegee Airman display at Moton Field, Tuskegee, Alabama during Black History Month. Several members felt the White crew chief was insensitive to the unit's needs and diversity efforts. After the dust settled, I met with senior leadership, including my Commander, who informed us of the Georgia Flag nose art update. The unit scheduled repainting of the nose art when the aircraft flew to the depot for regularly scheduled maintenance.

There, depot maintenance would replace the flag with another nose art.

While flying F-15 aircraft missions, my unit planned a TDY to Singapore. As in most cases, the planning takes place months in advance. The planners were full-time personnel, not weekend warriors like me. Although I served as First Sergeant of the maintenance Squadron, sometimes I was kept in the dark about things that happened during weekdays when I was not around. When I learned about the TDY to Singapore, I was shocked that my Commander had selected a white female master sergeant from his staff to serve as First Sergeant during the trip. His decision disappointed me, but I did not see it as a race issue. What bothered me was that he should have consulted me before deciding on someone to serve in my position and represent our unit. Over the years, I learned that full-time employees treated weekend warriors differently. Leadership made many decisions during the weekday involving traditional guardsmen, including preferential treatment, temporary duty assignments, employment, training opportunities, etc.

The guys who worked together each day of the week would look out for each other and "scratch each other's back." That is not necessarily racist. What is racist is when you deny other people, based on their race, the chance to serve in one of the positions where they can offer opportunities to the ones who are left out. Everyone wants to be one of the "good ole boys".

Despite the behind-the-scenes history of the 116th Fighter/Bomber and Air Control Wings, the unit, with its diverse members, has succeeded. The unit's history includes 23 Air Force Outstanding Unit Awards (AFOSUA) from 1974-2023. Black people first joined the Wing as full-time Technicians between 1974 and 79 with the arrival of F-100s. During my tour of duty from 1979-2003, we received eight AFOSUAs. In 1998, I was given the honor to read the Award as the Entire Wing, their families, General Officers from Georgia, the National Guard Bureau, and representatives from US Congress joined me on the temporary stage, a moment that will forever be etched in my memory. I am proud to have served with some outstanding individuals.

DIVERSITY IS GOD'S IDEA

As Paul preached to the Athenian philosopher, "From one man God made every nation of the human race, that they should inhabit the whole earth" (Acts 17.26)

Why do companies, including federal, state, local governments and universities embrace Diversity Equity and Inclusion (DEI)? Since 2014, America has started a culture change, partly due to one political party's leadership that trickled-down to companies and government agencies. Before 2015, organizations, including the military, used DEI to promote and ensure fair treatment and full participation for all people, especially those who have historically faced discrimination or underrepresentation. Companies implemented policies or initiatives to help people from diverse backgrounds feel welcomed and supported in the workplace. All those initiatives are now declining, a concerning trend that we must address with urgency.

Most people need to be more informed about human origin. However, if you believe a "Black" is a person whose DNA is of African descent, then the number of Black people in the world today is close to eight billion. This means that every person who is living today, regardless of their race, has African ancestry. It's a powerful reminder of our shared human heritage. For more information about DNA migration, refer to The Journey of Man by Dr. Spencer Wells, a National Geographic documentary.

Daily news reports indicated there is a decline of the Caucasian or White population in the United States due to several factors, which include the aging population, fewer births, more deaths, limited immigration, and the pandemic.

When we look at global demographic statistics, we see a diverse and interconnected world. The world's population is approximately 60% Asian, or around 4.75 billion people. The

Caucasian population worldwide is about 16%, or around 1.19 billion. These numbers remind us of the rich tapestry of human diversity that spans the globe.

Blacks or African Americans make up 13.6% of the U.S. population. Still, statistics don't accurately reflect the world's Black population because of the focus on African populations and do not include other countries with large Black populations, such as India, where Black people are included in the Asian statistics. One of my friends who is East Indian would be considered a Black person by anyone who met him. He presents himself as "Just another brother." Who is keeping the statistics?

Delving into the historical context of racial definitions reveals intriguing and often troubling stories. For instance, according to Immigrationhistory.org, in 1923, the Supreme Court decided in United States vs. Bhagat Sigh Thind that while anthropologists classified East Indians as Caucasians, people of Indian descent were not white by the common American definition and thus not eligible for citizenship. This case, and others like it, shed light on the complex and often arbitrary nature of racial classifications. Have you ever heard the words, "five-dollar Indian."

There was a time in our history when Whites paid five dollars and pretended to be native Americans to purchase land allotments under the Dawes Act. To keep the land, they pretended to have "Indian" blood and assimilated into their community.

While serving in the Georgia Air National Guard (GA ANG), I did my part to influence cultural change. According to the Diversity Education Plan, my duties included serving as Advisor to the Commander on issues enhancing the organization's culture and promoting opportunities for all ANG members to maximize their potential for success without regard to cultural differences to meet mission requirements. I also facilitated mentoring and diversity education training for the Georgia Army and ANG Personnel. During one session at an ANG facility in southeast Georgia, a young Airman asked, "Why do

Black people still have a Miss Black America Pageant?" "Good question," I said. Does anyone know the answer?" No one responded, so I took the opportunity to educate the group. The Miss America Pageant started in 1921. The pageant crowned the first Caucasian Jew from New York City in 1945. She was Caucasian in appearance, so her religion was not an issue. The racially segregated Miss America Pageant refused to allow Black people to participate, so Black people decided to form their pageant. This segregation was a result of the deep-rooted racism and discrimination that Black people have faced throughout history. In 1968, Saundra Williams was crowned the first Miss Black America. Her message was clear, "Black is beautiful." Therefore, the Miss Black America Pageant serves as a platform for promoting diversity and holds significant cultural value in the Black community. In 1971, Cheryl Browne, Miss Iowa, participated in the first Miss America Pageant. In 1984, a Black woman, Miss Vanessa Williams, was crowned the first Black Miss America.

In this case, let us use the Bowdoin's restaurant as a example to illustrate how people are treated based on race. If White Jews, White Hispanics, or White Latinos had walked into Bowdoin's restaurant, or the Woolworth's lunch counter, they would have been served. Why? They appear in the eyes of other White people as who they are, Caucasian. This analogy not only highlights the societal perception of race but also the profound impact it has on acceptance and discrimination. So, in my view, the answer is straightforward: Black and Brown people were, and in many cases, still are, primarily discriminated against because of skin color.

So why do Black people continue to support their own Miss Black America pageant? The answer is as clear as the sun on a sunny day: Blacks were not allowed to compete in the National pageant, so they started their pageant. Eventually, it became a part of Black culture. As we know, it is difficult to change cultural norms overnight. This underscores the pro-found influence of cultural norms in shaping our society.

The Civil Rights Movement, a testament to the resilience of the human spirit, significantly impacted the creation of a better world and more opportunities for all people of color, including women of all races. While living in Juliette, Georgia, and Monroe County, this part of the world did not expose me to people from other countries. The only students I recall seeing were either Black or White. Today, Asians own restaurants, people with Indigenous Native American ancestry own restaurants and other businesses, and East Indians own convenience stores (except for chain stores like Quick Trip), liquor stores, hotels, and restaurants all over America. The Civil Rights Movement paved the way for them to live freely as American citizens and enjoy many privileges still limited to Black people. However, the ancestors of these immigrants did not sacrifice for the privileges they enjoy today in America, my ancestors did the work. The new immigrants were not lynched in large numbers for spitting on the ground, looking at a White woman, dying for a crime committed by a White person and falsely accused, killed for their land, enslaved for over one hundred years, and prevented from earning an education. They did not experience separation of families and were not imals. Yes, my Black ancestors paved the way for people like Vivek Ramaswamy and Kashyap Patel, who would not have been allowed to sit at the Woolworth lunch counter or at Bowdoin's restaurant to enjoy a meal as an American citizen while surrounded by "Dixiecrats."

Understanding historical context is crucial in our quest for social justice. I've often heard people say, "We are the party of Lincoln." Please don't try to deceive me with lies and alternative facts. History clearly shows the former Confederate States of America, sometimes referred to as "Dixiecrats," changed from the Democratic Party to the Republican Party due to their opposition to the Civil Rights Movement. Furthermore, Black people changed from the Republican Party to the Demo-cratic Party during the 1930s after Presidential sevelt promised opportunities in the Federal workforce, such as jobs at the postal service.

America has provided many examples of slow change, whether deliberate or not. Many states were slow to change their culture regarding the use and display of the Confederate Flag, the desegregation of schools, churches, and businesses, the sale of alcohol on Sundays, and what scenes were allowed on television, including interracial relationships on TV shows and commercials. This slow pace of change reminds us of the need for patience in our efforts to combat discrimination.

In 1999, Former Secretary of State and Major General David B. Poythress, Adjutant General, encouraged a workplace that promotes trust, opportunity, fairness, and open communication in the Georgia Department of Defense (GA DOD). He said, "I firmly believe that our support for diversity will assist us in accomplishing our goals and reflect the character of our State and diverse communities.

General Poythress established the GA DOD Human Relations Team to create change in the Georgia Army and ANG. Our first task, in 1999, was to create a GA DOD Diversity Strategic Plan. We met quarterly at various locations throughout the state and produced the plan in October 2000.

Our Mission was to create an organization dedicated to mission effectiveness, valuing diversity, and ensuring everyone has the opportunity and means to reach maximum potential for the 21st century and beyond. Our vision was to achieve an organizational culture that values individual differences and similarities and understands the human environment and its impact on the Mission. Our values included Integrity First, Service Before Self, and Excellence in All We Do. The GA DOD developed the Diversity Strategic Plan to supplement and enhance the GA DOD Strategic Plan. In plan development, we decided the strategic focus areas are Commitment, Education and Training, Career Management, Policy Creation Process, Community Involvement, and Recruiting and Retention.

Goal One: Commanders and supervisors are committed to creating an environment that fosters diversity.

Goal Three: The Commander will ensure that every unit member can access a viable career management and mentoring program.

Goal Four: Review and update National Guard Bureau (NGB) and Georgia DOD policies to ensure fair and equitable treatment.

Goal Five: The issues of diversity will be reviewed and emphasized when planning and
conducting forum meetings within the Georgia Department of Defense.

Goal Six: Establish and enhance community relationships and partnerships through,
media advertising and active team participation in local events, youth activities, youth
mentoring, and other outreach programs.

Goal Seven: The recruiting and retention force will recruit a force that reflects the
diversity of its community.

Goal Eight: Establish highly visible recruiting in communities of underrepresented.
groups.

On February 28, 2023, Major General Konata A. Crumbly became Commander of the GA ANG, Assistant Adjutant General, the first Black person to hold that position. Before joining the 116th as a pilot, he was an Army helicopter pilot. His father-in-law, Chief Watson Fluellen, was my mentor, a person with experience and wisdom, and encouraged him to join the 116th Air Control Wing. Major General Thomas Grabowski preceded him. I vividly recall when General

Graboski first joined the unit as a Lieutenant and became Commander of the Communications Squadron. He requested that I conduct diversity education training for his squadron. I asked everyone to complete the Anita Reed Personality Trait Exercise during the session. Captain Grabowski scored high in the red category, indicating he is a purposeful person who is all action, short with words, and a workaholic. It is no surprise to me he rose in the ranks to become Major General. Moreover, he exhibited leadership and used the tools and resources available to improve the Communications Squadron and the GA ANG.

The GA ANG and its members have consistently demonstrated their commitment to service, excelling in natural disaster relief and community service. Their motto, "always ready, always there," truly reflects their dedication and preparedness.

Today, the GA ANG is a beacon of diversity, a testament to our collective efforts and commitment to inclusivity. This transformation would not have been possible without individuals like Percy Jewel, Watson Fluellen (First Black State Human Resources Advisor), Michael Rhett (Enlisted Council), Betty Morgan (First Black 165th Wing Command Chief), Billy Pinkney (State Human Resources Office), Stephen McClinic (Manager), Colonel Odom (First Black Officer in the 116th), and many others. Their dedication and support have played a pivotal role in shaping the GA ANG into a better and more inclusive place to serve. Aaron J. Layton, author of Dear White Christian, said, *"Diversity is God's Idea."*

As I have journeyed through life, traversing many parts of the world, I've seen how people live differently from day to day. In this North American country called the United States of America, we are not exactly united as of 2024. However, no matter what people are faced with, ultimately, some will survive to tell the story. These are not the stories covered by the media, but the personal narratives, the internal feelings and emotions felt during these challenging times and experiences, that truly connect us as human beings.

Life has been a masterclass in the diversity of human expression. On more than one occasion, I found myself at Hartsfield Jackson International Airport, sitting at a gate and captivated by the shoes worn by passing passengers. My initial goal was to identify the most popular shoes among travelers. I would spend up to an hour watching as hundreds of passengers walked by. What I observed was a testament to the unique ways in which we all express ourselves–not a pair of identical shoes, except for sports teams, fraternities and sororities, people in uniform, etc. Even after numerous observations, I have yet to spot two people wearing the same style and color of shoes. Considering the number of passengers walking on the concourse.

People are unique in countless ways, and life is shaped by a multitude of factors, some within our control and others not. Diversity, in all its forms, is not something to be feared or avoided. Just as we wear diverse types of shoes, we have diverse perspectives on work ethic, interests in various activities, and different lifestyle choices. This diversity is what makes life interesting and enriching, whether it's our passion for education, sports, gardening, golfing, camping, chess, music, fishing, diving, skiing, reading, carpentry, cooking, grilling, tailgating, or our choices regarding the consumption of alcoholic beverages, attending worship services, or traveling.

Diversity is not just a simple label, but a complex and rich tapestry that makes up our total identity. It's a collection of our thoughts, ideas, experiences, interests, goals, as well as religious and political views. This diversity is not uniform across the globe, but is shaped by our geography, the country where we live, the laws within that country, and the cultural norms and practices that we adhere to.

Equity, defined by Oxford Languages, as the quality of being fair and impartial. One well-known example shows people of different heights lined up behind a fence to watch an event. Equity is giving equal opportunity for each person to get a box to stand on to get a better view. When I became the first Black First Sergeant in the history of the 116th Maintenance Squadron, it allowed me to look over the fence and receive knowledge and exposure to the other operations and missions of the 116th Fighter/Bomb/Air Control Wing.

Inclusion is defined by *Oxford Languages Dictionary* as the practice or policy of providing equal access to opportunities and resources for people who might be otherwise excluded or marginalized, such as those who have physical or intellectual disabilities and members of minority groups.

I once attended a military conference, and the guest speaker was Jane Elliott, PhD. She spoke about her Blue Eyes/Brown Eyes experiment on racism with third graders after Dr. Martin Luther King, Jr. was murdered in 1968. Her powerful message left a lasting impact, inspiring me and many others to strive for a more just and equitable society. It was an awesome experience that will be etched in my mind forever.

"Workforce diversity is an organizational behavior that acknowledges and values differences and similarities among people and how the differences can work to improve the organization."

Major General A. Paul Weaver, Jr.

"I'm going to give you dignity and respect as an individual, but I expect you to do the same for me."
Lieutenant General Russell C. Davis

"Prejudice is an emotional commitment to ignorance. Ignorance and prejudice are the handmaidens of propaganda"
"The greatest weapon against prejudice is education."

-Jane Elliott-

"You are not born racist. You are born into a racist society. And like anything else, if you can learn it, you can unlearn it. But some people choose not to unlearn because They're afraid they'll lose power if they share with other people."
-Jane Elliott-

CHAPTER 5

LAW AND ORDER, TO PROTECT AND SERVE

In 1982, I joined the East Point Police Department (EPPD). East Point GA, which was closer to my residence, Atlanta College, and friends. Immediately, I was assigned training officers on the beat. I quickly learned that police officers perform their duties differently and use their discretion to apply the law. After graduating from Clayton County Regional Police Academy in 1983, I started patrolling the streets alone. The City of East Point is divided into four zones: Zone One included north of the city; Zone Two was east and south, including Virginia and Central Avenues, Sylvan Road, and Willingham Drive; Zone Three was the center of town, including Main Street, Delowe and Dodson Drives, and Redwine, Ben Hill, and Stone Roads; Zone four was the Southwestern part of the city that included parts of Washington Road, Camp Creek Parkway and a section of I-285.

While working at EPPD, I pursued a college degree at Saint Leo University's satellite campus on the grounds of Fort McPherson, Georgia, located next to East Point City limits. I would work the midnight shift, go home to College Park to sleep, and go to the library before attending evening classes. On days I did not participate in classes, I worked part-time police security jobs in uniform. In 1984 and 1986, I earned associate and bachelor's degrees in criminology. After leaving East Point in 1987, I attended Central Michigan University's satellite campus master's degree program in Public Administration at Fort McPherson from 1988 to 1989.

While there, I decided to pledge to Phi Beta Sigma, Lambda Sigma, a graduate chapter at the encouragement of one of my Saint Leo professors, John Turner. Hosea Williams and John Lewis were members of Lambda Sigma. Thanks to Robert Eason for his leadership at Lambda Sigma in the fall of 1989.

Five years later, in 1991, I earned another associate's degree from my technical experience in Munitions Systems Technology at the Community College of the Air Force.

In 1986, while serving as a police officer, I decided to start snow skiing again and joined the Atlanta Ski Club, which had about 10,000 primarily white members throughout the southeast. Although I never skied with the club, I learned about all the ski shops that offered discounts in the metro Atlanta area and places to ski nearby within an hour's drive, such as Sugar, Beech, Scaly Mountain, and Cataloochee Ski area in North Carolina. I recruited police officers and my friend George to ski with me. None of them had ever skied before. We took several trips to Cataloochee, and skiing became a part of my life again.

As an officer on patrol, I would stop at businesses during my shift to "check on their welfare." One of the businesses, a beauty salon, was located on Washington Road. The owner was named Lillie. She was very friendly and kept me informed about incidents happening in the community. One day, during a visit, I met a couple of flight attendants who told me about a majority-black ski club named Southern Snow Seekers, which was part of a larger group called the National Brotherhood of Skiers (NBS). I quickly joined the club and attended the first of several NBS Summits. My first was at Lake Placid, New York, in January 1987. Next was Steamboat Springs in 1989. Between 1987 and 2021, I skied at several locations, including Copper Mountain, Vail, Keystone and Beaver Creek, Colorado; Whistler/Blackcomb, BC; Jackson Hole, Wyoming; Alta, Snowbird, Park City, The Canyons, Deer Creek, and Solitude, Utah; Sunday River, Maine; Piancavallo and Cortina, Italy; Innsbruck, Austria; St Moritz, Switzerland; and Big Sky, Montana.

INTERNAL INVESTIGATION TO RECRUITING E MODEL

I experienced several incidents as an officer at the East Point Police Department (EPPD) that I will never forget. While serving as a "rookie," I worked the midnight shift most of the time. Police officers view the midnight shift as the most undesirable work. However, officers often rotated to all three shifts. There were options such as using seniority or swapping to change your shift. I enrolled in college and used the hours to my advantage. I attended classes during the day and evening. I don't remember the exact time of year during my first year, but my days off were Tuesday and Wednesday. I had just completed the midnight shift (Midnight to 8 a.m.) and started working the day shift from 8:00 a.m. to 4:00 p.m. I reported to work on a Thursday morning, and at first observation, I noticed several White police officers looking at me strangely. I had no clue what had happened but knew something was suspicious. During the morning "Roll Call," the Patrol Sergeant told me to report to the Deputy Chief's office. I immediately complied. Upon entering Deputy Chief Morris's Office, he told me I was under investigation. I guess he could see the look on my face when I said, "Excuse me, what are you talking about?" He asked if I objected to being escorted to the Georgia Bureau of Investigation (GBI) for a Polygraph Examination. I had no objections because the allegations dumbfounded me.

Before the visit to the GBI, on the way to the East Point Detective's office, I called my wife and told her, along with my sister-in-law, Ellena, and her husband, Chris, who was visiting, about the allegations. They thought it was a joke and laughed. I was shocked the department accused me of such a serious matter, and they thought I was joking. They knew I was not capable of such criminal acts.

Minutes later, I left EPPD in a city vehicle with an investigator who drove us to the GBI Headquarters on Panthersville Road in Dekalb County. The polygraph examiner asked a series of questions about a female who had reported to the police she was intoxicated and driving home one night on

Washington Road when a black police officer stopped her and told her she was driving under the influence (DUI), and that if she did not have sex with him, he would take her to jail.

After two polygraphs ended, I returned to the police department. The Deputy Chief told me he would contact me later after receiving a report from the GBI. At that point, I cooperated with everyone but was still shocked by the allegations. They directed me to go on patrol. After passing on that information, my sergeant assigned me to patrol in a "swing car." Two swing cars worked assignments on each shift, one for the east (Zones 1 & 2) and one for the west (Zones 3 & 4). They acted as backups to the respective assigned zones. That decision allowed me to respond as a backup for the remainder of the shift.

Can you imagine patrolling the streets, responding to calls, and not knowing what the future would bring to my doorstep? It was a stressful time. In my view, the city did not make a good decision. I should have been placed on administrative leave until the issue was resolved. As an innocent person, they did not care about my mental health. I should have sued them. However, since I knew I was innocent of the charges and a little naive about the process, I worked my shift and removed the issue from my mind as best I could. I had to stay focused to remain alive for my family.

Around 3:00 p.m., the Deputy Chief called me back to his office as my shift was about to end. After that event-filled day, he told me I passed the polygraph tests and was cleared of all allegations. He directed me to report to the Detective Division for a post-investigation interview. It was when I first learned the details of the ongoing investigation that occurred before my arrival for work on Thursday morning. After walking to the detective's office, investigators tried to play the "good cop, bad cop" routine with me. Major Gus Thornhill, in the role of the bad police officer in charge of the detective division, started questioning. At some point during the interview, one of the investigators showed me a picture of the alleged victim. My response was, "Oh, hell no, if I raped someone, it damn sure would not be an old ugly woman. Are you kidding me?"

There was an investigation of all the Black officers working at EPPD, College Park, and Fulton County Police Officers, whose territory connected to East Point southwest of the city. They narrowed the list based on work hours and assigned zones. On the night of the alleged incident, I was the only Black officer working in the Washington Road area. At the end of the interview, the investigators asked if I had any information that may be helpful with the case. At first, I thought you just accused me of sex crime and extortion; now, you want me to help you with your case. Then, I started thinking about everything that happened during my midnight shift. One night, I saw a College Park police officer pull over a female on South Main Street near College Park and East Point city limits. As a courtesy, I drove close to the traffic stop and parked as a backup for the officer. He allowed the driver to leave before walking over to my police car and told me he stopped her and smelled a slight odor of alcohol, but after speaking with her, he let her drive home about one block away. During the following week, someone told me East Point Detectives were investigating a Black College Park police officer about the same incident, using the information I provided about the traffic stop. For whatever reason, he resigned. I did not hear any more about the investigation until over twenty years later when one of the officers who had been promoted to the rank of Major, informed me the investigation revealed the alleged victim had some mental issues and the allegation was unfounded. The investigation turned out to be a tool used to go after me by a Black patrol officer who assisted with the investigation. As karma would have it, that officer and nine other employees, including five officers, two identification (Crime scene) technicians, and two Law Enforcement Certified Fire Marshals, were fired after failing a department-wide drug test.

After realizing the trauma and distrust I experienced and all the scrutiny during the investigation, the department decided to include my photo in its recruiting brochure. They tried to make me feel better as a "poster boy." They left a permanent scar that could not be erased. However, I would become a better investigator because of the experience.

"I RAN BECAUSE I WAS SCARED"

One incident occurred when East Point police received a fight call at a housing project operated by the East Point Housing Authority. "622, please respond to signal 29 at East Point Housing Authority, Norman Berry Parkway," replied the dispatcher. The officer assigned said, "622 clear." "625 clear," I answered. Upon arrival, all the kids who either participated or watched it ran from the police. As the officers arrived, not knowing all the facts, they started chasing whomever they saw running. Minutes later, Officer Riggs' voice came over the radio, "Radio, I got one running behind the abandoned school." "625 clear," I replied. Riggs chased the kid to a field behind an abandoned school but lost sight of him in the tall grass. At least eight officers arrived and started walking in the field, looking for the suspect. Suddenly, the kid stood up and said, "I'm here; I didn't do anything." Riggs, who initiated the chase, walked over and hit the kid under the chin—lifting him with his forearm and knocking him to the ground. Riggs placed the kid into his patrol car and returned to the housing area. The primary witness who called the police told us, "He was not involved; he just ran away like many others." The situation at that point did not sit well with me. I returned to the police station at some point after the incident and spoke with my Lieutenant concerning what I witnessed. I suggested he talk with the officer. I also told him I was not making a formal report. He insisted I draft a report, so I did. The Watch Commander was off duty during the weekend when the incident happened. When he returned to work on Monday, he told me his preliminary investigation revealed, after speaking with other officers at the scene, that I was the only officer who saw the assault. There was no further investigation of the incident. I told him my conscience was clear, and I would let it go. Within one year, Officer Riggs was shot five times but survived. One shot grazed her neck; one broke her arm, and three shots to the chest in her bulletproof vest. Shortly after that, the city terminated her following a pos-itive test for illegal drugs.

ROBBERY SUSPECT

While working the day or evening shift, I received a "be on the lookout" (BOLO) notice for a robbery suspect. I was driving southbound on Sylvan Road, approaching the Interstate-85 entrance and exit ramps near Owens-Corning Fiberglass Company. A Day and Night taxi drove approximately three car links in front of my patrol car. The passenger sat behind the driver and looked suspiciously out the back window several times. Before stopping the cab, I called the dispatcher. "622 Radio." Our dispatcher replied, "Go ahead, 622? "I am following a Day and Night Taxi with a suspect as a passenger heading south on Sylvan Road." I decided he could be the robbery suspect based on his actions. After I turned on the blue lights and siren to stop the taxi, he stopped near the I-85 southbound entrance ramp on Sylvan Road. The Black male in the back seat sprung out of the left rear door and started running down the ramp towards I-85. I pursued him with thoroughness, running after him until he ran across four lanes of traffic, crossed the median, and ran across another four lanes. The difference between him and I is that I was wearing a gun rig with a .357 magnum and holster, a bulletproof vest, handcuffs, an additional 12 rounds of ammunition, a walkie-talkie, and regular police patent leather shoes. He was wearing loose jeans and sneakers. I knew he had the advantage, and I assumed he could have pulled out a gun at any point during the case. As he gained ground, I ended the chase, returned to my patrol car, and drove to the other side of the expressway in the City of Hapeville. East Point notified Atlanta and Hapeville that the suspect had fled across the interstate, cleared a fence, and proceeded toward Hapeville. I made the right decision not to risk my life chasing that alleged criminal across four lanes of interstate highway traffic. Another one escaped arrest.

SAVED ANOTHER LIFE

Many incidents or 911 calls officers received during the evening shift (4:00 pm to midnight) involved domestic disputes. As I performed my routine patrol in Zone 3, I received a dispatch: "Unit 723, please respond to signal 29 domestic at 1234 Delowe Drive." I acknowledged by answering, "723 clear." Upon arrival at the apartment, a female resident met me and stated she had asked her boyfriend to get out because, as she said, "I'm done with him." I asked him to leave the premises, and he complied. Minutes later, I received another domestic violence and trespassing call to the exact location. Upon arrival, I saw the subject knocking on the back door. I placed him under arrest and took him to the station for booking. While there, he started acting strangely, so the desk sergeant advised us to put him in a cell with a full view of the camera and take away anything he could use to hang himself, including his clothes. Specific actions were required if a person was considered suicidal. I returned downstairs to complete the report when another officer ran in and said the guy was trying to hang himself. We both ran upstairs but did not have anything to cut the blanket. The other officer ran back downstairs to get a knife from the kitchen while I stood there holding the guy up, using my shoulders to prevent him from hanging himself. Once the officer obtained a knife, he returned and started cutting the blanket to release the prisoner. We learned the inmate received the blanket from the guy in the next cell. Imagine standing under a naked man with his balls on your shoulder while you are trying to hold him up, and he is pushing down. Imagine the odor of someone who had not bathed in a couple of days, with his balls touching your police shirt. We managed to save his life, but my police shirt died that day due to stench exposure, and it found its way to the trash can.

THE TRACTOR-TRAILER CHASE

My first "Smokey and the Bandit" type truck chase began when I received a call from the dispatcher reporting a tractor-trailer in pursuit by the GA Department of Public Safety (GA DPS). I parked my patrol car on the southbound entry ramp from Camp Creek Parkway near I-285. I waited for more information about the chase southbound on I-285 approaching Camp Creek. I waited while in contact with the dispatcher, and then finally, I saw a GA DPS Police vehicle with blue lights inside following a tractor-trailer. "624, Radio," I called. "Go ahead, 624." said the operator. "I am attempting to stop the "18-wheeler", but he is continuing south on I-285, traveling within the speed limit."

As I entered the slow-speed chase, I positioned my vehicle in the left center lane as the tractor-trailer continued southbound in the right lane. The rain had just started, which made the situation more dangerous. After turning on my blue lights and siren, the driver ignored them and continued traveling southbound on I-285. As we approached the exit for I-85 south, the driver acted like he was going south, then abruptly turned east on I-285. At about the same time, Fulton County Police entered the chase and followed in the right lane. At that point, East Point, Fulton County, and DPS were all involved as the truck driver maintained a speed of about sixty miles per hour (mph). When he approached the exit for I-85 north again, he pretended to continue, then turned abruptly to head north on I-85 at the last second. Before reaching this point, the driver swerved the truck several times to prevent my patrol car and Fulton County from pulling up beside him. Once we started north on I-85, near the airport, College Park Police entered the chase and became a victim of the truck driver as he attempted to hit the police car by weaving from lane to lane as the cars approached. We found ourselves in a more dangerous situation as the truck driver decided to drive towards downtown Atlanta and cause a significant accident. As we passed Virginia Avenue, I recall Chief McClendon asking if we could shoot out the tires on the truck. The officers in chase cars could not get close to the truck due to the dangerous weaving from lane to lane, while attempting to assault police cars with the truck. Next, we continued rolling northbound as Hapeville and the Georgia State Patrol (GSP) entered the chase. By this time, three EPPD cars were entering the chase from Virginia Avenue, and one College Park car was directly behind the truck, traveling between 60 and 70 mph. I continued to drive in the left lane as we approached the Cleveland Avenue exit. At the last minute, the truck driver turned to exit on Cleveland Avenue, traveling about 70 mph. I almost overshot the ramp, which caused me to turn immediately to the right and drive down a hill in the grass to return to the exit ramp. As I lined up behind the two East Point cars, I witnessed the truck run a stop sign and strike two westbound vehicles on Cleveland Avenue. The truck hit the first car, knocking it into a second car, and continued up the northbound entrance ramp. Officer Carlotta Harris, the current County Commission Chairperson of Henry County, Georgia, ran away from her police car to avoid a direct hit. The truck finally stopped after hitting the East Point patrol car parked on the ramp. As the chase approached that location, it had been pre-positioned on the ramp to prevent cars from entering I-85 northbound.

  When I saw the impact of two vehicles, I immediately stopped to render aid to the victims. I pulled one bleeding passenger from the back window as I could see smoke coming from the car. The situation was dangerous. As a result, I got blood all over my uniform. Oops, another shirt for the trash. I was so busy rendering aid to accident victims that I did not see what happened to the truck driver. The driver of the first car struck by the truck had to be removed by the "jaws of life."

  Someone told me College Park Police took the truck driver to jail. From what I witnessed, the truck driver was facing numerous charges, including assault on police officers, speeding, reckless driving, failure to maintain a lane, running a stop sign, and damage to government property. I did not receive an invitation, or subpoena, to go to court, and I do not know his fate.

After the chase, I decided to become creative in documenting these events. I built a portable platform to secure my handheld video camera on the dashboard inside my police cruiser. At that time, cameras in police cars did not exist. I never used it in court as evidence, but it highlighted the need for video evidence. Years later, a camera was invented specifically for police usage.

When computers were introduced to police departments across America, EPPD became one of the first, if not the first, to use the system in Georgia. It was called the Mobile Data Terminal (MDT).

DRUG-RELATED MURDERS

Murder and drug deals were standard in the eighties. It was no different in East Point, Georgia. One early morning, around 2:00 a.m., I received a call to a home near Washington Road and I-285. Several officers arrived at the same time because gunshots had been reported to 911. Our captain arrived at the front door to speak with the caller while we searched the premises. The caller, the wife of the missing person, reported that her husband's car was parked in the driveway after he arrived; she did not see him after he returned from a trip out of town. After hearing gunshots, she called 911. We started a search of the yard and found nothing. As I returned to the front porch, the light was on as our captain spoke to the missing husband's wife. The porch light cast a shadow over the flower bed in front of the porch, which was dark at 2:00 a.m. I looked down and saw a human body lying there in the flower bed with a fatal gunshot wound to the stomach. Everyone looked down, and the wife screamed out loudly. There, next to the body, was the sawed-off wooden stock from a shotgun. The victim received a close-range fatal gunshot wound.

Later, when I visited Lillie at her Beauty Salon, she commented. "That guy who was killed owned a boutique in

Washington Plaza, but you would never see customers going in the business." "I guess he was laundering drug money," I said. As a first responder and uniformed officer, I usually did not hear about the outcome of homicide investigations. As far as I can recall, the murder was never solved.

During the evening shift, I responded to a call reporting a person shot at an apartment on Desert Drive near Camp Creek Parkway. When I arrived, the wife said someone came into their apartment, went upstairs, shot her husband in the bedroom, and then ran out. I followed her upstairs and saw the victim sitting on the floor with his back against the wall and a gunshot wound to his forehead. It was a drug-related execution. A briefcase with an airplane ticket to Miami, FL, was on the bed. The wife was not harmed and did not recognize the shooter. Homicide investigators took over the crime scene, and after I had completed my report, I returned to the streets to serve and protect the citizens of East Point.

DOMESTIC CALL TURNED INTO FIGHT

During the day shift, Officer Anders and I responded to a domestic incident on Desert Drive. The female caller reported she and her husband fought, and she wanted to leave to get away from the situation. She met us in the parking lot and indicated she wanted us there while she packed some clothing. While there, we accompanied her inside the apartment so she could pack some clothing. As we stood in the living room, her husband went to the refrigerator and started drinking beer. Since he was home, there was nothing we could do about it. Unfortunately, the beer helped build his courage, but it was a wrong decision on his part. After quickly consuming at least two beers, he decided to go to the bedroom where his wife was packing. We asked if everything was okay, and she said yes. In hindsight, we should have accompanied her. She carried one large bag from the bedroom to the living area, and her husband said, "I will help you take your shit to the car." When he picked up the bag, he intentionally dropped it on the floor and caused it to open, resulting in her clothes falling. He quickly gathered the clothes, stuffed them back in the luggage, and proceeded out the door to her car. Next, he walked over to his car, opened the trunk, and pulled out a motorcycle tire and a shotgun.

Officer Anders checked the shotgun to determine if the gun was loaded. We ordered him to place the gun back in the car. As he leaned, Officer Anders noticed a concealed weapon in his waistband. We asked for his concealed weapons permit, and he produced a regular carry permit. Anders informed him he was under arrest for carrying a concealed weapon. Then, the subject started running towards his apartment door, followed by Anders and me. When we reached the door, it was locked, and he could not enter; Anders reached for the subject's gun before the subject punched Anders in the face and other places.

As Officer Anders attempted to reach for the suspect's gun again, I pulled my weapon and pointed at him. I realized he had a gun, but he never went for it, so I placed my weapon in its holster and prepared to make a physical arrest. The suspect swung at me, but I dodged it. Next, he tried to kick me and missed. He then started to run. I chased him until he missed a few steps and fell face down on the sidewalk. I leaped in the air and landed on top of him, simultaneously throwing punches to place him under arrest. Seconds later, here comes Officer Anders, whose glasses were broken and his uniform shirt torn. He hit the subject on the head with his flashlight, which caused bleeding. I grabbed the flashlight and stopped him; the situation was under control. I thought all was under control, but the subject's wrists and arms were so big I had difficulty placing handcuffs on him. At that point, both he and Officer Anders were exhausted. Finally, after I was able to handcuff the suspect, I took him to the patrol car and rushed him to the police station, where paramedics met me to treat his injury. On the way to the police station, the subject apologized several times, stating he works hard, but his wife likes to spend too much money.

After the incident, Officer Anders sued the defendant in Small Claims Court for damage to his uniform shirt, glasses, pain, and suffering. He was awarded a $5000 judgment in his favor.

DEALING WITH DRUNKS

Washington Road, located in Zone 4, runs southwesterly of downtown East Point from Main Street to U. S. Highway 29. Traffic is usually busy. One day, as I drove west on Washington Road approaching Redwine Road, I noticed cars moving over to the side of the road and stopping as if an emergency vehicle was on the road. A car was driving on the wrong side, forcing cars to move out of the way. I slowed down as I passed the car, turned around, and activated my blue lights and siren. The vehicle continued to move at a turtle's pace on the wrong side of the road. I exited my car, ran up to the moving car, reached inside, and slammed the car into the park. As I entered the vehicle, I could smell a strong odor of an alcoholic beverage. I opened the door and pulled out the driver, who turned out to be an 83-year-old Black man with a 36-year-old white female passenger, who was also intoxicated. I placed him under arrest for DUI, driving on the wrong side of the road, and reckless driving. When my white male sergeant arrived, he instructed me to arrest the female for public drunkenness; I refused because she was not in public until she got out of the car that was going to be impounded. I asked another officer to give her a ride to the police station, where she could call someone to arrange her transportation home. When the case went to court, Judge Barron took his driver's license for life.

In another incident nearby, I drove on patrol along Desert Drive in Zone 4 and noticed a car cross the centerline before turning into a parking lot. I initiated the traffic stop and checked for license and insurance. The driver said he had consumed a couple of beers. I monitored him as he stepped out of his car, and all seemed okay. I noticed the address on his license, and his apartment was only a few feet away. So, I issued a verbal warning to him before he walked to his apartment. Two weeks later, I received a call from Mrs. Winners on Camp Creek Parkway reporting a customer had fallen asleep at the Drive-thru window. When I arrived and walked over to the car window, I immediately noticed it was the same guy I had given a warning to two weeks earlier. I also smelled a strong odor of alcoholic beverages and noticed several beer cans on the floor. I placed the subject under arrest and transported him to jail.

BANK ROBBERY AND COMEDY OF ERRORS

On September 2, 1987, I was assigned to my first bank robbery case when two suspects robbed the First Atlanta Bank in East Point, Georgia. Officer Gibson, Unit #723, received a call about a bank robbery around 3:55 p.m. Upon arrival, he spoke with a teller who reported the suspect walked into the First Atlanta Bank and stood around for about two to three minutes to allow clearance of the teller line. He walked up to the teller's window, placed a bag on the counter, and said, "Fill it up," as he pointed a nickel-plated revolver at the teller. As the teller placed money in the bag, the robber said, "Hurry up, or I'll blow you away." The teller placed over $2000 in the bag. The robber grabbed the bag from the counter and ran out of the bank. Although the robber was dressed like a woman, wearing makeup, a wig, and a jogging suit, the teller strongly believed it was a man. Other witnesses reported to Officer Gibson that they saw the robber run across the street to a Waffle House rear parking lot and jump into an awaiting getaway car, described as a Silver Pontiac Grand Prix with a flat tire. The witness also made a note with the tag number.

I was in the East Point Detective's Office when I received notification of the bank robbery only three blocks away. I immediately rushed to my car and drove to the scene as Unit #759. When I arrived, Officer Gibson briefed me on the facts of the case. In the meantime, a BOLO was placed for East Point Officers to look for the Silver Pontiac Grand Prix. Within minutes after the robbery, a city employee reported seeing a silver Pontiac with a flat tire traveling on Irene Kidd Parkway, approximately one mile from the crime scene. Later, officers located the car at the intersection of Martin and Randall Streets around 4:11 p.m. Officers responded and saw a person matching the getaway driver's description. He was detained for questioning. Meanwhile, police officers and detectives interviewed several witnesses at the scene.

Witnesses, including Mr. and Mrs. Lewis, provided several descriptions of the robber, but all reported he was a man in disguise, pretending to be a woman. "He had large hands and feet," said Mrs. Lewis. "He was wearing a black wig, dressed in a light blue ski jumpsuit with white stripes down the legs, makeup, breasts, and carrying a brown pocketbook." Mr. Lewis said. "He had a male voice tone, and you could see veins in his arms." Officer Brazel recovered a black wig from Church Street near the intersection of Taylor Street. Officer Cherry recovered a considerable amount of red-stained cash from the ground near 1347 O.J. Hurd Court. While officers were securing evidence and gathering information from witnesses, I took action to locate and identify the robber. I drove to where we found the robbers' car and interviewed witnesses.

Witness Smith said she was "drinking alcohol" earlier with the two guys before they left together. Later, she looked outside and saw them running away from the Pontiac. The witness described Yarbrough, the suspect, as having nappy hair, big lips, a light skin complexion, and wearing cutoff blue jeans. "He was carrying a black bag held against his chest with both hands," she said.

Witness Terrell also lived on Randall Street and had known the bank robber for about a year. "Where did you meet the suspect?" I asked. "I met him through my mother; he stayed with her last year on Delowe. That is how I got to meet him," said Terrell.

After giving the suspect's age and birth date, Terrell said the following: "Well, actually, this morning, let me see, he came over and asked me if I wanted to get some money, and I said, Naw." He said, "Oh, you're scared." Terrell responded, "Yea, you damn right, I'm scared about that." The suspect looked at Terrell and said, "I'm going to rob a bank." Terrell said, "Ahh nigger, you know you ain't gon' rob no bank." According to Terrell, the suspect returned later to wait for his driver to pick him up. At that time, Yarbrough was dressed like a woman, wearing makeup, a black wig, a blue jogging outfit with white stripes, sneakers, and shades. He left shortly after that with another guy around 1:00 p.m. Terrell said he saw the suspect after the robbery and described him in a recorded statement. "He's about five feet nine, with a brown complexion. One of his eyes is messed up. It is closed. His left eye is dim like it has been hurt because he said he got hurt when he robbed a place the last time. One of his eyes is messed up, and he has short, low-cut hair," said Terrell. After Terrell identified Douglas Yarbrough in a photo lineup, I issued a warrant for his arrest.

After not locating any other witnesses, I returned to the station to interview the "getaway driver." Following a check of the license plate, we identified Gregory Hightower, the owner and driver of the getaway vehicle. Minutes after the robbery, EPPD located the getaway car and Hightower a short distance from the bank. It only took a few minutes for him to start singing like a bird. According to Hightower's account, as he drove away from the Waffle house lot, the dye bomb exploded, and red dye smoke floated out the car windows. As soon as they left the crime scene, Yarbrough threw his wig out the car window. Hightower went down East Point Street with a flat tire and continued to drive until it came off the rim. He was arrested, and we continued searching for the other perpetrator.

Once I learned the robber's name, I entered it into the National Crime Information System (NCIC). The next day, Dekalb County Police Department (DCPD) informed us Douglas Yarbrough was in custody based on the warrant I issued for his arrest on the bank robbery charges. They arrested him for stealing a television from a friend because he alleged she owed him money. When the police arrived at her apartment, she pointed out the apartment where Yarbrough was living. They arrested him after running a check of his identification and got a "Hit" from NCIC for bank robbery. When I picked up Douglas Yarbrough from DCPD, I noticed red dye was all over his hands and in his pants pockets. I closed the case on September 3, 1987. The following November, I left EPPD and began eleven years of employment at the Fulton County District Attorney's Office.

ARREST OF CURTIS ROWER, THIEF TO MURDERER

In 1987, while serving as a detective at the EPPD, I investigated and arrested Curtis Rower for eleven counts of auto theft. He was seventeen years old at the time. Following his arrest, he admitted to stealing the cars and rode with me to show me where he abandoned them. Little did I know this kid would later become a murderer in such a high-profile case. He is currently serving a life sentence in prison for murdering Fred Tokars' wife. Tokars is a former Atlanta Lawyer, part-time Atlanta City Judge, former ADA, and former Police Academy Guest Instructor.

Tokars hired and paid for the murder of his wife in 1992. A jury convicted him in March 1997, and he died in Federal Prison on May 13, 2020. He engaged in criminal activities, including money laundering. While serving as an investigator with the Fulton County District Attorney's Office (FCDA), I completed a White-Collar Crimes Investigation Course at the Georgia Public Safety Training Center, where Fred Tokars was one of my instructors. In another case I investigated at the DA's Office, Tokars was mentioned as a source of money laundering. I passed that information on to Federal Agents before Mrs. Tokars' murder.

In 1992, Tokars hired a hitman, Curtis Rower, to murder his wife. He kidnapped Sara Tokars along with her children Ricky and Mike, who were six and four at the time. Rower shot Sara Tokars in the head. Rower was 23 years of age at the time when he was arrested for the murder. After pleading guilty, he identified Fred Tokars as the person who hired him. During Tokars' trial, prosecutors said Tokars hired Rower to kill his wife after she discovered that he was laundering money for drug dealers through his law practice. She had threatened to turn him in, so her husband had her killed, prosecutors said. Tokars was convicted of racketeering in 1994 and sentenced to life in prison. In 1997, he was convicted of Sara's murder and given another life sentence.

Tokars died of natural causes at age 67 in a Pennsylvania prison while serving a life sentence.

SNAKE IN MY STEREO

One night, while working the midnight shift, I received a call to an address on Dodson Drive. It was a Signal 39 call, which meant "information for an officer." When I arrived, the middle-aged Black female resident came to the door and reported having a snake in her console stereo. I am not fond of snakes, so I remained at the door to obtain details about the snake's location. She said pleasantly, "I can't stay here with this snake in my house; what will you do?" I said, "Okay, ma'am, show me where the snake is. At about the same time, another officer, J. Fletch, arrived. We walked to her living room, and there was a small snake in the lighted area used to change the radio station. The snake was trying to keep warm from the light. There was no way to remove the snake, so I suggested we move the console stereo outside to the front porch. She agreed it was the best option at that point. After placing the stereo on the porch, we returned to duty. After approximately thirty minutes, I returned to the house as a courtesy and noticed the snake was not in the same location. Officer Fletch also returned. The resident told us to wait to take the stereo inside until we could ensure no snake was inside. I removed the back cover, looked inside, and saw the small snake clinging to some wires. I said, "Ma'am, do you have a set of pliers and some tape? "Yes", she replied. Seconds later, she returned with pliers and electrical tape. I walked outside and broke two branches from a tree, each about two feet long, taped them to the pliers, and used them to clamp down on the snake and remove it from the stereo. Since it was nonvenomous, a garter snake, I took it across the road and released it in the bush. Since we were not issued snake detectors, and she did not report other snakes, there was nothing else we could do for this citizen. Before leaving the scene, she hugged us, and we returned to duty as crime fighters.

DEATH ON THE BEAT

Police officers experience stress and trauma in the line of duty, and the impact can have negative implications on officers' health and well-being. Many officers never receive any professional help to deal with routine events that include traffic deaths, natural deaths, suicides, accidental deaths, and murders.

The first officer on the scene, sometimes called the "First Responder," is required to protect the scene until a police investigator can investigate if needed. Throughout their careers, most officers will be exposed to a minimum of at least one incident involving death. Police officers deal with death in diverse ways. I recall one incident while watching a scene on television when police killed an elderly female after serving a search warrant at the wrong house. Officers shot her several times. Officers stood around in groups when the media showed up to record the scene outside her home. Some were laughing and smiling. Why? To the onlookers, this behavior appeared inappropriate. The officers discussed some other experience or incident unrelated to the present crime scene. After encountering several deaths per week, you become detached from it and perform your duties, such as protecting the perimeter.

As a young police officer fresh from the academy and riding solo, I responded to a car accident on Camp Creek Parkway at the intersection of Interstate 285, Southbound Camp Creek exit. When I arrived, I noticed a dump truck traveling westbound on Camp Creek had struck a car attempting to turn left and head eastbound on Camp Creek Parkway. The crash killed the driver instantly. I approached the vehicle and noticed a white female wearing an Eastern Airlines flight attendant's uniform. When the truck struck the driver's side door, the force caused her head to violently contact the door, resulting in instant death. I noticed her blue eyes were wide open, indicating she was in fear before the truck hit her car. When the paramedics arrived, one of them placed his hands over her eyes and closed her eyelids. That memory is etched in my mind for life.

It was a typical night patrolling the streets. Police officers on the midnight shift respond to domestic dispute calls from midnight to about 2:00 a.m. Between 2:00 and 5:00 a.m., they check for business burglaries and occasional traffic accidents or theft. Periodically, they receive calls at all-night restaurants such as Waffle House and, during the eighties, drive-offs from gas pumps.

Around 2:00 a.m. on a Friday, I responded to a motorcycle accident on Cleveland Avenue near Norman Berry Drive. Upon arrival, I saw a motorcycle beside a utility street light pole. Next to the bike was a white male lying on his back. He was not wearing a helmet because it had split into two halves from impact with the pole. As I ran closer to the victim, I noticed blood coming out of his mouth, nose, ears, and eyes. He had lost so much blood; it was like a miniature stream flowing downhill next to the curb into a drain a few feet away. I could hear him gurgling and gasping for breath. Immediately, I knew he was approaching brain-dead due to the amount of blood loss. I felt helpless, even though we were two blocks from South Fulton Hospital. I reported my observations to the radio dispatcher, but I could do nothing except wait for an ambulance. While I waited, he breathed his last breath before me. I prayed for him. It was the only time in my life I watched a person die.

Law enforcement officers are trained to respond in most situations. However, until confronted with one of those situations, no one knows how you will react to a real-life incident. No one knows the short- or long-term impact these incidents have on your body mentally and physically. Numerous studies have been conducted on job-related stress and how it affects law enforcement personnel. Professional assistance is available for those who seek it. Most officers do not take advantage of it because of its stigma.

CHAPTER 6

District Attorney's (FCDA) Office, 1987-1996

After earning a bachelor's degree in 1986 and serving one year as an investigator at EPPD, I decided to move on to a different life. One of my professors at Saint Leo University, John Turner, an Assistant District Attorney (ADA) and DA Special Agent Bailey, also a student at Saint Leo, recommended me for the position. I was hired as a DA Special Agent in November 1987. My office was on the fourth floor of the Fulton County Courthouse, 136 Pryor Street, Atlanta, Georgia.

DA investigators were assigned to work with one or two ADAs in one of 12 Superior Court Rooms. I worked in the courtrooms of Judges Clarence Cooper (Retired), United States District Court, Northern District), Thelma Wyatt Cummings Moore (retired) and Edward Johnson (Georgia Court of Appeals, 1992-2004). My first assignment was in the courtroom of Judge Clarence Cooper where I worked with ADAs Harvey W. Moskowitz and Carol E. Wall, but not at the same time. I also worked with other ADAs during my 11 years in the office, who became State, Local, and Federal Judges, Assistant Attorneys General, Environmental Protection Agency (EPA) Regional Manager, GBI Director, District Attorney in surrounding metro counties, and one State Supreme Court Justice.

I enjoyed working in downtown Atlanta. We often walked to various locations for lunch. I sometimes jogged in the morning before work from the courthouse to Lenox Mall or 14th Street. It became a habit in preparation for the annual Peachtree Road Race, and at some point, ADA William Hawthorne would accompany me on the runs. I continued to jog and run the Peachtree Road Race and other races, including the

Cobb 10K Classic, Charles Harris Run, 100 Black Men 5K, Heart Trek 10K, U.S. 10K Classic, Corporate Challenge, Egleston Rainbow Run, Life College Run for Life, and the Peachtree City Classic for the next thirteen years. My best time running the Peachtree 10K was 43:39 in 1996; the Peachtree City Classic 15K, 1:14 in 1995; and the Half Marathon, 1:47:39 in 1996. Running was a stress reliever.

While working at the DA's Office, I assisted former prosecutor Nancy Grace in preparing at least one or two cases for trial. She worked as a prosecutor there from 1987 to 1996. Nancy grew up in Macon, Georgia, 23 miles from Juliette, Georgia, and attended Mercer University. My sister Carolyn Freeman Brown (not the Bird Lady) also attended Mercer, graduating in 1980.

PRIVILEGED USE OF COUNTY VEHICLES

I had not previously used my vehicle to perform work assignments for the county. Although they reimbursed us for our mileage, I found the policy ridiculous. However, some county cars were occasionally available for official business. The vehicle use policy created political issues and favoritism.

Lewis Slaton served for thirty-one years. I served in his office from 1987 until he retired in December 1996. On July 27, 1995, Investigations Managers Nelson and Miller and ADA Hadaway met to inform all investigators that the policy allowed for maximum mileage reimbursement for 571 miles when using a personal vehicle. Nelson also threatened fraud charges against those investigators he believed to have recorded questionable miles using their cars for county business. In 1995, there were about twenty-five investigators assigned to the office, and nine vehicles were in the assigned county fleet. However, Slaton and whoever else he would allow to use them, such as other ADAs, had two cars reserved for exclusive use. Investigators expressed several opinions about the meeting and asked why not purchase enough vehicles for everyone to use for official business. Given the criminal activity in the community, they also felt it was unsafe to drive a personal car.

On July 28, 1995, I took the initiative to create and issue a survey to my coworkers to find out their preferences from the following choices: Use of a flat rate of one hundred sixty dollars monthly, reimbursement of twenty-eight cents per mile with a maximum of 571 miles, or the use of a county vehicle. Nelson, who drove a county vehicle at his pleasure, said I disrespected him by issuing the survey. Again, this is the same guy whose brother owed me six thousand dollars from a loan three years earlier.

For my efforts to address the safety concerns of my coworkers, I received a letter of counseling. Nelson told me one of the employees gave him a copy of the survey. "Some folks don't like you," he added. "Well, obviously, they have a personal problem," I said. "You are a renegade; I will stop it," he said. Next, he told me I was causing friction in the office. I said, "You should take whatever action you feel is necessary; I will address the issue with Slaton." "You can't talk with Slaton," replied Hadaway. "He is the next person in the chain of command here, and I will speak with him over your objection," I said. In the end, Nelson showed everyone his poor management style and incompetence. On the same day, another manager, Ernest Miller, showed me an old mileage book from several years ago indicating nine hundred miles or more was common. Again, I thought using a personal vehicle in the criminal justice system was ridiculous.

Eventually, the DA's Office Administrator told Nelson he violated policy and should stop driving a county vehicle to his home. Well, it was about damn time; the rules apply to everyone.

THE DOOM GANG

During the early 1990s, a gang of thugs, four young men, three young women, and a fifteen-year-old girl who called themselves Doom, killed two young girls. The leader of the group was Armond Dunnigan, who kidnapped Nita Wall on or about August 1, 1993. His leadership role in the group was like Charles Manson's. Ahmond Sukarno Dunnigan, twenty-five, sometimes called "Mon" or "Mond" on the street, was convicted for ordering the torture of Nita Wall. She died on or about August 3, 1993.

One of the crime scenes was in an apartment near Cleveland and Stewart Avenue, now Metropolitan Parkway, where they tortured, beat, burned, and murdered Nita Wall. Doom members threw her body into overgrown kudzu in Southwest Atlanta. The grand jury returned true/accurate bills of formal accusation against the nine defendants—co-indictees on October 5, 1993. Marsinah Johnson, the other victim, was killed in East Atlanta, Dekalb County. While both girls were beaten and tortured by Doom gang members, they threw Johnson's thirteen-year-old body on railroad tracks near Dekalb Avenue. The Doom defendants were assigned to our courtroom with ADA Downs as the prosecutor. My primary role was to review all evidence, gather new evidence, re-interview witnesses, identify potential unnamed witnesses, subpoena, and coordinate witnesses for trial. We checked all leads for additional information once we determined the members involved were charged. In this case, it led to a witness from Birmingham, who met Dunnigan during one of her visits to Atlanta. She was extremely fortunate not to become one of the victims. I interviewed her and a radio personality, her outcry witness, in Birmingham, Alabama.

In February 1996, during the trial of three Doom Gang Members, Agent Nelson confronted me, alleging it was my responsibility to provide transportation for Nita Wall's mother to and from court each day. While sitting in court assisting ADA Downs with prosecuting gang members responsible for the death of Nita Wall, her mother, Ms. Cliff, who was seated several rows behind me, motioned for my attention. She was sitting with the Victim/Witness Coordinator. "Could you give me a ride home today?" She asked. The time was approximately 4:45 p.m. I looked at my watch and informed her to speak with the Victim/Witness Coordinator about her transportation needs. I was busy dealing with the court case and participated in carpooling with a coworker. Around 5:00 p.m., Judge Fuller announced the court would continue until 5:45 p.m. I requested assistance from a coworker, Investigator Don Scully, to remove evidence from the courtroom for overnight storage. Scully also agreed to remain in court until the end of the day's session. At around 5:16 p.m., I walked out of the courthouse and saw Ms. Cliff smoking a cigarette on the steps of the courthouse. At about the same time, Nelson and ADA Tanner drove up in a county-owned vehicle. Nelson rolled down his window and said, "I need to see you tomorrow." OK," I said.

On the next day, as Investigator Scully and I walked towards the seventh-floor elevator to go to court, Nelson said, "I need to see you two in my office right now." We followed him to his office, and he said, "I need you and Scully to pick up Ms. Cliff and take her home each day." He said he took her home the day before. Doesn't he realize I need to check with my assigned prosecutors in case we need to do a follow-up on the case on trial? I said, "She is not a witness for the state in our case, and she is not under subpoena." "If you don't plan to do as I ask, you should check off the clock and go home," he said. "I would like to address this situation with Mr. Slaton," I replied.

"No, you don't need to speak with Mr. Slaton.," he said. I reiterated, "I think it would be best for me to speak with him about this incident."

Immediately, we went to Slaton's Office. Nelson told Slaton he received a complaint that I was rude to Ms. Cliff when she asked me for a ride home, and I had upset her to the point that she was crying. He also told Slaton I informed Ms. Cliff I was carpooling and had to take someone else home. Nelson did not mention that I had children in daycare or that I asked Ms. Cliff to speak with the victim/witness coordinator for her transportation needs. He continued to allege I was more concerned about taking a carpooler home than showing concern for Ms. Cliff, the victim's mother. After listening to both sides, Slaton advised us to continue doing excellent work and avoid each other to avoid future conflicts. He said, "If future conflicts occur, we should address them with him directly. I said, "Yes, Sir," and proceeded to the courtroom, where I was involved as an investigator in a major murder case involving three defendants on trial. My responsibility was to assist prosecutors Joe Burford and Doris Downs in a trial. Transportation coordination was not my concern for the victim's parents, who were not on the witness list.

During the trial of three defendants, King, Hannibal, and Kenner, ADA Downs summarized the murder, stating the defendants tortured Nita Wall over three days. "Everyone in the apartment participated in the murder, and all should be held accountable," Nita begged them to kill her, and, in a final act, they drowned her in a cooler filled with water. Dunnigan held her head down. "You're dead," he declared. "Tell God that Doom sent you."

When the Judge read the verdict finding Kenner guilty of murder but mentally ill, Kenner held his head down for a moment and then lifted the defense table where he had been sitting during the entire trial. Immediately, courtroom deputies rushed in, surrounded the defendant, and restrained him as they led him through a door on the right front side of the courtroom. He yelled, "Don't let my mamma see this, don't let my mamma see this." While deputies removed Kenner, other deputies secured the two female defendants. Downs ran in the opposite direction, away from the incident. Investigator Scully, who was escorting Ms. Cliff, left his seat and moved quickly toward the action behind the deputies. Kenner's mother fainted as she watched her son slip into what his attorney described as the personality of Marcellus, the bad guy. Spectators ran from the courtroom as a local TV camera continued to roll and film the incident. Moments later, the Sheriff's Deputies allowed Ms. Kenner to visit with her son to help calm him; it worked. Kenner returned, and Marcellus left the room.

The Judge sentenced all three defendants after reading the verdicts the next day. Kenner and Hannibal received a life sentence plus twenty years, and King received life in Prison.
While the outcomes of trials can often be unpredictable, the subsequent parole of some defendants can still be a surprise. Hannibal, now forty-five, was paroled on April 17, 2019, a decision that may have raised eyebrows. King, now forty-nine, was paroled on September 3, 2019, adding to the unexpected turn of events. McCray, now forty-eight, was released on September 3, 1996, and V. Logan, now fifty-two, was released on August 31, 2008. Corey Gaither and Kenner, however, are still

serving life sentences, a reminder of the unpredictability of the justice system.

THE MURDER OF OFFICER NILES JOHANTGEN

The evidence showed Norris Speed was a drug dealer who sold drugs in the Thomasville Heights area of Atlanta. Officer Johantgen was a uniformed patrol officer whose regular beat included the Thomasville Heights apartments. On December 13, 1991, an Atlanta police undercover officer arrested José Griffin, who worked for Speed, after he had fled into Speed's grandmother's apartment. The police confiscated $2880 and one hundred grams of cocaine during this arrest. The police also noticed some marijuana on a table in the apartment, and they returned with an arrest warrant for Speed's grandmother. Although Officer Johantgen was not involved in the undercover operation, he accompanied the other officers when they served the warrant. Speed told his drug ring boss that he believed the raid resulting in the loss of the drugs and money was "influenced by" Officer Johantgen. Speed told someone that he planned to kill "The Russian" (Officer Johantgen's nickname).

On December 21, 1991, Officer Johantgen pulled into the parking lot of the Thomasville Heights apartments in the shadow of Atlanta Federal Prison, got out of his car, and approached several men standing outside. He detained one of the men and began to frisk him. Speed walked up behind Officer Johantgen and shot him directly in the back of the head with a 9 mm pistol, killing him instantly. Speed fired four more times at the officer while he was on the ground, but all the shots missed him and shattered on the pavement. Speed then fled the scene in a car. After Speed fled, he met with his drug-ring boss.

He told him that he had shot the Russian because Officer Johantgen had threatened to "catch him dirty" and because the officer was harassing people and searching them unnecessarily. Speed's girlfriend heard him tell his drug boss that he shot The Russian. Both Speed's drug boss and his girlfriend testified at the trial. Police arrested Speed two days after the crime, and he confessed to shooting Officer Johantgen, who was a United States Marine Corps veteran and had served with Atlanta Police for three years.

Once the case was bound from Atlanta City Court to the DA's Office, it was assigned to ADA Downs. I served as her investigator. While preparing for the trial, our investigation added information and drug connections associated with Speed. First, we identified one of his suppliers and his drug boss, Steve, whom the Drug Enforcement Administration (DEA) had recently arrested in Texas. I flew to Texas and interviewed him in prison. He cooperated, and we decided to fly him to Atlanta to be a witness in Speed's trial.

At trial, one witness testified that he saw Speed, who was well-known in the area, walk up behind the officer and fire the fatal shot into his head. Five more witnesses testified that they heard the first shot, looked up, and saw Speed shooting at the officer on the ground.

The Grand Jury indicted Speed for malice murder on January 28, 1992, and the state filed a notice of intent to seek the death penalty on February 10, 1992. The trial took place from September 7 to October 1, 1993. A Fulton County Jury convicted him of malice murder on September 27, 1993, and sentenced him to death. The court later reduced the sentence to life in prison. His Defense Attorney was Michael Mears.

USE OF INFORMANTS

A confidential informant, known as CL, provided information about Fred Tokars laundering money before he paid to have his wife killed and supplied helpful details on Jimmy Johnson, also known as "Little Jimmy," drug operations.

"How long have you been dealing in narcotics?" I asked. "About three years in Dekalb, Fulton, and Gwinnett Counties," he answered.

"Who is your source, and what amounts are you purchasing?" I asked.

"Red and Little Jimmy," he replied. "They live in Lithonia," he added.

CL admitted purchasing a quarter-kilo to a kilo (key) of cocaine, powder, and crack cocaine. He noted that his primary sales areas were Bankhead Courts, Thomasville Heights, Vine City, Fulton, and Dekalb counties.

"What is the most weight you ever sold?" I asked. CL said he purchased at least three kilos on more than one occasion. He further stated that he last contacted Little Jimmy on a Wednesday around November 25, 1992. He talked with Little Jimmy after calling to speak with someone else and Jimmy answered the phone. He said Little Jimmy and Red owned houses in Lithonia but kept their drugs at several locations in places off Candler Road and the Thomasville area. They kept their illegal drugs in a safe house off Daniel Avenue in Dekalb County.

"How much money did you make per week?" I asked. CL said he made thousands per week in one year. He made about a thousand per week and gave thirty thousand to Jimmy. "What did you do with all that money?" I asked. CL said he had planned to speak with Fred Tokars about investing some money in a downtown club on Peachtree Street. I asked CL to explain how he met Fred Tokars. CL said a man named Cannon told him he would introduce him to Tokars if he needed a lawyer. "How did Cannon know you were involved in selling drugs?" I asked.

"They thought I had murdered a girl and thought it was drug-related, but it was not drug-related; a guy named Renfro killed her because he was the only person who knew she had a lot of money." He said. CL also said a guy named Reggie had an addiction while trying to deal drugs.

According to CL, Cannon was the only person who talked about investing money in the club. However, Tokars was also present at the time but did not speak concerning the club owner's solicitation for investing. CL said he believed Tokars was part owner of the Penthouse Club. He said, "When I first met Tokars in 1989 or 1990, he talked with me about retaining him as a lawyer, stating that he would be available whenever I got into trouble and assured me that if I were arrested, I would not spend a weekend in jail." Tokars told him the minimum retainer fee was $5000.

The Atlanta Journal-Constitution newspaper article written by Anne Rochell reported, "Easter weekend begins with five violent deaths." Two of the deaths listed were Jimmy (Little Jimmy) Johnson and his live-in girlfriend, Precious Shivers Massey. Another article by Shirley L. Smith and Anne Rochell detailed what the police said happened in the house in Dekalb County off Wellborn Road, south of Marbut Road and North of Covington Highway. "The home is a lovely split-level house with wood siding, a two-car garage, and windows in each room facing the street.

Smith reported that it was Good Friday, and the rain poured most of the day. Neighbors passing the home had no clue there were two bodies inside, along with a four-year-old girl who had been alone for several hours with no food or beverages. The dead mother lay on the ground floor, strangled and bleeding from a blow to the head. The man, Johnson, was on the second floor, strangled and bleeding from stab wounds. The little girl, still dressed in pajamas, stood in the window, called out, and waved, but passersby did not understand her cries for help, which would continue for at least six hours. It was not an adult but neighborhood children who believed the girl was asking for help. When they opened the door, they saw blood all over the house. Smith further stated that now DCPD faced the possibility of having only a four-year-old as a witness to two homicides. Patrice Shivers Massey, 27, and Jimmy Johnson, 42.

A neighbor later reported seeing the little girl standing in front of the bathroom window around 1 pm Friday, but she did not realize anything was wrong. As she arrived home, the girl waved at her, and she waved back. Another neighbor reported she was suspicious of the unmarried couple who drove fancy cars, and often, there was a lot of traffic outside the home at night. Their suspicions were correct; Jimmy Johnson was a big-time drug dealer of enormous quantities of cocaine, earning several thousand dollars per week. The murder remains unsolved, as are many others related to dealing drugs.

Somebody spared the life of the four-year-old witness that day, and today, she would be in her thirties. We can only imagine how she has survived the trauma she experienced over 27 years.

MURDER AT INMAN PARK REYNOLDSTOWN

On March 1, 1990, a group of young Black males participated in the shooting of Marion Roberts at the Inman Park Reynoldstown MARTA station. Atlanta Police arrested several individuals, including Eugene White, Rodricus Glover, Juwan Robinson, Gilbert Stringer, and Aubrey Jackson. Eugene White was the alleged "trigger man," according to his co-defendants. During their investigation and arrests, the Atlanta Police did not recover the murder weapon.

Assistant DA Doris "Dee" Williams-McNeely was the prosecutor, and I was her investigator. After receiving several tips as to the location of the murder weapon, we executed a couple of search warrants to no avail. We worked tirelessly to follow every lead in this case. One day, I decided to go out in the community and hang out with young men we suspected had knowledge about the case, precisely the location of the murder weapon. I drove to East Atlanta near Cabbagetown and found guys playing basketball. I walked over and eventually ended up on the court to show them I was not just an investigator but a person who shared similar interests, the love of a good basketball game. After the game, I walked over to their house across the street and relaxed on the porch. The resident told me he knew why I was hanging around and knew I was a police officer. Minutes later, a young man arrived and asked for the resident by name and asked for some marijuana. The resident was standing near the door, so I looked at him and asked, "Are you selling marijuana? "I will take you to the gun," he answered. I immediately notified Williams-McNeely of my whereabouts and my intention to recover the possible murder weapon. I followed the young man to a house east of his residence. He walked to the door, and a young man appeared and asked, 'What's going on, man?" "Yo dog, Investigator Freeman wants that gun; you got it?" He said, "OK, I'll get it." I followed him to a room where he recovered the gun. It was an older 38-revolver with duct tape on the handle. After I took possession of the weapon into evidence, we sent it to the GBI Crime Lab for a ballistics test, which revealed the gun was used in another unsolved murder case under Atlanta Police authority. We conducted a follow-up on that case and found the connection with Eugene White as the suspected shooter. As a result, we solved another murder case.

The jury found all defendants guilty. Judge Edward Johnson was so impressed with the work involved in the investigation and trial preparation by me and the prosecutor that he wrote a letter to The Honorable Lewis Slaton.

RAPE OF A CONVICTED PROSTITUTE

I was an investigator for the late Alfred Dixon and Sam Lengen, Assistant DAs in one of Fulton County courtrooms. It was Christmas Eve, and the place was in Atlanta Overlook Apartments on Bankhead Highway. The victim lived there with her sister and mother in separate apartments. They would get together on Christmas Eve to cook dinner the next day. It became a family tradition. On this day, one sister began her walk to her mother's apartment and saw a guy standing outside one of the buildings. He spoke to her, and she ignored him and continued her walk. She presented herself as strong and confident. Her demeanor may have saved her from becoming a victim. When the guy spoke to her, she briefly conversed with him. She was more street-savvy and friendly than her sister. Minutes later, her sister walked the same route to her mother's apartment, and the suspect decided she was the one he would accost at knifepoint and forced her to walk to a vacant house nearby. The house was dark and cold, doors and windows broken. The subject forced her inside the house, which was used as a toilet by vagrants and smelled of urine and feces. The subject repeatedly raped her and kept her in the house for about four hours. She begged him to let her go to be with her family for Christmas Eve, but he refused. After four hours, he allowed her to leave. She immediately went to a nearby pay phone and called the police. When Atlanta Police arrived and began searching the vacant house, they found the suspect hiding in the attic.

While preparing for the trial, ADA Sam Lengen and I reviewed the facts. The defendant denied knowing the young lady and having sex with her. After an interview with her, we obtained a search warrant signed by Judge Moore for the defendant's blood and deoxyribonucleic acid (DNA). The test result proved he had sex with the victim. After receiving the results, the defendant changed his story and alleged he purchased sex from her and that she was a crack addict. The defendant's attorney learned the victim had been arrested for prostitution years earlier and tried to paint a picture of a business transaction by a convicted prostitute selling her body to purchase crack cocaine. After discussions with the defense attorney, Sam seemed reluctant to take the case to trial. I also sensed the judge did not want to deal with a jury trial. I suggested to Sam that we go to the crime scene on Bankhead Highway. After walking through the abandoned house, smelling urine and feces, we drove down the street. I spotted some Black senior citizens sitting outside in a parking lot playing checkers. I drove over to where they were seated. Sam and I exited our vehicle and approached the gentlemen. I asked a simple question. "If a crack addict was selling her body for five dollars to get another hit, would she stay with that person for four hours in a vacant house that smelled of urine and feces? "Hell no, she would be back on the streets to get more money," replied one gentleman. Another gentleman asked, "Did she leave and return for more money?" I told him she did not leave because she was held there for four hours. Another gentleman said, "That HOE would return to the streets after three minutes unless he had some crack." We left the gentlemen with what I hoped to be street knowledge for Sam Lengen. He said, "Percy, we need to interview her mother and sister." After interviewing the mother and sister, we learned the victim had a boyfriend of several years, so we arranged to interview him at the victim's apartment. He informed us they had dated for several years. He was aware she had a history of using drugs and an arrest for prostitution years earlier. He stressed that she was his girl and did not need to walk the streets for money. The mother and sister corroborated the victim's recent dating history.

During the trial, the boyfriend took the stand. Sam asked him about their dating history, and he restated that the victim was his woman and that if she needed money, he would give it to her. Sam asked him how much money he gave her. The boyfriend told the jury he would give her whatever she asked for and then pulled out a wad of cash from his pocket to show them he had money. He told the jury he loved her and that she was not a crack addict and not a street whore.

The defense attorney tried to convince the jury his client was merely purchasing sex and that the woman wanted more money. When he refused to give her more money, she called the police. His version of the story did not work. The jury found the defendant guilty of rape. I looked at the judge's clerk, who was in disbelief. At that moment, I wondered if the clerk influenced the judge's decision. I never understood why the judge sentenced the defendant to a halfway house.

If I had not convinced Sam to take the case to trial, another rapist would have been released back to the streets without a conviction. In this case, he was convicted by a jury but released back to the streets by a judge.

Agent Nelson took over as manager after Chief Ernest Miller retired. Our business and people management styles were vastly different despite our shared experiences, such as military service and attending the same college. The dynamics of professional relationships can become complex, especially when personal connections are involved. This was the case with Nelson and me.

POLITICS IN THE OFFICE

On April 4, 1991, I loaned Roger Nelson $6000. He signed the Promissory Note as Roger Nelson, President, Thirty-Two Degrees, Inc. I understood when Thirty-Two Degrees opened, Roger Nelson was to become 50% owner, and the other 50% would be shared by Eric Mole, L. Francis, C. Ward, and R. Crawford. I quickly realized Roger Nelson did not have the money he pretended to possess when he agreed with his co-owners. I learned he used my six-thousand-dollar loan to open a checking account with $2500 and to pay $3500 for the liquor license. I met Roger Nelson through his brother, who was my coworker. I loaned him the money because his brother asked and, secondly. After all, I would work security at the business along with his brother, Agent Nelson, as we had previously done at Fat Tuesdays. Thirty-Two Degrees was in the same spot as the former Fat Tuesday's. When it closed, former employees Mole, Francis, Ward, and Crawford planned to open their business selling frozen daiquiris with additions to slightly change the recipes and names.

The business was booming and making a lot of money. It became one of the most popular spots on Old National Highway and South Atlanta Metro. There were guest performances by Bobby Brown and other celebrities. Professional athletes also frequented the spot. I recall meeting Evander Holyfield and Otis Nixon there. I also remember a young lady who modeled Playboy lingerie. I was standing outside working in uniform when Ms. Paula walked outside to get some air. We started talking and became friends. We are still friends after over thirty years.

On one occasion, I recall a young man named Kevin driving up in front of Thirty-Two Degrees in a Datsun 280Z. Next, several young kids exited the vehicle and proceeded into Thirty-Two Degrees. Within the hour, the kids performed, and the crowd loved it. Kevin explained he was their manager. Little did I know these kids would later get a contract and become well-known as the group ABC.

Thirty-two Degrees later closed due to disputes and disagreements between Roger Nelson and the co-owners. R. Nelson settled after the co-owners filed a suit. In his settlement agreement, R. Nelson failed to repay my loan. As a result, once he was out, the new owners filed Chapter 11 bankruptcy, which created a $6000 loss for me.

After I filed a suit against R. Nelson, his brother, my co-worker, E. Nelson experienced a personality change toward me. When he became a manager, he acted out against me in ways I thought were petty and unprofessional and appeared in the form of retaliation. As they say, sometimes, do your best to avoid those who act like the devil. As a result, I dropped the civil suit and took the loss. However, the unprofessional actions continued until the newly elected DA removed him from a management position.

WORKING A DUAL ROLE DURING THE 1996 OLYMPIC GAMES

On September 18, 1990, I was in underground Atlanta with thousands of people, including Maynard Jackson, when the Olympic Committee selected Atlanta as the host city for the 1996 Summer Olympic Games. Jackson accepted the Olympic flag at the 1992 closing ceremonies in Barcelona, Spain. While working downtown at the DA's Office, I saw the city's transformation as it prepared for the 1996 Games.

As a member of the Georgia ANG., I soon became involved in planning from a different position. Colonel Jimmy Davis selected me to serve as one of three Assistant Military Venue Officers (AMVO) for military security at the Georgia Dome. The position would last forty-five days, including before and after the games. The official dates for the games were from July 19 to August 4, 1996. In my security role, I served as manager of military security operations from 2:00 p.m. to 10:00 p.m. each day. Several military units rotated tours of duty during the 45 days. The DA's Office operated on a minimum schedule because the court system had closed temporarily for the games. There was a period when I arrived for work at the DA's Office
at 6:00 a.m. and worked until 2:00 p.m. I skipped lunch to leave thirty minutes early to report for military duty. The office allowed a flexible work schedule and fifteen military days off to work all forty-five days without interruption. My office was in a temporary building on the north side of the Georgia Dome, several feet from the building. The building also housed a room where military and law enforcement personnel monitored activities in and around the Dome with sophisticated camera sys-

tems. My role was more about dealing with conduct and discipline, welfare, and needs of the soldiers and Airmen from military units all over the United States. It was an exciting time; one I will never forget.

On July 27, 1996, a bombing in the Olympic Park changed the way we conducted security operations during the games. I would learn later that my high school friend and former roommate, Larry Bowden, was in the park during the blast and was struck in the face by shrapnel, causing damage to his jaw to the point where, even now, the scar is visible on his face. After he recovered from the injury, he moved back to his hometown in fear of returning to Atlanta. Eventually, he got over it and returned to everyday life. Ironically, he married a nurse involved with his recovery.

The explosion happened after 10:00 p.m., and I had left to go home for the evening. I learned about it the following day. When I returned to work, I created an Air Force Security Forces team, which escorted the *Magnificent Seven* gymnastics team from the Dome to the media tent after each session.

After reporting for work one day, I learned that some guys from one of the visiting Army Guard units, whose job was to patrol the Dome on foot for eight hours and function as the eyes and ears of law enforcement, needed to take their job seriously. They had used an unauthorized golf cart connected to an overnight recharging unit for personal use. The next day, the battery died when staff came to use the cart. Later, we learned the staff had tried to stop the unauthorized usage by attaching a chain to the steering wheel. That action did not deter the soldiers; they drove around with the chain still attached while draining the battery. When we identified the soldiers, the Georgia Dome Army leadership wanted to punish them severely, but I recommended we move them to another facility. On the same day, I requested reassignment of the soldiers to the Georgia World Congress Center.

Each day, when soldiers and Airmen reported for duty, Colonel Jimmy Davis and I would hold a formation and roll call outside in front of the Dome. It was a reminder that we were a military operation.

William Jefferson Clinton was President of the United States in 1996. While performing a walk-thru of the Dome near the lower level where VIPs and other dignitaries arrived, I spotted Secret Service Agents running behind Chelsea Clinton and her girlfriends. It must be a tough job to allow these young girls to act like regular kids while protecting them in a very public environment. Then I thought that was precisely why we were there to protect the public. I will speak more about Colonel Davis later; he was an inspiration and mentor in my life.

During the Olympics, the Air Guard allowed me at least three days off during my forty-five-day tour of duty. Before the Olympics, I entered my name in bidding for four Olympic event tickets and successfully obtained tickets for basketball, baseball, and track and field events. I attended with my wife Ellen and my six-and nine-year-old daughters. I was proud for them to experience the opportunity of a lifetime.

OFFICIAL BUSINESS IN JULIETTE

All felony cases committed in Fulton County are bound over for presentation to the Fulton County Grand Jury. Cases are randomly assigned to one of the Superior Court Judges after there is an actual bill or formal accusation. Two or more ADAs work in the courtrooms. Moreover, each court is assigned one investigator. The cases are usually randomly distributed to different judges. We received the murder case involving defendant James L Clanton, "The one-eyed monster." When I reviewed the case file and learned Clanton fled Fulton County after murdering a 24-year-old female, Dawn Kruk, traveled to Macon, Georgia, assaulted a Macon resident, stole his vehicle, then drove to Monroe County where they captured him after a statewide search, the case got my full attention.

Dawn was a beautiful young lady, born in Harris County, Texas, in May 1969. She became another victim of homicide in this world by a person with evil intentions. Clanton broke into her apartment, stabbed her repeatedly with three knives, and slashed her throat.

After a full review of all the evidence, it was time to schedule appointments to interview witnesses in an unrelated case. First, we interviewed Mr. Sidney Hall, Sr, near Arkwright Road in Bibb County. We drove to his home and sat with him in his living room. He reported that Clanton surprised him, hit him over the head with a pipe, and stole his vehicle. Sidney ended up in the hospital with severe head injuries. However, he survived and would be able to testify if needed.

Next, we drove about five miles north on Georgia Highway 87 and US Highway 23 to the home of 76-year-old Thomas Fletcher. I mentioned to the ADA that my sister was building a new home in a subdivision connected to the north side of Fletcher's property. I contacted my sister, who said someone had visited their home that was under construction, and they discovered someone had stolen a pair of her husband's shoes. I said, "I'm just thankful neither you nor James were at the house that day."

When we arrived at the Fletcher residence, he came outside to greet us. Instead of going inside his home, we wanted him to show us where he first spotted Clanton in the tree.

Fletcher reported hearing his dog "Eeny" and two other dogs barking in the yard. He had heard them barking before in the same manner and did not pay much attention to it because it could have been a possum or some other critter. Looking out of the second-floor window, feeling something was wrong, Fletcher watched his smallest dog running back and forth from the old walnut tree to the driveway. After walking outside to investigate, he spotted a leg hanging from the tree. He went back into his house and retrieved his 22-caliber pistol. Fletcher said, "He kept telling me, don't shoot, I ain't got nothing." Cautiously, pointing his 22-caliber at Clanton, Fletcher directed him to get down from the tree and hold his arms up. Fletcher maintained about twenty-five feet from Clanton for his safety. He beat on the side of the house to get his wife's attention and asked her to call 911. In the meantime, Fletcher's wife called their son Tommy, and he immediately rushed over to the house with his 45-caliber pistol. Moments later, Bibb County Sheriff Deputies arrived, followed by Monroe County Deputies. Clanton was arrested and transported to Bibb County to face charges of assault on Sidney Hall, Sr.

James Luther Clanton entered a plea in Fulton County Court, and the Judge sentenced him to the Georgia State Prison System, where he died.

JAMAICAN YELLOW GIRL

In early U.S. Census records, light-skinned Black women were often listed as Mulatto or Yellow Girl. Today, they are sometimes referred to as Redbones. In his 2007 book *Redbone*, Ron Stodghill wrote about one of the high-profile murder cases in the history of Fulton County, Georgia. Lance Herndon, a millionaire, and successful Atlanta businessperson who owned a computer consulting company, was murdered by his lover, Jamaica-born Dionne Baugh, in 1996. He lived in an exclusive neighborhood north of Atlanta, where he operated his business. His bedroom became the crime scene of his violent murder at the hands of Baugh, who bludgeoned him to death with a heavy-duty object. The weapon used was never found.

Before I left employment with the Fulton County DA's Office in 1998, I received an unusual assignment involving the Herndon murder case. Howard was concerned that Baugh, a Jamaica native, might try to leave the country to avoid prosecution. One year after Howard's Inauguration, a Roswell Municipal Court Judge signed an arrest warrant for Dionne Baugh. The affidavit read: Personally, appeared the undersigned prosecutor, Detective W.E. Anastasio, who under oath says that Dionne Baugh, a/k/a Dionne Nelson, did commit the offense of murder in violation of Georgia Law at Bluff Trace, Roswell, Georgia.

After the Judge signed a warrant for her arrest, my supervisor approached me with my new assignment. He called me into his office and handed me a copy of the arrest warrant. Attached was a photocopy of Dionne Baugh's driver's license and a booking photo from July 6, 1996. On the back of the second page was a handwritten note: Percy, page Bill Anatasia when the subject leaves. She may be going to Marietta to drop her child off. If not, then she will go up 85 north to 316 to the Gwinnett County courthouse. She lives on Roswell Road.

I arrived early to start surveillance on Baugh. It reminded me of my college days when I worked as a private investigator. Sitting in a car for hours requires patience while monitoring the surroundings. You notice things that most people do not notice because they are too busy going about their daily lives and don't pay attention to details. We often hear the words "remain vigilant," which means to be careful and look for indications of danger. Within 30 minutes of my arrival, I watched Dionne as she exited her residence and walked towards her Mercedes Benz. As I observed her, I wondered how this petite woman could be a violent killer. She entered her car and headed towards the streets of metro Atlanta, with me following her in a low-profile unmarked county vehicle. She traveled to I-285 and headed north to the Gwinnett County Courthouse. After exiting her car, she walked towards the courthouse entrance. At that point, she was not aware she was under surveillance. I briefly stood outside and watched her start her passage through security before entering the building. Once inside, I followed her to the courtroom and contacted Detective Anastasio as directed.

In 2001, she was convicted of murder and received a life sentence. Two years later, the Georgia Supreme Court overturned the conviction. However, she remained in jail as the legal process continued. In 2007, she pled guilty to voluntary manslaughter and received ten years to serve and ten years on probation. In 2005, the case was featured on an episode of Snapped, an Oxygen television crime series about female killers.

CHAPTER 7

DISTRICT ATTORNEY, 1997-1998

Paul Howard, Jr. succeeded Lewis Slaton and served from January 1997 to December 31, 2020. District Attorney Howard had also worked as an assistant for Slaton from 1980 to 1988. Howard assumed the role of the first Black District Attorney in the history of Fulton County and the state of Georgia. I worked with him when he served as an ADA at Fulton County and served as his investigator on a murder case that happened on Georgia Avenue near Grant Park. I recall he loved to add unique displays to his trial to help convince jurors who were more visual learners. Later in life, I understood that some people learn by listening while others learn visually, so we painted a picture for them. From my experience, I became an investigator/media specialist and illustrator for the case. While preparing for the Georgia Avenue murder case, I walked to Kessler's store, one block from the courthouse, and purchased materials to create a 3-D crime scene using toy vehicles, buildings, and plastic people. Later, when Howard became DA, he hired a full-time media specialist. No surprise there. I agreed with him because we continued to perform our duties with ideas and equipment from the past. It was time to upgrade and start using innovative technology in the courtroom.

When he started his reign, I sensed some things would change, but I did not know which direction the changes would take us. Early on, I realized I should start preparing for a different career. First, there was E. Nelson; now, I had to deal with a personality distinctly different from DA Slaton. I had heard stories about his management style from investigators in the Solicitor's Office. Now, it was my turn to experience his management on a personal level. Shortly after Howard began serving, he authorized brief space sharing with other agencies at the Fulton County Courthouse. He filled positions with investigators, attorneys working for him at the Solicitor General's Office, and his political supporters. What I witnessed appeared to be political favoritism towards those employees. In words from an old familiar line, "The writing is on the wall." Things had become more political, and it was time for me to seek other employment.

While Howard did not personally do anything directly that affected me negatively, he issued a policy that if you wanted a promotion and were a civil servant, you had to give up that status. While working in Howard's office, I designed the official shoulder patch and a new badge. The patch was modeled after the US Capitol police patch and the Los Angeles Police badge. The badge remained in use until Fani Willis became District Attorney in January 2021.

I attended several group meetings and training activities as a Special Agent and sworn officer. One group was the Georgia Crime Information Network (GCIN). It was a group that shared information about criminal activity in Georgia and specific criminal activity that was on the rise. There, I encountered Thomas Bloomberg, whom I had known for several years as a member of the GA ANG. I served as his First Sergeant from 1994-1997. The FAA hired Bloomberg as a Special Agent with the FAA Security Division, Drug Interdiction Security Program 1998. While working for the GA ANG, his military duty included working with the FAA Internal Security Program.

After two interviews, the FAA hired me in September 1998. Initially, I accepted a pay cut to escape the county work environment as it began to change. Some changes were significant, while others were just too political for me. Eventually, it became one of the best decisions I made in my life. Another big decision-maker for me was after Fulton County requested $17,000 to buy back my military time. The Federal government requested around $800 for my five years of active-duty military service. It was an easy decision. After one year at the Agency, I exceeded my Fulton County salary and added five years of federal service.

MURDERS AT THE COURTHOUSE

2005 I returned to the Fulton County Courthouse to obtain records for an FAA internal affairs investigation. Each time I visited the courthouse after employment with the FAA, I would seek out old friends and professional colleagues to chat about our current lives and any news about mutual friends or employees. I arrived early in the morning, so I walked over to the Fulton County Administration building cafeteria across the street from the courthouse on Pryor Street. I was familiar with the area after working there for eleven years.

I purchased coffee and walked to the dining area in the Atrium. There, I noticed Julie Brandau, a court reporter whom I had known for several years. At that time, she worked in the courtroom of Superior Court Judge Rowland Barnes. "Hi Julie, how are you this morning.?" "Great, how are you?" she responded. "Do you mind if I join you?" I asked. "No, no, please join me," she said. We chatted for about 20 minutes. I noticed she ate her cereal from a coffee cup during the conversation. After eating the cereal, she drank the remaining milk. Within two or three weeks after our unscheduled meeting, a tragedy would remove her physical being from this earth.

On March 11, 2005, a deputy escorted Brian Nichols to his retrial for the rape of his girlfriend and other charges. While Nichols was in a holding cell at the courthouse, changing from his jail uniform to a suit for court, he overpowered the deputy and stole her gun. Nichols decided to flee the courthouse and would kill anyone who got in his way. He walked across the bridge of the new courthouse to the old Pryor Street building into the courtroom and continued to the Judge's private chambers, demanding to see him. An employee pressed the panic button for assistance. When a deputy arrived, Nichols handcuffed him and took his weapon. Now armed with two weapons in the courthouse, he locates Judge Rowland Barnes, presiding over an unrelated case in another courtroom. When he sees the Judge, he shoots him and Julie Brandau, the court reporter. Sergeant Hoyt Teasley pursued Nichols out of the building to Martin Luther King, Jr Drive, where Nichols shot him several times in the abdomen. An ambulance took Teasley to Grady Hospital, where they pronounced him dead a brief time later.

In 1994, I began serving as First Sergeant for the 116th Aircraft Maintenance Squadron, GA ANG, Dobbins ARB, Georgia. My duty required me to get to know each member of my unit. One of the members was Sergeant Hoyt Teasley. I knew more about him than other airmen in my unit because I saw him often at the courthouse. He worked as a Fulton County Deputy Sheriff at the Fulton County Courthouse. Throughout his years of service there, he was assigned various duties responsible for securing the courthouse. In 2005, he was on duty when he responded to an incident that took his life.

As an investigator at Fulton County DA's Office, I worked cases in several courtrooms to assist in other cases not assigned to my courtroom. As a result, I would meet and work in the courtroom of different Judges. The Honorable Rowland Barnes was friendly, professional, and very approachable. He always spoke with a smile. Before becoming a Superior Court Judge in 1998, he had served as a City and Magistrate Court Judge. His birthday was one day before mine. When people enter our lives, we never know what will happen the next day, week, month, or year! Therefore, we must enjoy our time on this earth. Treating people with dignity and respect must become more commonplace. It does not hurt to smile or speak to someone. I will always remember my time with Julie Brandau, Judge Rowland Barnes, and Sergeant Hoyt Teasley. They all entered my life for a season. I mostly remember their pleasant personalities.

CHAPTER 8

INTERNAL AFFAIRS INVESTIGATOR

I joined the Agency in September 1998 as a Special Agent assigned to Internal Investigations focusing on employee, contractor, and background investigations. I had served as a special agent with the DA's office for eleven years, working on criminal cases. Initially, as an FAA Agent, I worked as an 1811 Series Federal Criminal Investigator in criminal cases. Within two years, our position classification changed to 1801 Series, which authorized us to work only on Administrative and Regulatory Investigations.

During my tour of duty, I worked in several cities throughout the United States, including Seattle, Washington; Fort Worth, Texas; Islip, New York; Oklahoma City, Oklahoma; Chattanooga, Knoxville, Memphis, Nashville, and Tri-Cities, Tennessee; Washington, DC; Joint Base Andrews, Maryland; Culebra, San Juan, and Vieques, Puerto Rico; Columbia, Gulfport and Pascagoula, Mississippi; Fort Lauderdale, Fort Myers, Jacksonville, Melbourne, Miami, Myramar, Orlando, Panama City Beach, Pensacola, Sarasota, Tampa, and West Palm Beach, Florida; Bessemer, Birmingham, Huntsville, Montgomery, and Vestavia Hills, Alabama; Charleston, Columbia, Greenville, and Myrtle Beach, South Carolina; Charlotte, Durham, and Raleigh, North Carolina; Dulles and Leesburg, Virginia; Philadelphia, Pennsylvania; Atlantic City, New Jersey; Louisville, Kentucky; Atlanta, Augusta, College Park, Hampton, Macon, and Peachtree City, Georgia; and the United States Virgin Islands.

The FAA Regional Office is in College Park, Georgia, about one block east of the MARTA station. The building is red brick, and the windows appear dark outside. A second building, the Campus building, is on the east side of the main building. A large parking lot surrounds both buildings in a fenced-in, secure area. Armed Security Guards are positioned at the north and south entrances. The view from my fourth-floor office was great. During my twenty years at the FAA, I investigated several exciting cases and became the subject or target of investigations and complaints myself. I will share some of these cases.

TECHNICAL OPERATIONS INVESTIGATION

I was assigned to investigate an employee working at a Technical Operations facility at a small airport in Tennessee. The employee was accused of ethics violations for signing a contract to perform excavation work for the government while serving as an employee with the government. Since this was a possible criminal case, I contacted the Department of Transportation, Office of Inspector General Investigations (DOT-OIG). They agreed to accompany me on the investigation to decide whether to accept the case based on the information we found during my administrative investigation. The DOT-OIG Agent and I traveled to a small Tennessee town and started the investigation by obtaining bank and equipment rental records and identifying potential witnesses, such as employees. First, we visited the work site and interviewed an actively working employee. He cooperated and confirmed that his boss, the Subject under investigation, hired him to help with the assigned contract. He further reported that his boss had not paid him in a couple of weeks, which caused him concern. He named a second employee who lived in the area. We pursued another witness with that information and later learned they had a criminal past. As a result, we contacted the local police to accompany us to his residence, which was a single-wide mobile home. The potential witness was well known to local law enforcement, was a previous owner/operator of a juke joint, and was also known to sell drugs. When we arrived at his trailer, the local police officer announced that we were there to interview him.

He told the officer that the Federal Agents could come inside, but he could not enter without a warrant. The local officer left us to conduct the interview. Special Agent Steve, who was armed, and I walked inside, and my first observation was a line of boxes against the hallway walls. I asked him why he had boxes in his home and what he intended to do with them. The guy showed us his easels and canvases used for painting. He further stated that he is not a real artist but would throw paint on a canvas and call it abstract art. "People on eBay will buy anything, and so far, they are buying my paintings, which is legal," he said. He told us he had worked for the Agency manager at the excavation site but did not like how he treated him.

Next, we met a young Black man at the equipment rental company. What was different about him was the way he spoke. I have traveled worldwide and heard different dialects in other countries. This brother was a Black man who sounded like his culture was of someone living among people from the rural backcountry in the hills of Tennessee or West Virginia. I do not emphasize his speech to make fun of him in any way, but it was very amusing to us at the time. He helped provide the information we needed to show that our subject had rented the equipment at the work site. After completing the investigation, the Department of Transportation-Office of Inspector General (DOT-OIG) decided not to prosecute the employee criminally. However, the FAA terminated the employee. Interestingly, the Technical Operations manager attempted to regain his position ten years after his termination. He was denied re-employment.

PERIODIC MAINTENANCE REQUIREMENTS

Sometimes, our investigations required us to read technical manuals to become familiar with terms, procedures, and equipment before starting interviews and identifying evidence to be used in the investigation. I was assigned a case in North Carolina that required technical assistance, so I solicited a technician to accompany me for the inquiry. The employees had allegedly falsified maintenance records to cover up a lack of periodic maintenance performed on backup generators located at various sites in and around a 25-to-30-mile radius of the international airport. I had to become familiar with glide slopes, inner and outer marker beacons, localizers, Instrument Landing Systems (ILS), and Visual Flight Rules (VFR). A marker beacon is a type of VHF radio beacon used in aviation, usually in conjunction with an ILS, to give pilots a means to determine position along an established route to a destination, such as a runway.

We visited each location, typically a small building in and around the airport. We checked the maintenance and visitor logs and the work performance records of each person responsible for the facilities. Backup generators are vital to maintaining power during an electrical failure. After each employee was interviewed, we found instances of people needing to follow the correct procedures, but no significant violations were found. During several investigations, I learned that many of the alleged incidents are reported to create changes in the work environment, such as an attempt to eliminate certain management officials who have allegedly created a moral problem or showed favoritism in the workplace.

PUERTO RICO OPERATIONS UNDER SCRUTINY

According to Wikipedia, Puerto Rico (P.R.) is a Caribbean Island and an unincorporated U.S. Territory with a population of approximately 3.2 million as of 2020. Almost 50% of the population consists of residents of two or more mixed races.

Puerto Rico's residents have been U.S. citizens since 1917. However, they cannot vote for president or vice president while living on the island.

The Puerto Rican Trench is located north of Puerto Rico and is considered the deepest part of the Atlantic Ocean (5.2 miles). A 4.8 earthquake happened there in 1987, a 6.4 in 2014, and a 6.0 in 2019, making the island susceptible to tsunamis.

I was assigned a significant investigation in Puerto Rico involving allegations against Operations and Maintenance Inspectors receiving rewards and benefits from a charitable event held each year at a golf resort. Employees solicited money from companies regulated by the Agency.

Once again, I solicited assistance from Agency employees assigned to Puerto Rico; since there was a language barrier in some cases, I obtained donation records from the employees who hosted and managed the event. They collected over $23,000 but only donated $2,300 to a charity. Much of the money was spent on gifts, rental cars, hotel rooms, and other employee benefits. The donors cooperated and indicated they were unaware that donating was wrong; however, they felt they needed to donate to remain in good grace with the inspectors. This acceptance of donations was totally against Agency ethics rules. One of the exhibits always used in an administrative investigation is the training records that specifically show the date of ethics training. After three weeks of interviews on the Caribbean Island, I found several violations. Now, things were beginning to heat up.

While in Puerto Rico, I visited two islands, Culebra and Vieques, to interview owners of small commuter airlines. The owners cooperated without problems. I learned that the islands have a unique culture that practices a form of mutual aid, often expressed as, 'You scratch my back, and I will scratch yours.'

This cultural norm fosters a strong sense of community, where people look out for and help one another.

As you may know, Vieques was the island the United States Navy used for bombing practice. For several years, the residents complained about the bombing and its impact on the increase in cancer among residents in the surrounding area. There were often protests on the island and at the military installation near the East end of the island named Roosevelt Roads Naval Station. Jesse Jackson, Al Sharpton, and Robert Kennedy, Jr. protested. In 2004 the bombing stopped, and the residents thought it would make them happy and safe. However, the closure of the Naval Air Station had a devastating impact on the local economy. When a military installation closes, many people lose their government jobs and revenue from various businesses, including property rentals, dry cleaners, restaurants, car sales, auto service repairs, barber shops, etc. This economic fallout was a stark reminder of the far-reaching consequences of military actions.

One night, I was in my hotel room at the Embassy Suites in Isla Verde when someone placed a brown envelope under my door. I first noticed it when I arrived in the room. Upon opening it, I saw several pictures of inspectors at a party in an aircraft hangar. There was a note attached that said the inspectors often frequented the airline owner's home in the Dominican Republic, where they played golf at a nine-hole golf course on his property. Moreover, the inspectors would also attend parties there regularly. This information raised concerns about the impartiality of the inspections, especially considering that the airlines operated between the Dominican Republic and Puerto Rico.

After completing the investigation, we learned that three of the employees under investigation developed cancer, and two of them died. Within two years following my investigation, the FAA closed the Flight Operations Inspector's Office in San Juan and moved it to Miramar, Florida, leaving only General Aviation inspectors. The Agency decided there was too much "back-scratching."

On another occasion, while in Isla Verde, Carolina, PR for work, I stayed at the Embassy Suites near the airport, approximately three blocks from Isla Verde beach. Walking towards the Beach, I crossed Avenida Isla Verde and continued to Jose M. Tartak Avenue. On the right side of the street, the sidewalk spans between the street and a concrete wall securing condominiums on the right.

As I came within twenty-five yards of the Beach, I encountered a large group of 12 or more people who appeared to be a Puerto Rican family leaving the Beach. I continued walking on the right side of the sidewalk and noticed they were determined not to break ranks. They were spread across the sidewalk on both sides, about six feet. I maintained my pace as the distance between us lessened. I wondered if they would move over as most people would, but they continued walking in my direction. I asked myself if these people were just rude or testing me because I was alone. As I continued walking, I noticed the group, which included primarily people under forty with kids, males, and females, continued walking towards me. I remained on my path until I was within three feet of the group. At that point, they parted slightly to allow my passage. One of the males, late twenties, or early thirties, said, "Really, man." I said, "In America, we move to the right when we encounter pedestrian traffic while walking on a narrow path; Puerto Rico is part of America." He looked at me strangely and said, "That's f##ked up, man." As I continued walking, I uttered the words of the late Marvin McDowell, "Merry Christmas." This encounter highlighted the need for mutual respect and understanding of accepted norms in American society.

THE EMPLOYEE PYRAMID SCHEME

The drive from College Park to Hampton, Georgia, is about twenty-five miles. The Atlanta Air Route Traffic Control Center (ARTCC) operates near the Atlanta Motor Speedway. The Agency operates from a secure facility that controls all air traffic in a defined area. Their primary responsibility is sequencing and separating flights, arrivals, and departures to provide a safe, orderly, and expeditious flow of aircraft. The ARTCC covers an area of 129,000 square miles in the Southern United States, which includes Georgia, Alabama, South Carolina, North Carolina, Tennessee, Kentucky, West Virginia, Virginia, and parts of Florida and Mississippi. Other ARTCC locations include Houston, Jacksonville, Washington, Indianapolis, New York, Boston, and Memphis. I have worked at all the above locations listed except Indianapolis.

A scheme was masterminded and used employees' retirement funds unsuspectedly. Several employees filed a complaint alleging they invested money from their 401K retirement accounts in a company owned by two air traffic control employees to receive higher and quicker turnaround payouts. I conducted a thorough Administrative Investigation of two employees, interviewed several witnesses and victims of the fraud, and later referred the cases to the Florida Department of Law Enforcement (FDLE) and the Futures Trading Commission.

In July 2011, The U.S. Commodity Futures Trading Commission (CFTC) filed charges against Louis J. Giddens, Jr. of Fayetteville, Georgia; Adam W. Dutton of Peachtree City, Georgia; and Michael Gomez of Valrico, Florida for operating a fraudulent off-exchange foreign currency (forex) scheme in which they solicited millions of dollars from working people.

TARGET OF INVESTIGATION

According to an FAA Order that established the Accountability Board (A.B.) in 1998 and expanded it in 2000, the scope of the Board included allegations or incidents of verbal, written, graphic, or physical harassment and other misconduct that creates or may reasonably be expected to create, an intimidating, hostile, or offensive work environment based on age, color, disability, gender, national origin, race, religion, genetic information, sexual orientation, sexual misconduct, reprisal and management's failure to report. The order prescribes procedures for reporting, investigating, processing such allegations, and analyzing data to identify trends to support Agency leadership in addressing harassment claims.

In August 2015, I received a letter of reprimand for disparaging references and expressing a stereotypical view that had a detrimental impact. A Black female FAA employee accused me of saying, "If it weren't for the women's rights movement, you wouldn't be working."
On March 25, 2015, I attended a ceremony celebrating Women's History Month at the regional office auditorium. After entering the auditorium, I chose to sit close to the front, a few rows from the stage. Seated in a row behind me were two familiar faces: a supervisor and an Administrative Assistant from Human Resources.

The honorees included Millie Strickland, Director of the Office of Civil Rights; Winsome Lenfert, Airports Division Manager; Mary Sherer, Director of Operations Air Traffic Services; Dannette Giles, Technical Operations Manager; Randy

Hyman, Regional Counsel, Southern Region; and Kathleen Bergen, Communications Manager, Eastern Services Area.

During my 20 years as an investigator, I conducted investigations involving employees in each of the honorees' departments and offices. Hosea Williams' daughter, Elizabeth Omilami, was listed to be the guest speaker. I turned towards two females sitting behind me. I wanted to include history in my comment. Since Hosea was my fraternity brother and a civil rights activist, I said, "The Civil Rights Movement has had a major impact on the gains of Blacks, Hispanics, women, and especially white women in the workplace." In her statement to the investigator, the Black female supervisor reported that she told me, "Percy, sometimes you can say things that are offensive to others." I responded, "If anyone is offended by the truth, they are ignorant of the Civil Rights Movement." I recognized at that point there was no need to enter a conversation with her. I turned toward the stage as the PowerPoint presentation started. The slides included a photo of each honoree and summarized their accolades. In the slides, each honoree was asked to comment on the challenges faced as a female manager in a male-dominated industry. When I saw the responses, I turned to the females behind me, pointed to the screen, and said, "That is what I'm talking about." I turned around and continued to watch the program. As I scanned around me, I noticed the supervisor was texting. Later, I learned from an exhibit in the investigative file that she texted her manager to report me for making an alleged borderline offensive remark. After the program ended, I left the auditorium and returned to work.

After a week on a cruise, I returned to the office and learned I was under investigation for allegedly making disparaging remarks in the presence of two employees during a Women's History Month Program. As a result, an investigator from our Washington D.C. office, Ann Branch, arranged to interview me regarding the incident. This investigation was an education in human behavior for sure. Sometimes, it is not what or how you say something; it depends on how it is received or interpreted. In my case, the listeners were not good listeners, so at least one of them exaggerated the facts to fit her perceptions. Moreover, by her admission, the supervisor visited the witness in her work area and planted thoughts in her head, thus tampering with the investigation and suggesting her version of the facts.

In a statement to an FAA investigator, Cal Dumas reported she was a manager on March 25, 2014. However, the correct date was March 25, 2015. Dumas reported attending the Women's History Month Ceremony in the auditorium and sat next to Erin, a Clerk in the Personnel Division. She said, "Percy came down and sat one row in front of Erin, faced the PowerPoint slides, then turned around to face Erin and said something to the effect that if it were not for the women's rights movement, you would not be working." In her statement, she also said Erin looked at her in shock. She continued and said, "Percy repeated himself."

Dumas admitted that my comment tested her as a new manager. Truthfully, she could have been a better listener and understood the purpose of my comment. Dumas thought I said something negative, so she elevated the incident and reported it to her manager. She reported it because she was not sure if Erin would report it. At that point, she had been a supervisor for three years and did not want to be investigated if Erin had reported the incident to her manager. Because of Dumas's insecurity and lack of listening skills, she elevated the incident to the point where an investigation was required, whether frivolous or not. This unnecessary investigation significantly impacted the workplace dynamics, highlighting the need for a fair and thorough process.

Dumas was aware I served as an investigator, which made her nervous about what she perceived I said. She feared she could have been disciplined if Erin had reported the incident, and she did not report it. As a result, her immediate action was to report the incident to her manager as required by FAA policy to cover her butt. Her insecurity, fear of investigation and punishment for not reporting an incident, and poor listening skills led her to report the incident. However, due to her exaggeration and misunderstanding of the facts, she tried to cover up by going to the only witness to plant thoughts in her head. This incident underscores the importance of a fair investigation, ensuring transparency and accountability in conflict resolution. Dumas was so out of focus that she did not even understand my comments were not directed towards one person; it was "small talk" for her and Erin.

In her statement, Erin said she was not shocked or offended by my words. She said, "There was a PowerPoint presentation on a small screen that ran before the ceremony started about women in the FAA. Somewhere in the presentation, it spoke about women's lib or something like that. Mr. Freeman then just turned around and said something to the effect that women's lib helped women get jobs; I wasn't upset or offended by what he said."

In three rebuttal memorandums to my manager, I identified all the inconsistencies in the witness statements, the influence of the witness by the supervisor, and the poor investigation conducted by the assigned agent. Dumas as a supervisor, intended to influence the witness, which I pointed out in my rebuttals. Initially, my division manager asked if I would fly to

New York City for mediation with the Deputy Director. I booked a flight and a one-night stay in a hotel near the airport in Jamaica, NY. After checking my bag at the airport on the day of the flight, my division manager called and asked me to cancel the flight because the mediation was changed back to Atlanta. I told her I was traveling to New York with my checked luggage. I flew to New York, spent the night, and returned to Atlanta the next day. While there, I visited the hotel bar and met the sister of a Board Chairperson and President of an NFL football team. We chatted over drinks, and she told me how it felt hanging out with her sister at NFL football games. Sometimes, you will only get to know who sits beside you at a bar if you start a friendly conversation. I had a long conversation with her about family history research. The next day, I returned to College Park, Georgia. The Assistant Division Manager asked me what I wanted from the mediation. "I want the letter of reprimand removed from my file immediately," I said. She said, "Okay." In the end, I participated in mediation via teleconference, resulting in the removal of the Letter of Reprimand from my file

CLOWNS CONTROLLING AIR TRAFFIC

In January 2007, the Agency, a reputable investigative body with a proven history in handling such cases, dispatched me to conduct a crucial investigation into two incidents at the Tampa Air Traffic Control Tower. The gravity of the situation was clear, and the primary goal was to produce a formal report of the investigation, which would serve as a critical document for management and stakeholders involved in the investigation and workplace policies.

In December 2006, a local newspaper interviewed the Tampa Airport air traffic manager regarding air traffic issues. The interview appeared in a local newspaper with her photograph. This photograph was later acquired, laminated, and placed in the men's bathroom urinal on the ground floor near air traffic management offices at the tower's base. The second incident involved someone allegedly deflating tires on the air traffic manager's privately owned vehicle, parked near the building at the government facility. At the same time, she traveled out of town for a meeting. These incidents, which posed a serious threat to her safety, may have resulted from her involvement in national contract negotiations with the National Air Traffic Controllers Association.

One of the critical issues discussed during the investigation was the need for a revised and more stringent dress code for air traffic employees. The previous dress code, which allowed too much flexibility, had become a tool for mocking the rules, leading to significant employee unrest.

Upon my arrival at the facility to commence the investigations, I observed several controllers wearing what could only be described as clown outfits. These outfits were designed to resemble clown costumes, with employees wearing mismatched patterns, prints, and colors and older clothing such as bell bottoms. They even went as far as wearing bright-colored suspenders and multicolored socks and shoes. They would bring their 'clown suits' to work and change before reporting for duty, using these outfits to protest the dress code and irritate management.

I meticulously developed leads during my investigation and identified employees I believed had access, opportunity, and motive to commit the two acts. Based on the information provided by security personnel, I determined that Patrick, President of the local union, was a suspect in the tire deflation incident. However, I needed leads concerning the placement of laminated pictures of the manager in the urinals. Thus, I decided to conduct interviews with bargaining unit members on shift the day security discovered the photos in the urinals, ensuring a professional and thorough approach.

I interviewed thirty-four employees while investigating the two incidents; most were bargaining unit members. Of that number, only one was allowed to have a union representative present during his interview. At least four bargaining unit members, Paso, Formosa, Parsons, and Buck, requested union representation at their interviews and were denied because there was no evidence indicating they were involved. Some employees also asked me to execute a statement documenting their request and its denial, stating that their participation resulted from an order to do so. I conducted the interviews at the control tower facility in a private office away from the employee's workspace. The thirty-four interviews were conducted under oath, resulting in signed, sworn statements.

After I completed the investigation, management took no disciplinary action against any employees. However, the union filed a complaint with the National Labor Relations Board alleging the employees were authorized to receive union representation. During my many years as an investigator, I realized that employees would often share information after interviews, and union representatives could not be trusted to not share information during an ongoing investigation. Logistically, the government could not afford a different representative for all thirty-four interviewees.

When the investigation went to court in Central Florida, the evidence submitted revealed that while I told employees they were not the subject of the investigation, they could become the subject depending upon what was discovered. Furthermore, we did not give interviewees any oral or written assurance they would not be disciplined based on the investigatory interview. The two employees testified at the hearing that their superiors instructed them to participate in the investigatory examination, that they requested a union representative near the start of the interview, and that I denied their requests. During his interview concerning tire deflation, I allowed the representation of one suspect, Patrick, the local union president. Since I interviewed all the union officers during the investigation, no one could represent the other employees.

I subsequently told the employees that if the investigation did not result in discipline of the culprit responsible for the pictures, we could conduct another inquiry, and any discipline imposed after the second investigation could be more severe. In preparation for my interviews, I prepared a list of questions to ask each interviewee and conducted each interview similarly.

The questions for each employee interviewed about the two incidents included the question, "Did you do it?" I testified that any FAA employee who worked at the facility when the pictures showed up in the urinals was a perpetrator. However, I only asked if they did it after the interview ended. I knew no one would cooperate truthfully and honestly, so I asked specific questions after the official interview to observe their nonverbal communication. The union decided my method was unfair treatment and filed a complaint.

The ultimate purpose of this investigation was to create a formal report, which management could use to take administrative action against the employee(s) responsible for the incidents. Management did not take administrative action since no evidence specifically identified a suspect.

After a few days in court and thousands of dollars spent ferrying witnesses from Tampa and Atlanta to court in Orlando, the judge ruled in favor of the union. Again, no one received disciplinary action before the union filed a complaint. The complaint is listed in court as follows:

The complaint, AT-CA-07-0210, Federal Aviation Administration, Tampa Air Traffic Control Tower, Respondent, and National Air Traffic Controllers Association, Charging Party, October 29, 2007.

The Federal Labor Relations Authority has found that the Department of Transportation, Federal Aviation Administration, Tampa Air Traffic Control Tower, Tampa, Florida, violated the Federal Service Labor-Management Relations Statute and has ordered us to post and abide by this Notice.

WE HEREBY NOTIFY OUR EMPLOYEES THAT:

WE WILL NOT require any bargaining unit employee of the Tampa Air Traffic Control Tower, represented by the National Air Traffic Controllers Association, to take part in any examination in connection with an investigation, whether as a subject, suspect, or witness, without union representation when such representation has been requested by the employee and it is reasonable to believe that the examination may result in disciplinary action against the employee.

WE WILL NOT, in any like or related manner, interfere with, restrain, or coerce our employees in the exercise of their rights assured by the Federal Service Labor-Management Relations Statute.

WE WILL establish that no discipline to employees occurred as a result of their interviews with Percy Freeman that took place on January 22 and January 25, 2007, respectively, and that the information from those interviews was not relied on or will not be relied on to adversely affect any bargaining unit employee in the future; and that nothing has been retained in their personnel records as a result of the interviews that could adversely affect them

I'VE FALLEN, AND I CAN'T GET UP

The Agency assigned me to an investigation in Mississippi at a federally controlled facility—an employee who was approaching retirement filed for disability after allegedly falling downstairs. Someone reported to the Agency that he faked the fall and fraudulently filed for disability for a hurt back and spine. In the complaint were photographs of the subject with his daughter on his shoulder legs draped around his neck. The complainant also reported the subject worked out regularly at a fitness gymnasium two to three times per week and played golf several days each week at The Oaks Golf course in Pass Christian, Mississippi. These regular activities raised suspicion and piqued my curiosity. I drove to the golf course and sat in the patio area enjoying morning coffee near where the golfers arrive to prepare for tee off. When the subject arrived, I became more relaxed and blended into the scene. I wore clothing like what is worn by most golfers. I was armed with a tiny camera in my pocket to memorialize the subject's activities. The subject signed out his golf cart and proceeded to the teeing hole. After a few minutes, I casually walked over to the teeing hole and saw him pull out his driver. I started taking random pictures and videos of the subject as he struck the ball. I completed my Report of Investigation (ROI) and did not conduct a follow-up to find out the results of my investigation. Usually, if there is disciplinary action, the appeals process can take months and sometimes years to resolve.

As I drove towards the golf course, I passed several beautiful homes in the subdivision at The Oaks, where home prices range from $400,000 to more. Upon my return, my wife shared an exciting piece of information. She had spoken with her childhood friend Jennie from the Virgin Islands, who operated her insurance company. Jennie mentioned that Ellen's goddaughter, Charlotte, lived near a golf course in Pass Christian, MS. We obtained the address and learned that I was working on an investigation at a golf course in the subdivision where Charlotte lives. Charlotte, a graduate of the University of Georgia (UGA) and UGA Law School, became a Legal Counsel for an insurance company after graduation. The company had relocated Charlotte and her family to Mississippi. The discovery of this personal connection added an intriguing twist to the investigation, making the world seem surprisingly small.

THE DAY ALL PLANES WERE GROUNDED

It was a typical workday, and the investigators were scheduled to participate in a 9:00 am teleconference on the fourth floor of the FAA building in College Park, Georgia. We started arriving just before 9:00 am when one of our agents assigned to Miami, FL, asked if we had heard about the airplane crash into the World Trade Center. Since most of us started working as soon as we were seated at our desks, no one had heard the news. Several Agents walked briskly to the main conference room to view the television coverage. Sitting there glued to the television were Special Agents Jack and Joseph. There were also two employees from the Hazardous Materials Division. After entering the room, I was there just in time to see the second plane fly into the second tower. I thought immediately we were under attack and had no plan. While we sat contemplating our next course of action, I recall seeing a supervisor named Demi, who received the text about the alleged derogatory remark, gathering everyone in a circle to pray together. It was a moment of shared vulnerability and uncertainty when we all felt the weight of the situation. It was time for management to decide our role or course of action for the remainder of the day and the days to come. Our director was stuck in Puerto Rico after the FAA stopped all flights. However, the FAA Administrator accompanied him, so he was in good company. This type of company would allow them to secure a flight back to Atlanta and Washington, DC. These personal reflections on the crisis testify to the human experience in the face of such a significant event.

On the other hand, I just wanted to go home and be with my family since we had not received any directions, and I was not privy to management's decisions. Either the next day or a day later, I joined other investigators to assist our building security force by checking identification cards and conducting vehicle inspections of cars entering the facility. In the days that followed, the event's magnitude became clear as we realized the need for drastic changes in airport security. Since all investigators were trained to conduct airport security inspections, we were reassigned to temporary duty at the airport. Other agents who previously worked as air marshals were reassigned to air marshal duties after completing training and use of weapons on aircraft. The changes were significant and would alter the way we approach our work in the future.

As management continuously updated enhanced security measures, the Security Division directed us to assist at all levels. I was assigned to conduct inspections at several gates, including all Delta flights to Washington DC metro airports and all South African Airlines, Air Jamaica, and Lufthansa Airlines flights.

As the days progressed, I was assigned to inspect a South African Airlines flight scheduled for an afternoon departure. My assignment was to ensure that the airline followed FAA guidelines on random checks of passengers using a metal detector. Secondly, I monitored the primary flight crew's required briefing of air marshals. Shortly after arrival at the gate, I noticed they were not conducting random passenger security checks. I requested that all passengers deboard the plane and that they needed to follow FAA rules in the Notice to Airmen (NOTAM). The pilot or captain advised me that he only had a nineteen-hour window to complete the flight, and they needed personnel present to perform the checks. The actual flight time to Johannesburg, South Africa, is sixteen hours. I told him that his airline was a partner of Delta Airlines, so he should contact them for help. Within a few minutes, Delta aided them, and the South African flight departed on time.

Another day, I monitored a Delta flight to the District of Columbia (D.C.) and noticed Georgia Congressman Sanford Bishop standing near the gate. There were other people with him, none of whom I knew. I asked one of the gentlemen if he was an assistant to the congressperson. He smiled at me and said, "I'm just like him." I did not think about it immediately but realized I had unknowingly insulted a congressperson and embarrassed myself. The "assistant" was ranking South Carolina Congressman James "Jim" Clyburn, the Minority Whip.

PART THREE

Ledbetter Roots

Darden Swan Roots

CHAPTER 9

VOICES OF MY ANCESTORS

During the early 1990s, I became involved in efforts to change the Georgia State Flag. This was a significant moment in my genealogy journey as the flag, from 1956 to 2001, displayed the State Seal and the Confederate Battle Flag. This sparked my interest in studying Civil War history, leading me to read numerous books and articles and watch the Civil War Documentary by American Filmmaker Ken Burns.

My research uncovered Georgia's rich Civil War history, a tapestry that includes General Sherman's March to the Sea, the Battles of Atlanta, Chickamauga, Griswold, Kennesaw Mountain, and Peachtree Creek, Georgia, Allatoona, Ezra Church, and several others scattered across the state. With its historical markers, Georgia became my guide as I embarked on a journey to visit and photograph as many significant battle sites as possible, from Chattanooga, Tennessee, to Savannah, Georgia, following the trail of Sherman.

Georgia historical markers report Sherman's Right Flank, led by General Kilpatrick's Cavalry, crossed the Towaliga River on Highway 42 after a skirmish at that location. General Sherman's Right Flank at Indian Springs marched from McDonough to Jackson, then to Indian Springs, and camped there before crossing the Ocmulgee River, six miles to the east. Indian Springs is also where Chief McIntosh (Creek Indians) signed a land treaty with the United States in 1821, giving the U.S. all land east of the Flint River, thus sending the Creek Indians on the Trail of Tears to Oklahoma.

My determination to find out if the enslaved from Monroe County, specifically my relatives, fought for the Union or Confederate Armies led me on a journey that would change my life forever. I became diligently involved in learning about my family roots in Butts, Bibb, Monroe, Jasper, and Jones Counties. Initially, I would spend two to three Saturdays per month reviewing records at the State and Federal archives, mostly reviewing census records. Today, due to efforts by Ancestry, Inc. and other companies, records are more easily accessible online. It was a lot of work for me. Records were stored on microfiche and recorded in books. At one point, I felt it had become an addiction or an obsession because I was yearning for knowledge of family history. Several genealogy books suggested I interview as many of the oldest living relatives as possible because when they are gone, so would much of our history. This journey was not just about uncovering facts but also about connecting with my past and understanding the struggles and triumphs of my ancestors.

My grandaunt, Mrs. Carrie Gilmore (age 87), departed this life in Atlanta, Georgia, on Thursday, October 31, 2019. She was born in Juliette in 1932 to the late Willis Freeman, Jr., and Mattie Grier Freeman. She graduated from Hubbard High School in Forsyth. Eventually, she moved to Atlanta, where she enjoyed working for the Friedman family for over sixty years. She was proud to be a family historian and shared history with anyone with a listening ear. She would gladly pick up her phone to check on those she loved and leave them with a story of her youth or a tale about Juliette or Forsyth. Her stories centered around her church family at the St. Paul AME Church, where she was a faithful and dutiful member for over 70 years. I made regular visits and phone calls to Aunt Carrie when I had questions. Most times, she gave more information than I expected. I placed a notepad and pen in my vehicle just in case when I visited her, I would never be disappointed.

Early Census records only listed the head of the household, usually a male, and listed the wife by her first name only. Aunt Carrie helped me identify many female maiden names. Her assistance was appreciated, and she helped me connect with families through marriage. Black people did not appear in census records before 1870 unless they were free. Aunt Carrie provided information from her memory based on exchanges her relatives passed on to her.

Nonetheless, she provided valuable information over the years, which I had no problem corroborating. However, I learned later that deoxyribonucleic acid (DNA) is far more accurate than the word-of-mouth history passed on by family members. Once I became engrossed in genealogy research, I became fully dedicated to finding my roots.

In 2003, I embarked on a journey to trace my family history using the power of modern DNA technology. This involved participating in several DNA analyses, including those offered by Family Tree DNA, Ancestry By DNA, African Ancestry, Incorporated, Ancestry.com, and 23andMe. I also enlisted the help of several cousins, including James Freeman, Sr, Forsyth, Georgia, to submit a DNA sample. The results were profound. James's test revealed the Freeman male lineage from the Ewondo People of Cameroon. Mary Gordon, Gladesville, Georgia, discovered her maternal lineage, which included her mother, Hattie Sands Gordon, and Hattie's mother, Mary Eliza Brisker Sands, which was traced to the Tikar People of Cameroon. Vernon Sands, born in Monticello, Georgia, grandson of

Jessie Sands and great-great-grandson of Hance Sands, had his lineage traced to the Ibo People of Nigeria and Mbundu People of Angola. I also submitted my DNA test and traced my mother's female lineage, maternal (Ruby L. Freeman), which included her mother, Mary Freeman Boozer; my great-grandmother, Mattie Grier Freeman; my second great-grandmother, Carrie Swan Dillard; and my third great-grandmother, Martha Shannon to the Fulani People of Northern Nigeria.

I also purchased and submitted tests for my daughters. My biological daughter's maternal test revealed Mende, Sierra Leone, and my adopted daughter's maternal test revealed Tikar People of Cameroon. I purchased several tests from African Ancestry, Inc. between 2003 and 2004. In 2014, I submitted a DNA sample to Ancestry.com. This company maintains a database and connects participants with their relatives through historical records and DNA results. The comprehensive DNA analysis provides the donor/participant with a detailed percentage of their DNA makeup. My test revealed the following results: 75% African, 24% European, and 1% Asian or Indigenous American.

The most recent advanced analysis of my Ancestry.com DNA results in 2024 revealed a more detailed and diverse description of my genetic makeup. It further divided the DNA origin between maternal and paternal ancestry, displaying the rich tapestry of my genetic background.

Percy Freeman's African results in 2024 show a diverse range of origins, including:
24% Nigerian (14% Maternal and 10% Paternal)
12% Benin & Togo (Maternal)

10% Ivory Coast and Ghana (1% Maternal and 9% Paternal)

8% Western Bantu Peoples (4% Maternal and 4% Paternal)

7% Cameroon (2% Maternal and 5% Paternal)

5% Mali (4% Maternal and 1% Paternal)

4% Senegal (2% Maternal and 2% Paternal)

2% Central West Africa (Maternal)

2% Central Nigeria (Maternal)

1% Yorubaland (Paternal)

Percy Freeman's European Ancestry is equally diverse:

8% England and Northwestern Europe (Paternal)

7% Germanic Europe (Paternal)

3% The Netherlands (Maternal)

2% Portugal (Maternal)

2% Wales (Maternal)

1% Scotland (Paternal)

1% Ireland (Paternal)

1% Indigenous Americas. (Paternal)

Around 2011, I started planning a Juliette Roots Reunion after accumulating many records from branches of the Darden and Swan family trees. That reunion was held in 2012 at Stone Mountain Park and The Doubletree Hotel in Tucker, Georgia. It was a joyous occasion where family members from Georgia; Huntsville, Alabama; Detroit, Michigan; Tampa, Florida; San Francisco, California; Washington, DC; Nashville, Tennessee; North Carolina; and other locations came together, reinforcing our shared roots and connections.

During the planning before 2012, I started contacting family members and gathering information to complete the family lineages accurately. At one point, I began hearing rumors that I had stolen family history information from someone else. Someone alleged I attempted to take over or replace the Darden Rooks Johnson (DRJ) Family Reunion. Someone in the family had either fueled or created the fire. I had no such intention. When I learned about the DRJ, I did not participate in any of their events. Later, I realized that a family who relocated to Detroit, Michigan, all of whom had roots in Juliette, Dames Ferry, and Bolingbroke, Georgia, started DRJ. Since there was no connection to the Lettie Swan lineage, my family did not participate in the Darden Rooks Johnson reunions. However, later DNA results would change that belief. Once I established the marriage between Ethan (Eden) Darden and Lettie Swan, I began creating the family tree. However, I set out to identify the person spreading rumors to clear the record. Although unsuccessful, I identified one family member whose father allegedly maintained family records. I invited her to my home in Stone Mountain, and we discussed the allegations. I showed her my collection of documents and provided details of my numerous trips to the library, and records reviewed at Federal and State archives. When she left, she assured me the people who informed her were mistaken. This experience taught me the importance of people verifying information before spreading rumors.

In 2013, we witnessed a momentous event as The Blalock, Darden, Jackson, Grier, and Swan Reunion held its gathering in San Francisco, California. This was followed by the Darden Rooks Johnson (DRJ) Reunion in Chattanooga, Tennessee, in 2015; Detroit, Michigan, in 2017; and Forsyth,

Georgia, in 2019. These reunions were not just gatherings but testaments to the enduring bonds of our shared history.

I also learned my maternal great-grandfather, Willis Freeman, Jr, served in World War I. His father is Willis Freeman, Sr, and his grandfather is Jack Freeman, all from Monroe County, Georgia. Willis Sr. married Lugenia Colbert (born in Crawford County, Georgia), daughter of Mary Ishe (Ishee). Their only child, Willis Jr., was born in 1893 and served in the United States Army, Quartermaster Corp, Camp AA Humphreys, Virginia, from August 8, 1918, to November 1918. While serving his country, a mule kicked him on his head. The doctor placed a silver dollar in his skull to cover the hole. Despite this life-altering injury, he showed remarkable resilience and had no problems showing it to anyone who wanted to see it. However, he did not receive disability compensation for his injury. He received an Honorable Discharge after this short tour and returned to Juliette. The Army discharged him on November 30, 1918, with his final cash payment of $38.10 and $25.51 travel pay, totaling $63.61.

Willis Jr. worked briefly at the Juliette Milling Company, pictured on the cover, before returning to farming on rented land near the Towaliga River and Highway 87 (U.S. Highway 23), now Newton Road. A visit to his home was like visiting the farmer's market. He loved cultivating his garden and growing fruit trees like apples, pears, peaches, and plums. But he cherished his family. He married Mattie Mae Grier, daughter of Carrie Swan Dillard. That union produced three girls, Mary Sue, Carrie, and Annie. Dorothy was Carrie Swan's oldest daughter from a previous relationship. Later, after the divorce, Willis Jr. married Lettie Myrick of Juliette and remained with her until his death in Berner, Georgia.

In 2017, I completed the third edition of my family history book *Roots from Jasper, Jones, and Monroe Counties*. The book contained 671 pages of family lineages, short stories, a history of local churches in the Juliette community, a list of military veterans, family connections, and family lineages. Copies of the book are on display at the Monroe County Library, the Black History Museum at the Hubbard Complex, and the Monroe County Historical Society Museum. Since completing the book, several lineages have changed due to new DNA information. It revealed the identity of my DNA makeup, conflicting with information that family members circulated. During my research, I learned that there are secrets in family trees, and at the same time, people just believed what someone told them. Now, accepting the truth is only sometimes a pleasant experience for some people. "You can choose your friends, but not your relatives."

Over several years, I searched for my father to no avail. The emotional toll of growing up not knowing my father or anything about his family was significant. There were always questions. What type of person was he? Where does he live? Is he still alive? Does he have other children? As I continued to search, I thought I would never receive an answer. But sometimes mysterious things happen.

During the early 1990s, I became interested in genealogy research and set out to find my family. I began with what information I had at that time concerning my father. My family told me his name was Percy Hughley, and he was allegedly about 16 years of age in 1955 while living in Chattanooga, Tennessee. My mother visited Chattanooga during the summer of 1955. That is where she met Percy and where they conceived me. She returned to Georgia after the summer, and I was born the following year in April 1956. She would have turned twenty years old in July 1960. She died in March 1960 at age 19. I was three years and ten months old. My grandmother adopted me, and I lived with her, my aunts, uncles, and friends until age eighteen.

During research, I questioned my grandaunt, Dorothy, who provided a little information about my father. She was the person whom my mother visited in Chattanooga during the summer of 1955. She described my father's physical appearance but could not provide any details of his family, except that he lived near 13th Avenue in Chattanooga, Tennessee. I searched school and census records in Chattanooga, Tennessee, and tried to find one person named Percy Hughley. Years later, in 2006, I found Percy Lee Hughley on the Social Security Death Index. He died in Los Angeles, California. He was born on July 21, 1941, one year before my mother, in July 1940. The information was too close to be a coincidence, but I checked it out anyway. I located and contacted Percy's widow, his son, brother, and sister. None of his family was familiar with Percy ever living in or visiting Chattanooga, Tennessee. They had lived in Arkansas before Percy moved to Los Angeles. I concluded this person was not my father, so I continued my efforts in another direction. I checked the phone directory of all Hughley families living in Chattanooga and sent a letter to each one, asking if they knew Percy Hughley. I never received a response from anyone. I visited the Chattanooga library and sought assistance from staff members to no avail. At that point, I decided to let the issue rest.

After completing DNA tests with African Ancestry Inc. (2003-2004) and Ancestry by DNA (2006), respectively, that identified my paternal roots as European, I decided to take another test with the National Geographic Genome Project, The Journey of Man, tracing the migration of humanity through DNA. After receiving a copy of my results, I became more interested in DNA and its usage in genealogy research. National Geographic suggested I transfer results to Family Tree DNA (FTDNA) to match with others in their system. I agreed to transfer my results. After learning about this new Family Tree DNA matching of participants, I sought more expert information. I was new to this DNA revolution and unsure exactly what it meant, so I sent questions to Geneticists Dr. Rick Kittles, African Ancestry, Inc., and Dr. Mark Shriver, Penn State University. Both experts indicated the matches showed close connections within four generations. Next, I contacted the person whose email was listed for all three closely related matches (exact matches) and sent a copy of my biography with a photo and phone number. Ralph William Wyatt responded and described himself as a white male, the grandson of Ralph W. Wyatt, AKA Joseph J. Ledbetter. Ralph served as a Probate Judge in Bakersfield, California, appointed by Governor Jerry Brown. He stated that his father, Ralph Tozier Wyatt, retired from the Los Angeles County Sheriff's Office as an Inspector, and one son, Ty, at that time, was a student at Brown University and is now a physician in San Diego, California. His other son, Ray, attended Baylor University and resides in San Diego.

  Ralph conducted family history research, attempting to find his father's roots. Since he was unsuccessful in finding information about his grandfather, Ralph W. Wyatt reviewed his grandmother's marriage certificate. That is when Ralph W learned Joseph J. Ledbetter became Ralph W. Wyatt. Judge Ralph William Wyatt's father, Ralph Tozier Wyatt, was alive and commented that he knew there was something secretive about his father. Once Ralph William Wyatt learned about his grandfather's name change he researched to identify his blood relatives. He found them in Georgia and Alabama. Joseph J. Ledbetter, a/k/a Ralph W. Wyatt, was born on July 28, 1872, in Talladega County, Alabama, and died November 19, 1955, in Los Angeles, California, under the name of Ralph W. Wyatt. In 1874, his family moved to Lafayette, Walker County, Georgia, in the northeast section of the state, directly across the state line from Chattanooga, Tennessee.

According to my research and the information provided to Ralph William Wyatt by a distant relative, between 1901 and 1912, Joseph changed his name to Ralph W. Wyatt. Military records revealed Joseph enlisted in the U.S. Army on September 7, 1899, in Kansas City, MO, and the Army discharged him on November 20, 1900. He changed his name to Ralph W. Wyatt before he married Leona Melissa Beavers in 1912 in California. Leona was born August 23, 1885, and died November 1962. While living in Los Angeles, they had four children: Lillian L., Ralph T., Gwendolyn E, and Eva Mae Wyatt.

Judge Ralph William Wyatt informed me that one of my cousins, Wayne Ledbetter, lived in Decatur, Georgia, and another, William "Bill" Ledbetter, lived in Auburn, Alabama. We matched DNA through Family Tree DNA, uncovering our shared family history. Bill now lives in Huntsville, AL. I arranged to meet Wayne for lunch at The Depeaux Restaurant (former Decatur Train Depot), which serves Cajun food. We enjoyed a great meeting and Cajun-style lunch. Wayne gave me a Ledbetter family photo taken in Walker County, Georgia. Joseph Ledbetter was not in the photo with his parents and siblings. Wayne explained that Joseph had left Georgia and that no one in his family knew what had happened to him until Ralph William Wyatt had contacted the family. Wayne also explained that the family told him Joseph had left Walker County during the early 1900s because he had "gotten in trouble with a girl." He did not know what happened; it was only speculation. As far as he or other family members knew, "Joe just disappeared." Our family history, with all its mysteries and connections, is a significant part of our identity.

MEETING THE LEDBETTER FAMILY

In 2010, en route to Alabama for work, I met Dr. William 'Bill' Ledbetter for breakfast at a Waffle House in Auburn. When I arrived, the server asked if I wanted to order. I told her I just wanted coffee; I would wait for my cousin to arrive before ordering food. Later, when Bill walked through the door, we saw each other for the very first time, except for photographs, we hugged. As she stood in disbelief, the server asked, "Is that your cousin?" "Yes," I said. We laughed about it and proceeded to a table. Also, in 2010, I attended my first Ledbetter Family Reunion in Lake Guntersville State Park, Alabama. It was there that I met more members of the Ledbetter family. I am pleased to announce that I was well received and felt amazingly comfortable with my family.

The following year, 2011, we attended the Ledbetter Reunion at Amicalola Falls State Park in the North Georgia mountains, followed by a reunion in Huntsville, Alabama, in 2012 and back to Amicalola Falls again in 2013. The 2014 family reunion was held in Lafayette, Walker County, Georgia. In 2015, I hosted the Ledbetter Reunion in Chattanooga, Tennessee. I selected Chattanooga because of its proximity to Walker

County, Georgia, and because it is where my parents met, a place that holds a special significance in our family history. The Reunion occurred at the Chattanooga Choo-Choo Hotel between June 19 and 21, 2015. It was well attended and included a boat ride on the Tennessee River. We continue to hold reunions each year. In 2020, due to the COVID-19 pandemic, the Ledbetter reunion was virtual via Zoom. The 2021, 2022, and 2024 reunions were at Amicalola Falls State Park. In 2023, the Ledbetters hosted the Reunion in Gulf Shores, Alabama.

In April 2023, Joan and I were excited as we prepared to attend the 20th Annual Ledbetter Reunion in Gulf Shores, Alabama, hosted by Julie and Louis McRae. We rented an Airbnb in Gulf Shores on the main highway across from the beach. It was a four-unit apartment building with adequate parking and was exceptionally clean and comfortable. Surprisingly, it was about one hundred yards from Julie and Louis's summer home, where the family held some of its meetings. Ralph Wyatt and his sons Ray and Ty attended the reunion, adding to the event's excitement.

In June 2023, we received heartbreaking news. Wayne Ledbetter had passed away in Jacksonville, Florida, and in the same month, Judge Ralph William Wyatt left us in California. Ralph was the first family member I spoke with after receiving DNA results from Family Tree DNA. He was the one who encouraged me to attend the first Ledbetter reunion in 2010, a significant event that brought our family together and enriched our shared history. On the other hand, Wayne was the first family member I met in person. He lived in Decatur, GA, close to his grandchildren and his son, who worked at Emory University. Wayne retired as a Navy Lieutenant Commander of the Hurricane Hunters in Jacksonville, Florida. Wayne and Ralph were regular attendees of the Ledbetter reunion, and I will always cherish the great times and conversations we had during our reunions. Wayne was indeed a conservative in his political views, but I learned to respect and love our family bond, regardless of our differing opinions.

My first reunion was a moment of unexpected discovery. A relative handed me a copy of my great-grandmother's lineage dating back to the 1400s in Urach, near Stuttgart, Germany. They also shared the Ledbetter lineage from the 1500s in Durham, England. The shock and surprise of this revelation were palpable. I was now connected to my father's roots and a family history that spanned between five and six hundred years. This newfound connection filled me with a deep sense of belonging and a desire to learn more.

Later, a relative approached me during the same reunion and asked if I was familiar with Nathan Bedford Forrest. I told her I knew him because I studied Civil War history. I told her he was a Confederate General and Commander of the unit that massacred three hundred members of the United States Colored Troops after they surrendered at Fort Pillow, Tennessee, on April 12, 1864. I also told her he was the first Grand Wizard of the Ku Klux Klan in 1867. She said, "Percy, there is a possibility he is your distant cousin." I was in temporary shock. The emotional impact of this revelation was profound. I told her something I had often heard: "You can choose your friends, but not your relatives." Records from Ancestry confirmed Nathan Bedford Forest's third-great-grandfather Shadrack Forrest married Jane Ledbetter, who is listed in the *Ledbetters of Virginia*, a family history book that traces Ledbetters' roots to Durham, England.

This year, 2024, following Ralph William's passing in June 2023, his son invited our cousin Steve Ledbetter and me to his San Diego, California home. He explained that he was in the process of decluttering and was considering discarding a sizable portion of the family history records accumulated by his father over several years of research. He asked us to review the documents and decide what we wanted to keep, with the rest to be discarded.

Ray entrusted us with the important task of reviewing the documents, deciding what to preserve, and leaving the rest. He entrusted the family photographs to his brother, Ty. On a memorable Saturday morning, April 26, 2024, Steve and I delved into the records stored in 16 to 20 banker's boxes, neatly stacked in Ray's garage. As we sifted through the boxes, I stumbled upon a clear folder containing all the email exchanges between Ralph, Steve, Bill, Wayne, and myself, dating back to the very beginning.

Email From a William Ledbetter to Ralph William and Wayne, September 9, 2009

"Hey guys! Just a heads-up on our DNA match with Percy Freeman. I did a Google search and learned a lot about him. He is a Black guy. A CMS with the GA ANG. (Chief Master Sergeant with the Georgia Air National Guard). I had communicated with him in one email after our 25-marker match (and copied to Wayne) before I knew any background. I will check first in the future. I thought we only matched at the 25-marker level, but lo and behold, he matches at the 67-marker level! I told him I knew no Ledbetters in Chattanooga, knew no one named Hughley, and couldn't help him with his search."

"I don't intend to pursue this further, but I wanted to let you know the status. There is no way of knowing where our blood intersects, but as early as our grandfathers or much later. I will assume much later, during the slavery era, as there was much crossover. His research has shown that about 30% of blacks in this country have European Ancestry." "I should add that I have always been known as a liberal on racial matters. I taught at two historically Black colleges during my long teaching career, and I have close Black friends, etc. I am not a racist. I do not know what good can come from further pursuing this information. If you feel differently, please pursue this as you see fit."

Email From Percy Freeman to Ralph, September 30, 2009

"I have been very unsuccessful in searching for my paternal lineage until now. After receiving the results from DNA testing, I felt a sense of new hope in locating information on my father."

Email From W Ledbetter to Ralph, October 18, 2009

"Ralph, I had lunch with Percy Friday. He was interested in the pictures I had. Upon seeing the picture of my grandfather and your father, he commented, "Now, I know where I get my large ears. He is very interesting and was intrigued that our relatives were from Tennessee and Alabama."

Email From Steve Ledbetter to Ralph, October 18, 2009

"Hey Ralph, Thanks for all the updates via email. Percy sounds a lot like you when you were searching for your past. I will email Percy to see if he wants to visit Mount Carmel Cemetery. I know you have given him a lot of insight into how to find his past relatives. I hope you are doing well. We may need to go to the next family reunion. It seems to be growing."

While in San Diego, Ray invited us to stay at his home, a few miles from the airport, near Corona. It was my first visit to San Diego. I was struck by the breathtaking beauty of the city's weather and landscape. Ray's home is near the westbound air traffic flight path. During our visit, Ray and his wife were wonderful hosts. We did not need to drive while there, although they offered a car for our use anytime. We ate out for breakfast, lunch, and dinner. Since Ray drives a Lucid, we went to lunch one day and charged the car while dining nearby. It was also the first time I witnessed the power of an electric car. When Ray pressed the accelerator, the car sprang forward so fast that I was surprised at how powerful this electric car was. It also reminded me of years earlier when electric cars were toys. Since I was there for my birthday, we ate dinner at a seafood restaurant near the downtown Bay Area. Ray's mother joined us. The harbor view was terrific, and the conversations were relaxing and entertaining.

THE OCTOBER SURPRISE

After months of contacting family members, I finally found a DNA match. Kimberly Sanders, from Detroit, Michigan, gave me a photo of a partial family tree. A sense of connection quickly replaced the shock I felt when I saw the name

Percy Heulett. My aunt had always said my father's name was Percy Hughley, and now, we had confirmed that my father was Percy Heulett. There was a profound sense of relief. But I knew the Percy she mentioned couldn't be my father due to his age. This realization led me to do further research, and I discovered a son of Percy named Henry Heulett, Sr; his son, Percy, was born in 1935. My mother was born in 1940. Additional research revealed Percy (1935) moved to Chattanooga, Tennessee, around 1950. I later learned he had brothers Archie Lee, Henry Jr., Walter Sr, and half-brother James Hall, who also lived there. At that moment, at age 66, I was certain Percy Heulett was my father. My mother became pregnant at age 15, around July 1955, close to her 16th birthday, and I was born in Georgia in 1956.

After reviewing all evidence, we concluded that Joseph Ledbetter returned home to his father's funeral in Walker County, Georgia, around 1909. Travel by train was routine between Chattanooga, Tennessee, and Huntsville, Alabama. Henry Heulett was born in Huntsville, Alabama, in 1910. While these facts support Joseph as Henry's father, the only other evidence is the DNA connection. The other possibility was that Joseph could be the father to Percy Heulett, born in 1889 in Huntsville, Alabama when Joseph was seventeen. Strangely, Mattie, mother of Percy Heulett (1889), was listed as divorced in the 1900 census when Percy was ten years old. His two older brothers were born in 1882 and 1883. Black women seldom divorced during those years in America. What happened to cause the divorce?

Over the next few months, my mission was clear: to uncover my family roots and build a comprehensive family tree.

I began by contacting Kimberly Sanders for additional information about her lineage. Each day, I dedicated two or three hours to researching Ancestry.com. I started by identifying Percy's siblings, their children, and Henry's children. I learned that Jessie Heulett, brother of Henry Sr., moved from Huntsville, Alabama, to Kentucky and started a family there. His grandmother Mattie was born in 1860 in Alabama. She was married to Robert Heulett (Uless) and was mother to Percy (1884 or 1889), Oscar (1882), and Robert (1883). However, the 1900 Federal Census lists Mattie as divorced. Percy is ten years old in 1900, with a birth year listed as 1889 or 1890. This journey of discovery was not just about uncovering facts but also about personal growth and understanding.

My great-grandparents, Percy Heulett (1889) and Rena Jones produced the following children: Jessie (1905-1953), Oscar (1909-1949), Henry Sr. (1910-1950), Olivia (1913-1992), Sallie Mae (1913-1975), James (1916-1969), Laverta (1920-2009), Lyla Mae (1925-1996), Lottie (1927-2007), Thomas (1929-1998) and Dora (1931-2013). Research revealed Thomas died in October 1998, a few days after I began employment with the FAA. He lived near Cascade Road in Atlanta, Georgia, and operated a metro Atlanta restaurant. Coincidentally, Pastor Dale Bronner, my wife's cousin, officiated the homegoing service.

The second Heulett descendant I contacted was in Decatur, Alabama—near Huntsville, the hometown of Percy and Rena and the city where my Black paternal roots started. As I delved into the Ancestry census records, I was fascinated to learn that Rena, age 65, lived with her son Jessie and his wife Mattie in Louisville, Kentucky, after Henry died in 1950. Jessie was 44, daughter Barbara was 8, and sons Alfonzo and Ernest were 14 and 13. Through additional searches, I found Barbara, who is now eighty and living in Decatur, Alabama. It was a stroke of luck that I was still in contact with a military friend from Aviano, Italy, Hal Swoopes, who lives in Decatur, Alabama. He was a talented basketball player for the Aviano Eagles. I asked him to visit Barbara's house and determine if she still lives there. When he arrived, he called me. I spoke to someone from my father's lineage for the first time. Barbara is 80 years of age. She was born in Louisville, Kentucky, and knew nothing about her Alabama Heulett family roots. After retirement, she moved from Kentucky to Decatur, Alabama. However, she said she did not know any relatives there. She was surprised to hear from me and said she would happily meet me in person. Since the phone call with Barbara, the tree has grown beyond my belief in such a brief time. I am filled with anticipation and hope she will be pleased when we meet. Both of her brothers are deceased.

My research into Henry Heulett, Sr. and his wife Sophia's family unveiled a web of connections. Archie Lee, Walter Jr, James Hall, and Percy all made their way to Chattanooga, Tennessee. Shirley Caudle, from a different mother, lived in Huntsville, Alabama; Detroit, Michigan; and Powder Springs, Georgia before returning to Detroit in 2023. My uncle, Archie Heulett (1938-2017) found his home in California after enlisting in the Navy from Chattanooga. His widow, Sherri Heulett, was last known to live in Highland, California and Tampa, Florida. Olivia (1913-1992) and Sallie Mae (1913-1975) made their lives in Detroit, Michigan, and Lyla Mae Heulett found her place in Huntsville, Alabama, where she married Frank Robinson. These connections, though distant, serve as a reminder of the vast Heulett family network.

In March 2023, I visited Mrs. Perlena Kight Heulett Sanders (1936-2024) in Chattanooga, Tennessee. She was the wife of my uncle Walter Heulett Sr. (1933-1972). She died on July 4, 2024. I met her son, George Heulett, and daughter, Linda Heulett, my first cousins. Walter and Perlena's sons Walter Jr. (1952-1981) and Tyrone are deceased. Perlena lived in a modest, well-decorated home on the East side of Chattanooga, where gentrification happens daily as the city changes from downtown outwards. One week before traveling to Chattanooga, I communicated with another DNA cousin, Terrance Jefferson. Terrence is a racially mixed son of April Backus and Terrance Jefferson, Sr., son of James Hall. Terrance Jr. visited Chattanooga from Minnesota to seek out members of his family. While there, his father, Terrance Sr., who lived in Atlanta, visited him in Chattanooga. He visited Mrs. Perlena Heulett Sanders and her family.

In March 2023, I learned James Hall's father is Henry Heulett, Sr.; therefore, he is my uncle. Henry also fathered Shirley Caudle either before or after marriage. Before visiting Chattanooga, Tennessee, I connected with another DNA cousin, Terrell Douglas, who is the son of Sharon Montgomery, daughter of Shirley (Caudle) Montgomery, daughter of Henry Heulett, Sr. Shirley recently moved from Powder Springs, Georgia, back to Detroit, Michigan. She has two sons, Jackson, and Gordon Montgomery, who live in Michigan.

In April 2023, I located my uncle Archie Heulett's family. He lived near Los Angeles, California. After searching relentlessly for contact information through the internet, I finally located one of his daughters, Dee, a lawyer residing in the Virginia, Washington, DC area. I sent letters to her and her mother who are now living in Florida. As of today, I am still waiting to hear from her mother. When I communicated with Dee via text messages, she verified James Hall is Henry's son. She seemed very friendly but a little skeptical of my intentions. I explained that I knew nothing about my father's family until Kim Sanders, a DNA match, informed me Percy Heulett was in her family tree. With that information, I started researching and identifying members of the Heulett family. I informed Cousin Dee that my goal is to learn as much information as possible about the Heulett family tree and obtain a photograph of my father.

During my research, and after locating several members of the Heulett family, I learned they knew little about the Heulett lineages and had yet to speak to each other. The ones who maintained contact in the past were all deceased. The current generation had only contacted each other once I made the connections. My involvement in this process has been crucial. I continued communicating with Walter Heulett's family in Chattanooga; Terrance Jefferson in Minnesota; Kimberly Sanders and her family in Detroit; Shirley Caudle Montgomery's Family in Detroit; and Barbara Ingram in Decatur, Alabama.

In August 2023, I contacted the National Archives in Morrow, Georgia for military information on my Uncle Archie Heulett. Archie enlisted in the Navy on August 12, 1955. His home of record is listed as Chattanooga, Tennessee. Percy was born in 1935. Archie, whose middle name is Lee, was born in 1938 and was just two years older than my mother, born in 1940. Although I have not found a photograph of Archie or Percy, I was shocked to see the resemblance between me and Archie Lee Heulett's daughters, my cousins. I have not found any siblings or descendants of Percy Heulett (1935-1960), who died at age 24. Dee decided not to share a photo of her father and has distanced herself from me since our last text communication. On August 6, I received a copy of Archie Heulett's DD-214. I immediately noticed he once lived in Chattanooga, Tennessee, at 1416 Baldwin Street. This connection to Chattanooga, a place of significant family history, is a powerful reminder of our roots. Military records helped to confirm my father and his family's residency in Chattanooga, Tennessee. This information is significant because my Grandaunt Dorothy told me my father lived near 13th Street or Avenue, where she and my mother met Percy Heulett. After checking the map, it appeared Baldwin Street once intersected with 13th Street and was separated by train tracks. 13th Street still exists north and south of the Chattanooga Choo-Choo Hotel.

WHO IS YOUR GRANDDADDY?

In October 2022, I purchased an Ancestry DNA kit for my cousin Vernon Sands. He declined to take the test, so I asked his sister, Vanessa. She gladly accepted and completed the test. Surprisingly, the results did not show a connection between Vanessa, me, and my sister Carolyn. The surprise arose because I have known Vanessa all my life as my mother's niece through her father, my uncle, Otis Fred Sands. Vernon and Vanessa are twins.

As a result of the DNA match with Cullen Walton, Jr., son of Cullen Walton, Sr., and Lilly Belle (Moore) Walton, which indicated Cullen Sr. is my grandfather, I needed to gather additional information. The match suggested Cullen Jr. could be my uncle while sharing 739 centimorgans (cMs). It created doubt that Jessie Sands was my maternal grandfather. Moreover, I matched DNA with Shamarion Marcus, whose father is

Charlie Hall. She shares DNA with Cullen Walton, Jr. Her second great-grandmother, Sallie Cabiness, is also the great-grandmother of Cullen Walton Jr. Cullen's Grandmother is Lizzie Mae Ford, half-brother of Luther Hall, Sr., and both are children of Sallie Cabiness. The generations are as follows: (1) Sallie Cabiness, (2) Luther Hall, Sr., (3) Luther Hall, Jr., (4) Charlie Hall, and (5) Shamarion Marcus.

For Cullen, it shows as follows: (generation 1) Sallie Cabiness, (generation 2) Lizzie Mae Ford, (generation 3) Cullen Ford Walton, Sr., (generation 4) Cullen Walton, Jr.

YOU ARE THE DADDY

In November 2022, I asked my sister if she had taken DNA tests. She stated she had taken 23andMe but had yet to receive results. I suggested she contact them directly to find out what happened. Within a few days, she received her results and learned she had another half-brother, Jeffrey, born in Jones County or Macon, Georgia. At that time, the three of us started searching for her paternal roots—with the information given to us from family, we had thought Marshal Blalock was Carolyn's father for all these years. DNA proves he is not her father. We followed the given clues, such as shared matches. In the meantime, I sent her an Ancestry DNA kit to follow up on Cullen Walton, Jr.

In March 2023, we narrowed the list for her father to either Clark, Toles, or Redding from Juliette, Georgia. Historical records and kinship between the Toles, Redding, and Clarks narrowed the field. Suddenly, Ancestry.com revealed a new DNA match. We shared the information with several members of the Toles and Redding family. One family member told us the name listed is the son of Pete (Redding) Myrick; therefore, Pete must be Carolyn's father. Howard Pete (Redding) Myrick's father is Anderson Redding. Once the results were shared with one of Pete (Redding) Myrick's known children, Trina Lamar, she revealed now he has a total of ten children: Trina, Brandon, Gregory (Same mother), Carolyn, Jeffrey, Cornelius; Celeste, and Clayton (same mother), Felicia and Samuel.

MURDERS IN CHATTANOOGA

In 2023, I traveled to Chattanooga, Tennessee, to seek police records about my father's death after reading an article in the Chattanooga paper that he was murdered by a shotgun blast to the head during an argument on February 15, 1960. He died approximately eighteen days before my mother died. When I arrived at the police department and told the receptionist I needed to speak with an investigator about a sixty-three-year-old case, she gave me a strange look. "Just a moment, sir; I will check to see which investigator is in the office; please have a seat," she said. Within a few minutes, an investigator said, "I understand you are looking for records in an ancient case." I said, "Yeah, my father was murdered in Chattanooga years ago, and I am trying to locate a photo of him." "Well, sir, here is the problem: years ago, the older police records were stored in a warehouse poorly maintained or temperature controlled, and unfortunately, those records deteriorated over time." "I suggest you check next door at the Medical Examiner's (M.E.) office," he said. The ME's office is three blocks from the police department. I drove there, walked inside, and requested to speak with someone about the death records of my father. The receptionist told me she would check on it. She walked through a door and returned a brief time later. "Sir, we don't have any records going back that far; you may want to check with the District Attorney's Office of Hamilton County." "Do you know where it is located?" she asked. "No, but I will find it. Thank you for your time," I said. At that point, I decided to seek those records another day.

The Chattanooga newspaper article reported the headline: Shotgun Fire Strikes Percy Heulett in the head. Percy Heulett, 1400 block of Rossville Boulevard, was shot and seriously wounded after an argument with Sam Edwards, 30, of 11 Johnson Street, at about 9:00 p.m. Sunday, police reported. Heulett was in critical condition at Erlanger Hospital late Sunday. An assailant shot him in the head with a 12-gauge shotgun. Homicide detective Pat Rowe arrested Edwards on a charge of felonious assault. Pat Rowe retired from the Chattanooga Police Department in 2000 and died after a car accident in 2006. He was the longest-serving officer in the history of the department.

On February 29, 2024, I contacted the Criminal Records Division of the Hamilton County Courts and inquired about the records. As the days passed in March 2024, I continued researching to find more information on Mattie Heulett, mother of Percy Heulett, Grandmother of Henry, and grandmother of my father, Percy. Following a long day of research on Ancestry.com, I finally 'struck gold.' It's often the case that we need to pay more attention to documents when researching family history records because the names differ. The 1900 census indicated that Mattie was thirty-nine years old, divorced, and raising three sons alone. The only information available was marriage records for Mattie Pope and Robert Uless. As I previously stated, census takers would write what they heard and only sometimes spell names correctly. Since I could not find another

Robert Uless (Heulett), I searched Mattie Pope and found Martha Pope and Mattie Pope as the same person on different records. Jackson Pope is her father, and Nancy Smith is her mother. Siblings included Adam, William, John, Isaac, Annie, Susie, and Henry Pope, Sr. All members of the family were documented as 'Mulatto.' Records show Henry Pope, Sr. was born in Huntsville, AL, in 1862, and at some point moved to Chattanooga, TN, where he died in 1942. His death certificate lists his occupation as a train porter. During the 1940s, porters worked on railroad trains. Their role was greeting passengers, carrying baggage, making up sleeping berths, serving food and drinks, shining shoes, and keeping the cars clean. Most of the Pullman porters were Black men who were a source of cheap and abundant labor. Henry is buried at Pleasant Garden Cemetery, Chattanooga, Tennessee. His sister, Susie Pope, moved from Huntsville to Chattanooga, where she married George Williams. Records reveal she died on September 20, 1937, and is buried at Pleasant Garden Cemetery in Chattanooga.

Coincidentally, Joan and I visited Pleasant Garden Cemetery in 2022. I had previously read a book about Ed Johnson, a Black man falsely accused of raping a white woman in 1906. He was convicted and sentenced to death. The United States Supreme Court issued a Stay of Execution; however, a local mob, with assistance from the sheriff, pulled him from jail and hanged him on the Walnut Street bridge in downtown Chattanooga. The story is documented in the book *Contempt of Court* by Mark Curriden and Leroy Phillips.

We drove through the mountains to an unpaved road, with overgrowth on both sides leading up a hill into the cemetery. There was a chain across the entrance to keep vehicles from entering. We parked in front of the chain and walked through the graveyard, searching for Ed's gravesite. We walked three-quarters of a mile on different connecting dirt roads in the cemetery, still searching. There were better times of year to visit. Mosquitos were in abundance, and they attacked constantly. It seemed like a cloud of mosquitoes surrounded me as I walked, which made it uncomfortable. Soon, after not finding Ed's grave, we returned to our vehicle. We noticed hundreds of graves in the neglected burial ground. At the time, I did not know any of my relatives had been buried in Pleasant Garden, rest in peace, Henry Pope, Sr., and Susie Pope Williams. Moreover 1942, Dr. Edel F McIntosh, Sr., a prominent physician in Chattanooga, married Mattie L. Pope, my first cousin, three times removed. Edel and Mattie were also buried in Pleasant Garden Cemetery.

In March 2024, while reviewing Facebook, I saw that someone had posted a video named, Lionel Richie Roots to Chattanooga, Tennessee, by Ivan Cousin. Immediately, I started viewing it. He went to Chattanooga after discovering that his great-grandfather, J.L. Brown, lived there. After a visit to the local library, he found John Lewis "J.L." worked past the age of ninety as caretaker of Pleasant Garden Cemetery, which is twenty-three acres, where he was laid to rest. He also found J.L.'s death certificate listed his father as Morgan Brown, with no mother listed. Next, Lionel visited the Pleasant Garden Cemetery. I can only imagine that he felt the same as me, about twenty-three acres of African Americans buried in a neglected place for many years.

Later, after visiting Nashville, Tennessee, where J.L. had previously worked, Lionel learned J.L. served during the Civil War, and Morgan W. Brown listed himself as J.L. 's owner. His death certificate lists Morgan Brown as his father. Next, he visited the Nashville Library and learned Dr. Morgan Brown was the enslaver of a plantation on the Cumberland River. A diary of Dr. Brown revealed his slave, Mariah, had a baby in 1840. In 1839, while Mariah was pregnant, Dr. Morgan documented his request for Mariah and her child to be set free in the event of his death. Moreover, he left her land and paid for JL's education. Since Dr. Morgan Brown was eighty years old in 1939, it is unclear if he or his son Morgan W. is the father of John Lewis Brown. I have something in common with Lionel Richie; we have relatives buried in the Pleasant Garden Cemetery, whose roots include Caucasian Ancestry.

FINDING MY ROOTS

In July 2004, Atlanta Good Life Magazine published an article on page 14 entitled, *Searching the Roots and Branches of the Family Tree* by Kathy Mitchell. The article focused on using historical records and DNA to trace my roots. I mentioned documenting over two thousand people in my database when the article was published. Since that time, I have documented over 11,000 people (family) in one of several Ancestry.com family tree files. This increase is primarily due to the green leaves, hints, and lineage connections offered by Ancestry. Amazingly, DNA databases help to connect thousands of people to their families. However, I still need to make the connection to include them in my tree.

Moreover, there are also branches in the tree that I have yet to follow up on. If I devoted eight hours daily to research, I could add another ten thousand people. Technology has changed since the times when I spent my Saturdays at the Georgia State Archives reviewing census records on microfiche.

After attending the Ledbetter Family Reunion in 2010, following DNA matches linking my English and German roots and probable kinship with Nathan Bedford Forest, I sought assistance from Dr. Henry Louis Gates, Jr., a well-known historian who produced the African *American Lives* television show. The show ran from 2006 to 2008. I knew he had the resources to help identify my father using the Family Tree DNA (FTDNA) connections information. Again, that is why I reached out to him for assistance. To the best of my recollection, I sent a copy of my PowerPoint presentation to Gina Paige at African Ancestry, Inc., and Dr. Gates. I was immensely proud of my work and shared it with others at every opportunity. I presented PowerPoint presentations to members of the Georgia Air National Guard, Neighborhood Associations

(2004), family, coworkers, friends, and the Monroe County Library (2006). The PowerPoint presentation, Finding *Your Roots, From Africa to the America*s, ' uses historical records and DNA to trace roots. I got the idea to name the PPT from a book entitled, *Finding Your Roots- How to Trace Your Ancestors at Home and Abroad* by Jeane Eddy Westin.

In 2009, after Dr. Henry Louis Gates, Jr. was arrested at his home in Cambridge, MA, for allegedly breaking into his own home, he visited the White House with the arresting officer to drink a beer with President Obama. Following the detention or arrest, I learned where he lived and sent a copy of my PowerPoint presentation on DVD to either his home or Cambridge University seeking assistance with these fascinating lineages. He never acknowledged receiving the DVD and never responded. Two years later, in 2012, he started the TV show, *Finding Your Roots*.

Dr. Benjamin Carson, Neurosurgeon, Retired Author, and former Secretary of US Housing and Urban Development is not just a public figure, but also a member of our shared maternal family tree through the Darden Swan connection. As I delved into our family's history, I unearthed a surprising connection to Dr. Benjamin Carson, born on September 18, 1951, in Detroit, Michigan. His father, Robert Solomon Carson, was born in Monroe County, Georgia, on December 27, 1914. He married Sonya Copeland from Harris County, Georgia. Solomon's father, Robert Carson, Jr., was born in Monroe County on October 4, 1881, and married Anna Lee Gordon. Robert Carson, Sr. was born in December between 1853 and 1856 in Monroe County. He married Amy Darden, daughter of Eden & Letty Swan Darden. Robert Carson, Sr's father, William Carson, was born about 1789 in Wilkes County, Georgia. He married Amelia, born in Jones County around 1820. William Carson was enslaved by Adam Carson in Jones County, Georgia, before 1843.

Dr. Ben Carson ran unsuccessfully for President of the United States in 2016. I met him at Hartsfield Jackson International Airport in 2016, where we briefly discussed the family tree. He was involved in a campaign at the time, and his schedule was busy. I received one communication from his office indicating he received a copy of the family tree. We have not communicated since that date in 2016. I also mailed a copy of the family tree to his retired brother, who lives in Fayetteville, Georgia. Like Ben, they are not interested in their paternal side of the family. This became more evident when I watched Dr. Gates's TV show covering the life of Dr. Carson. They did not research his paternal side of the family. The show was aired between 2006 and 2008. The information was available, but they chose not to include it in the show. It would be years later before I learned about his paternal roots from Juliette, Georgia.

A

CHAPTER 10

THE VIRGIN ISLANDS AND METRO ATLANTA

While working in the National Bank of Georgia (NBG) building, I met George Sturgeon, a Southern Bell employee who had moved to Atlanta from Virginia in 1979. George and I became best friends and continued to hang out and play basketball every weekend. He married and moved to an apartment across the street from Piedmont Park. I visited him periodically, and sometimes we played football in the park. Within a year or two, George and his wife moved to a community off Old National Highway in unincorporated College Park, Georgia.

While sharing an apartment with Larry Bowden, my high school friend, he introduced me to a young lady he knew from managing Woolworths near Campbelltown Road and Delowe Drive. I contacted her, and we met for the first time at the apartment where Larry and I lived. After that day, we started dating. Due to my financial situation, I was not looking for a permanent girlfriend. Soon, I visited her residence, Franciscan Apartments, on Allison Court near Stanton Road.

After dating for about one year, Ellen and I married in 1981. Before the marriage, I visited her mother, sisters, and brothers in St Thomas, United States Virgin Islands. It was my first time traveling to the Caribbean.

Ellen's mother lived in a duplex in Contant, Charlotte Amalie, northwest of Frenchtown, on a street just off the main highway between downtown and the airport in the US Virgin Islands. When I arrived at the house, I noticed a pastel green block wall about eight feet tall with a gate entrance. After walking through the gate, I saw a huge avocado tree, providing shade for the kitchen window, with hundreds of avocados hanging. The yard was tiny but beautifully maintained with various local plants and flowers. Since we were not married, and after meeting her mother and brother, her brother Calvin guided me to my room in his apartment upstairs on the second level. Ellen stayed downstairs with her mother. My first impression was good. Everyone was smiling and seemed happy to see me.

On the other hand, I was delighted to meet my future mother-in-law and brother-in-law. Florence had retired as a salesperson, working at a jewelry store in Charlotte Amalie, primarily selling to tourists. I immediately felt comfortable in that environment. Later, I met her brother Melvin and his fiancée, Veronica. We drove up the winding roads the next day toward "Mountain Top," north on Crown Mountain Road, to the home of Ellena and Chris, my future sister-in-law, and her husband. They built their home high on the island with the view people would pay millions for. Their house was designed with a balcony offering breathtaking views of the southwestern Caribbean Sea. On a sunny day, one could see Saint Croix in the distance. At that altitude, the weather is much more relaxed than downtown. They don't have heating or air conditioning. However, there is a moisture problem and a constant fight to prevent mold. The windows are wooden louver types that allow continuous airflow even when the louvers are closed. Ellena and Chris greeted us at the door, and to my surprise, Chris looked East Asian or Indian. He has a mixture of French and African ancestry. At the time, they were living downstairs because the upper portion of the home was still under construction. When finished, they would live upstairs and rent the one-bedroom apartment downstairs. Chris is an outdoorsy person and showed me his bird and turtle collections. There were iguanas of all sizes sunning in the trees around the house. Once the house was constructed, Chris created a beautiful garden with various plants, including banana, mango, and avocado trees.

While visiting Saint Thomas, Virgin Islands (USVI), we traveled around the island to Mountain Top Restaurant, which offers a panoramic view of Magen's Bay and the North Atlantic. We visited Red Hook, on the island's east end, where you load your vehicle onto a ferry and transport it to the island of Saint John. After arriving, we visited my other future sister-in-law, Carla. Trunk Bay is the primary site for snorkeling. A third of Saint John belongs to the National Park Service.

Back in Saint Thomas, we visited the University of the Virgin Islands, Foliage Hotel, Paradise Point, and Coki Point Beach, a beautiful place for snorkeling. One of the best highlights was visiting the Boschulte Family's isolated beach on the island's north side, Santa Maria Bay. Years after my first visit to the island, a scene from the movie Christopher Columbus was filmed there.

I visited the British Virgin Islands (BVI) several times to see my wife's childhood home. She moved to the USVI as a child after receiving her green card. While in the BVI, I met her cousin, Cyril Romney, who was Chief Minister there from 1983 to 1986. He died in 2007 in Florida at age 76. He received a master's degree in economics from Syracuse University and returned to serve in his community. According to the BVI Board of Tourism, Chief Minister Romney spearheaded efforts to start cruise ship service to Tortola, BVI. He was also a businessperson who invested significantly in equipment and services to meet the needs of cruisers and other overnight guests. His investments included boats, yachts, buses, properties at Peter Island, White Bay, and Dolphin Discovery. Mr. Romney fathered five daughters, who continue operating the businesses he created. In 2019, the cruise ship pier in Tortola was officially named Cyril B. Romney Tortola Pier Park.

During one of our initial visits to the BVI, we met Chief Minister Romney at the Prospect Reef Resort, where we stayed for a couple of days and visited my wife's family. We walked out to the dock, where he told me to choose a lobster from the basket lowered into the water. Before entering the restaurant for beverages and lobster, we toured the property, including Dolphin Discovery. After eating and having an enjoyable conversation, we settled into our room. It was unique in that the courtyard was in the middle, surrounded by the kitchen, living room, dining room, and bedroom. In the middle of the courtyard was a coconut tree. It was a wonderful time!

Cyril's daughter, Debbie, is the oldest of five girls. She decided to attend college at Georgia State University in Atlanta, Georgia. Since she only knew her cousin, my wife, she asked to come live with us briefly until she learned more about the city. Sometime around 1984, Debbie moved in with us at our modest home on Deerfield Trail in unincorporated Fulton County, College Park, Georgia. She lived with us briefly until she found a lovely apartment in northeast Atlanta. After Debbie graduated from Georgia State with a Hotel and Restaurant Management degree, she returned to the BVI to help manage her father's businesses. Now, she lives in a beautiful home surrounded by homes owned by her sisters. Her parents' house is less than 50 yards away, farther up the hill. Each home has a beautiful view of the Caribbean Sea and Prospect Reef. Debbie's home was designed and built with a 180-degree view.

Ellen's mother was born in Tortola, BVI. Her birth name is Hodge. Her father, Garty Hodge, was also born in the BVI. Garty Hodges' lineage is associated with the plantation owner, Arthur Hodge. Cyril Romey also has Hodge roots. According to Wikipedia, Arthur William Hodge (1763–1811) was a Tortola-born planter, alleged serial killer, and politician who was executed by hanging in 1811 for the crime of murdering one of his slaves. He was born in the British Virgin Islands. After attending college in England, he returned to Tortola in 1803 and settled down to a life as a plantation owner. In 1811, Hodge was found guilty of murdering an enslaved person he owned and became the first British white man executed for such a crime. The evidence presented against him proved he committed cruel acts towards enslaved people. The report described him as a sadistic, disturbed, and evil man. One witness testified that, in three years, at least sixty Black people had been buried on the property, and only one had died from natural causes.

During the first year of marriage, we took responsibility for the physical care of Ellen's brother, Calvin, as the HIV epidemic was starting in America. Calvin visited Atlanta and stayed with us briefly until the hospital admitted him for diagnosis and treatment. Initially, he was at Crawford Long, but they could not diagnose the problem, which led to his transfer to Emory University Hospital, where he passed away after a few months.

After Calvin's death, we purchased our first home on Deerfield Trail, west of Old National Highway. It was a one-level ranch-style home valued at about $66,000, with three bedrooms, two baths, and a one-car carport. My wife worked as a social worker, and in 1982, I became a police officer with the City of East Point. We lived just a few miles from my friend George Studgeon and his wife, Bessie.

After my brother-in-law passed at age 36, my mother-in-law lived alone in the downstairs unit of her son's duplex in Charlotte Amalie, Saint Thomas, United States Virgin Islands. When I first met her, she was a beautifully aging woman. She had divorced her husband many years earlier and raised two girls and two boys alone. Her ex-husband, like my father, was murdered. He died suddenly while working as a security officer in Saint Thomas. Her oldest son, Calvin, drove a Taxi in Saint Thomas. He divorced his wife a few years after fathering two sons. Her other son, Melvin, attended aviation school in New Jersey. He became an aircraft mechanic for the Aero Virgin Islands, and after moving to Orlando, FL, he worked for Trump Airlines and AirTran. When AirTran moved its operations from Orlando to Atlanta, he decided to change his career. He teamed up with his wife's business and started cleaning companies such as banks, apartment offices, clubhouses, mansions, vacation homes, and other rental homes. As an additional service, Melvin became the fix-it guy. He would make himself available 24 hours a day to address any problems at properties they cleaned. Ellen's sister, Ellena, received her master's degree from the University of the Virgin Islands and worked as a manager for the Virgin Islands Social Services Department until she retired. Her husband, Chris, worked as a Special Assistant to the Office of the Governor for several years before retiring. He served in that position for five or six different Governors.

The very first time I met someone with the official medical term Alzheimer's was my mother-in-law. One of the most common signs of Alzheimer's is forgetting or retaining recently learned information. Other signs include forgetting important dates or events. Some examples are not remembering the name of your best childhood friend, confusion with time or places, difficulty completing tasks, challenges in problem-solving, vision problems, communication problems, misplaced objects, poor judgment, withdrawal from social activities, and changes in mood and personality. More common issues include forgetting to pay bills or take prescribed medications.

While living alone in Saint Thomas, she began to show signs of forgetfulness. Thankfully, her daughter Ellena and son-in-law Chris had closely monitored her. When neighbors reported odd events, they moved her to their home. However, they continued to work each day, and she was home alone. Soon, they realized she could not be left home alone. They placed her in a nursing home in the Virgin Islands but soon became disappointed in how they cared for her. She remained in bed most of the time and developed bed sores. At that point, they moved her to a nursing home near her son Melvin's home in Orlando, Florida. After a while, Melvin became disappointed, yet again, with the services and care of his mother. The family met and collectively decided to move her from Orlando to a nursing home in Dekalb County, Georgia so that she could be near her daughter Ellen and hopefully a better nursing home. After moving to Dekalb County, GA, Florence died approximately one year later.

In 1983, I purchased a six-week-old Fury Chow from a shop in East Point. Her name was Princess, and she had a very dense, smooth hair coat. Her fur was thick in the neck area, giving her a distinctive mane appearance like a lion. Her eyes were deep set and almond-shaped, with a unique purple/blue-black tongue and a black nose. She was a wonderful dog, but my wife did not want a dog inside the house, so she lived outside. Living outside made it difficult to maintain her grooming. Before Debbie moved into her apartment, my little Princess destroyed several pairs of her shoes.

Life was good in the second year of marriage. I purchased a Ford Ranger pickup truck, and everything went well. After about a month at our new home, we decided to get the furnace checked and serviced before the winter season. Our neighbor was a heating and air technician, so he was the choice to perform the work. The decision to select him was one that we would later regret. Shortly after he repaired our furnace, someone burglarized our home and stole all our jewelry, including an 18-carat gold necklace given to me by my mother-in-law. We suspected it was our neighbor, the heating and air technician. One day, his six-year-old child had just arrived home from school and was alone, a "latchkey" kid. He came to our front door and yelled, "Mr. Freeman, my room is on fire." I ran outside, looked towards my neighbor's house, and saw flames from the upstairs bedroom window overlooking Deerfield Trail. Immediately, I called 911. According to 911.gov, the first 911 service call in the United States was made on February 16, 1968, in Haleyville, Alabama through the Alabama Telephone Company.

The Fulton County Fire Department arrived and extinguished the fire. The police came and charged the parents for leaving a child home unattended. Before their arrival, I asked the kid what had happened, and he told me he was playing with matches and had set a clothes basket on fire.

Most of my neighbors were friendly and maintained their homes and yards. Our house was on a dead-end street, so there was little traffic. I could walk through the woods to Burdette Road, where I played basketball regularly at Burdette Community Gymnasium, operated by Fulton County Parks and Recreation.

In 1986, we moved to Kings Forest Subdivision in Clayton County. The home was a split level with four bedrooms, a dining room, a living room, and three bathrooms. There was a fenced-in yard with a large in-ground swimming pool and a screened-in- deck outback. No neighbors were in the back of our home, only a natural wooded area. Our neighbor to the right was a single white female named Patsy; on the left was Ron, an insurance salesperson, and his wife, Alicia, a schoolteacher. Across the street was an East Point police officer, Rome Hairston, and his wife, an Atlanta police officer.

In 1986, I was promoted to investigator at East Point and completed my bachelor's degree in criminology at Saint Leo University. I became involved in the community and created the Neighborhood Watch program in the Kings Forest Subdivision. After moving to Clayton County, Princess became pregnant by our neighbor's dog, a German Shepherd. Only one puppy survived. We gave that puppy to a member of my Georgia Air Guard unit at Dobbins. Princess remained in the family and lived outside until she died years later in Stone Mountain, Georgia. At that point, I decided I would never own another dog that lived outside. After Princess died in Stone Mountain, we purchased our next dog, a Jack Russell Terrier, TJ, who lived for nineteen years after surviving a vicious attack by a pit bull.

After a five-year marriage and moving into our second home, we tried to become parents, but it did not happen. In 1986, we contacted Families First, an adoption agency associated with United Way. They required us to allow them home visits for an analysis of our living environment and to complete a series of classes before we could adopt a child. Once we successfully passed all requirements, in December 1986, we adopted a four-month-old girl. Her name at the time was Krystal, given to her by her biological mother. During the adoption process, we changed her name. In 1989, my wife became pregnant with our second child, Kari. The kids enjoyed the large in-ground swimming pool.

As the kids grew, it was time to consider their education. At the time, the Clayton County School System seemed undesirable for the needs of our children, so we started looking for a new home in Fayette County. We did not find a suitable one for the right price, so we turned to Dekalb County. Fortunately, we found a beautiful Water's Edge subdivision with new homes. During this time, the Veterans Administration (VA) had increased its loan amount to veterans. I left EPPD in November 1987 and began service as an Investigator with the Fulton County District Attorney's (FCDA) Office. In 1992, we moved from Clayton County to Dekalb County, Georgia.

LIVING ON THE WATER'S EDGE

1992 We purchased a home in Dekalb County's Water's Edge subdivision. It was a beautiful home with five bedrooms, three full baths, a full basement, and a two-car garage. The community offered a 145-acre fully stocked lake, fourteen tennis courts, two swimming pools, a clubhouse, a basketball court, and a volleyball court. We moved into the new home in February 1992 when Kari was twenty-two months old, Krystal was four years and seven months old, and Princess was nine years old.

Like many parents, we expose our kids to experiences to enhance their education. They visited Disney World, the Virgin Islands, Hawaii, the Museum at Tuskegee, the Chattanooga Aquarium, Hilton Head, SC, Las Vegas, Hoover Dam, California, Utah, Arizona, Washington, DC, and they enjoyed a Disney cruise. Krystal attended Space Camp at Cape Canaveral, FL. Kari spent a couple of weeks with her aunt in the Virgin Islands and played in the band at Stephenson High School. Both girls graduated from high school and continued their education. Krystal graduated from Georgia College and State University, and Kari from Strayer University. After being accepted at four colleges, Kari became pregnant as a high school senior. I was disappointed, but we offered her assistance with our grandchild. She promised to attend college after her child was born. True to her words, Cami was born in November 2008, and Kari started college in January 2009. Cami was born on November 4, the day Barack Obama was elected President of the United States of America, and on her grandmother's birthday.

When we first moved to Water's Edge, the community was changing, as many of the first residents there, who happened to be white, decided to move–White Flight–but some remained. Our neighbors, two houses north of us, Robert, and Sherry Burgess, became friends. Robert, called "Bob," worked for Georgia Power. He and Sherry owned a home decorating business. Sherry was also an accountant. I also learned that one of the guys who played on the same high school football team with me lived in the neighborhood—Deck Neisler, now a dentist, class of 1973, and his wife, formerly Brenda Bowen, my classmate from Mary Persons High School in 1974. We would occasionally see them during PTA meetings or events at the school.

During my first thirteen years at Water's Edge Subdivision, I was active in Neighborhood Watch. After my second year, I became the Neighborhood Watch and Security Committee Chair for the Neighborhood Association. Under my leadership and direction, we installed security cameras in all amenity areas, purchased covers for the swimming pools to be used when they were closed during winter months, added security gates with a card entry to the amenity areas, hired a part-time security officer to patrol the amenity areas during evening hours, placed security gates at boat ramps, placed volunteers at all street entrances to the subdivision during Halloween to act as observers, record tag numbers of every vehicle entering and exiting the community, and performed motorcycle patrols of the neighborhood on Halloween during peak hours between 6 and 9:00 p.m.

In 2003, the Dekalb County Police Department recognized me with a plaque for thirteen years of service as Chair of Neighborhood Watch, the longest-serving person in that position. They also selected me as the only civilian to serve on a selection panel for the newly formed Dekalb County Community Service Police Officers (CSPO) Division. After thirteen years of serving on Neighborhood Watch, the community selected me to serve as Treasurer on the Water's Edge Board of Directors. Our budget ranged from $700,000.00 to $1,000,000.00. The Water's Edge Neighborhood Association included five different communities: Water's Edge, Harbor

Point, Lakeside, Dockside, and Hidden Hills, totaling about 1,200 homes, a clubhouse, a 145-acre lake, tennis courts, swimming pools, basketball and volleyball courts, and a boat dock. After one year as Treasurer, I served as vice president for two years on the Board.

In September 2009, Water's Edge, like most of Georgia, experienced a five-hundred-year flood. It was a time when "the heavens opened up," creating heavy rainfall over several days that impacted creeks and rivers, causing waters to rise anywhere from twenty to forty-three feet above flood stage in several areas of the state. Like many communities in metro Atlanta, the flood impacted our Water's Edge community in Stone Mountain. The 145-acre lake receives water from two creeks, one flowing south from Stone Mountain Lake, Ramsden Lake, and runoff from West Park Place and other higher grounds north of the subdivision, and near Highway 78.

When I moved to the subdivision in 1992, residents included Brian Jordan, former Atlanta Falcons Safety, who played Major League Baseball as an outfielder with the Atlanta Braves, Los Angeles Dodgers, and Saint Louis Cardinals. I often played basketball with Brian as a teammate or opponent at the local fitness center on Rockbridge Road near Highway 78 in Gwinnett County. Brian was an incredibly talented basketball player. When we think of gifted athletes in multi-sports, we think of Deion Sanders and Bo Jackson. When Brian played basketball, he would dunk the ball with ease. His calf muscles were the size of my thigh muscles. This brother exhibited a power dunk, and you had better move out of the way as he glided toward the rim. Brian's wife also played with us and was an extremely competitive player. She contributed to her team's wins.

Dallas Austin, a songwriter, and record producer who later became a filmmaker, briefly lived on Waters Edge Drive with his mother. In an interview on a local radio talk show, he stated that he moved to College Park, Georgia, with his mother after she decided to sell her restaurant in Columbus, GA, and move to Atlanta to support his dreams. After moving to College Park, Dallas' mother worked as a cook at Po Folks restaurant on Old National Highway. From 1982 to 86, I lived off Jerome Road, which runs west of Old National Highway near Po Folks. I occasionally ate there, not knowing Ms. Willie Bell had worked there as a cook.

While living in Water's Edge, I frequently walked the neighborhood and would occasionally see Ms. Willie Bell outside. I spoke and continued my walk. It was not until later that I learned her son Dallas Austin was living or visiting there while quickly impacting the music industry. Eventually, as her son's income and popularity increased, Ms. Willie Bell moved from Water's Edge.

In February 2023, I embarked on a heartwarming journey to Stone Mountain, Georgia, to pick up my granddaughter from her grandmother's home. As I pulled into the driveway, I was greeted by a scene that filled my heart with joy. My two daughters and granddaughters were engaged in a lively conversation with my ex-wife. Three-year-old Bri, upon seeing me, dashed towards me with unbridled excitement, calling out, "Papa." In that moment, the sheer delight of grandparenting washed over me: the simple pleasure of spending time with the kids and then returning home, leaving them in the care of their parents.

I reached down and scooped her in my arms to receive the hug. She held me tightly until I placed her back on her feet.

Next, I walked over and hugged both daughters. It was a beautiful sunny day, adding a touch of warmth and comfort to the moment. Lastly, my ex-wife looked at me with a smile and then walked over to hug me. Again, unlike other divorces where formerly married couples are constantly battling, it was amicable. My wife and I divorced in December 2019. There were no issues that required months of back-and-forth negotiation with lawyers.

THE LOW COUNTRY BOIL

Between 1995 and 1998, I attended the National Guard Association of Georgia Conference in Jekyll Island, Georgia. One of the scheduled events was a Low Country Boil, held in an outside picnic area under trees. The caterer used a large pot to boil the red potatoes, onions, sausage, corn, and shrimp. I'm not sure what Cajun seasoning was used, but it was delicious. It was my first time eating a Low Country Boil. Years later, I invited friends to our home in Stone Mountain, Georgia, for a low country boil that I would prepare. Dr Brock Bowman and Polly arrived, and we sat in the family room chatting and enjoying some white wine. At some point, I started the boil on my back deck. As time passed, I completely forgot about the time limits on cooking seafood. As a result, the shrimp, scallops, and crab legs were overcooked. While Brock and Polly did not mention it, I was very aware of what happened, and it was not my best boil. They were genuinely nice and pretended the food was great. However, I admitted my error and apologized for the overcooked seafood. The sausage, corn, and potatoes were delicious. That experience taught me not to get distracted while cooking and to watch the time and cooking process constantly. It was a valuable lesson that I carry with me every time I cook.

Atlanta Magazine describes Brock Bowman, M.D., as follows. He is the Associate Medical Director of Shepherd Center and Assistant Medical Director of the Spinal Cord Injury Program. He treats individuals who have sustained brain and spinal cord injuries concurrently and heads the dual diagnosis team, which focuses on caring for these individuals. He graduated with honors from Johns Hopkins University in Baltimore, obtained his medical degree at Duke University School of Medicine in Durham, North Carolina, and completed his transitional medicine internship at Atlanta Medical Center in Atlanta. He received his specialty training in physical medicine and rehabilitation at Baylor College of Medicine, where he also served as the chief resident in his final year.

Brock is originally from Los Gatos, California, where he was a star football and baseball player in high school. He also played football and baseball at California Polytechnic State University, San Luis Obispo. I met Dr Bowman through my wife Ellen who worked on his team at Shepherd team as a Case Manager. After meeting his fiancée Polly, they decided to marry in Los Gatos, California. Ellen and I attended the wedding and reception at a Golf Club in Los Gatos, where we were warmly welcomed into their circle. Brock's college friend from California Polytechnic University was one of the Gallo brother's grandsons, possibly Tom Gallo. One of the grape suppliers for Ernest and Julio Gallo Wineries was seated at our table. It was a fantastic event. We stayed in the Toll House Hotel in downtown Los Gatos. Walking around the area near our hotel, I noticed expensive cars. After walking up the street about two blocks to a local bar, I conversed with the bartender. He asked, "Do you know the guy is sitting over there?" No, I said. "He owns many of the Outback Steak Houses in California." Well, he piqued my interest, so I looked at the guy again to see the demeanor of a multi-millionaire sitting in a bar. He was dressed in khaki short pants and a khaki shirt, the crocodile Dundee fashion. "So, how much does a house cost in this community? I asked. "Well, let's just say I can't afford to live here." He spoke. "A two-bedroom, one-bath home is about 450,000.00," he said. "Most of the people who work here live several miles out of town where the prices are lower." "If you are lucky, you may find a single wide mobile home for about $145,000 about 15 to 20 miles away. It was my first visit to California. We flew to San Jose, rented a car, and drove to Los Gatos. While there, we visited Dr. Bowman and his parents' house. They were delightful. Their backyard was one of the most beautiful places, well-designed and well-manicured with fruit trees. During our stay in California, we drove to San Francisco, The Golden Gate Bridge, Fisherman's Wharf, Pebble Beach Golf Course, Carmel-by-the Sea, and Monterey Bay Aquarium. During our stop at Pebble Beach Golf Resort, we ate lunch, walked out to view the ocean, and took a photograph on the 18th Green.

While serving as Neighborhood Watch Coordinator for Water's Edge Subdivision, I would host National Night Out on the first Tuesday in August each year. As Chairperson of the Security Committee, I suggested we cook a low country boil, invite residents, law enforcement, and firefighters to celebrate the occasion, and allow the residents to speak with local government and law enforcement leaders. It was a tremendous success and became an annual event for the next 13 years. I served as the main Chef and was assisted by members of the Security Committee. The first year, I received a budget of $650.00. It increased over time to $800.00. Serving 150 to 200 people was the norm. However, I never spent the entire amount, and the balance was returned to the Water's Edge Homeowners Association (WEHOA). We would use three pots each year and cook continuously until all the food was done. Guests included Hank

Johnson, several Dekalb County CEOs, Commissioners, police chiefs, sheriffs, police officers, deputies, and firefighters. On at least two occasions, the Dekalb County Police helicopter landed, allowing children to view the aircraft closely. They also received closeup views of fire engines. One CEO said, "This is the best corn I have ever eaten."

VISITING HAWAII

According to his current website, Clark.com, Clark Howard is a leading consumer advocate and money expert and has been sharing practical advice to help people save more and spend less for more than 30 years. In 2008, I listened to Clark Howard's program on WSB Radio, where he often shared information about travel deals. Well, on that day, he spoke about a great deal on airfare from Atlanta to Hawaii via Northwest Airlines. The fare was listed as $337.00 roundtrip. You would fly from Atlanta to Detroit, then to Seattle, and on to Hawaii. All flights included what is commonly referred to as "red eye" flights, which are overnight flights that can be a bit tiring but are a terrific way to save on accommodation costs. At the time, Detroit and Seattle were Hubs for Northwest Airlines, with continuous flights departing those airports each hour. This incredible deal made the dream of a Hawaiian vacation a reality for us, and it can be for you too.

I consulted my wife before extending the invitation for other family members to join us. We were a family of four at the time. Chris and Ellena were a family of four, along with one of their daughter's future husbands, Olin. I arranged to secure three rooms at the Hale Koa Military Hotel in Honolulu, Hawaii, for a rate of $120.00 per night. I found out that the rates are based on a person's military rank, and after providing my military credentials, I secured the rooms at a significantly discounted rate.

After about an hour of layover in Detroit and Seattle, we arrived in Honolulu. On the first floor of the hotel, there was a travel office that arranged paid tours for guests. We took advantage of the opportunity and signed up for a Luau at Paradise Cove, a visit to the Dole Pineapple Plantation, Black Sand Beach, Hilo, Kilauea Volcano, and Parker Ranch. For the trip to the big island, we met on the bus in front of the hotel at 5:30 a.m. and traveled to the airport to board a Boeing 737 to fly about 165 miles from Honolulu to Kona. After a full day of activity, we returned to our hotel around 8:00 p.m. These unique experiences, from the vibrant Luau to the awe-inspiring Kilauea Volcano, allowed us to delve into the rich culture and natural beauty of Hawaii, making our trip truly unforgettable.

We spent a lot of time on Waikiki Beach, which is about 50 yards from the backdoor of the Hale Koa Hotel. The weather was perfect, with sunny days and always a nice breeze to cool the air. On at least two days, we would relax among the palm trees in the grass near the beach to avoid direct sunshine.

My daughters were eleven and fifteen during their first trip to Hawaii. I am truly thrilled that we could provide this type of exposure to our kids, something we could never experience during our youth. It was a privilege to be able to share such enriching experiences with our children, and I'm grateful for the opportunity to have done so.

FRIENDS FROM DUGANS

In 2009, a Dugan's Bar and Grille group of friends set out on a skydiving adventure. On April 26, 2009, we decided to check this thrilling experience off our bucket list. While many were initially interested, a smaller, close-knit group finally gathered at the event. Our team of five was ready for the adventure: Tracy, Mike, Leona, Keesha, and me. The thrill of the impending jump was palpable, and we were all excited. Mike, a retired APD Police Officer, and I rode our motorcycles to Rockmart to begin another adventure.

We had purchased a bottle of champagne to celebrate the event after the jump. Mike, Keesha, and I were the only ones who skydived that day. Tracy and Leona became spectators and supporters. After we completed a required thirty-minute class that included a video and completed tons of paperwork, Keesha announced she needed to go to the restroom. After a few minutes, she returned. I glanced at her and said, "Keesha, your butt has gotten bigger." She laughed and said, "I am wearing Depends." "Oh, are you afraid you'll pee on yourself?" I spoke. "Ah, yeah," she said. We all laughed and waited for our Tandem Instructor. Minutes later, we walked outside, up the steps to the observation platform, to watch other skydivers as they landed in the field adjacent to the main building.

As several skydivers began to touch down on the field near the observation deck, we cheered for them. There was a group of female college students skydiving for the first time. As one of the young ladies removed her parachute, I asked, "How was it?" "It was effin' awesome." She spoke. "I'm going up again." She yelled with joy. I told my friends that her dad must have a lot of money. Minutes later, we were notified to join our instructors donning our harnesses before walking toward the tarmac to board our airplane. As we prepared to board the plane, the instructors directed us to sit in front of them so they could attach to the harness behind us. There were two rows of aluminum frame bench seats with polyurethane foam attached. The photographer/camera operator boarded behind each person who paid for the video footage of their skydive. When it was my turn, the camera operator stood, bent over near the side exit door, and jumped out of the aircraft ahead of us. I moved closer to the door as my instructor had already attached himself to the Tandem safety harness wrapped around my upper body.

The instructor meticulously reviewed the steps I needed to perform after exiting the aircraft, emphasizing the safety measures in place. His thoroughness and attention to detail reassured me. He asked, "Are you ready?" After my affirmative response, he guided me forward, and we jumped out of the aircraft. We plummeted at around 120 miles per hour, but I felt secure with the instructor strapped to my back. He tapped me on the shoulder, and I followed his instructions for the freefall and the parachute opening. When the chute opened, I felt a quick jolt as the air pulled out the parachute. At that moment, we started floating, and I could see the horizon, the forest, and the cows in the pasture. The instructor assured me of a gentle landing, and we descended to the grassy field near the observation deck. As we approached our landing site, the instructor guided me to lift my legs, and we landed softly on the ground. It was a perfect landing, and I felt a surge of accomplishment. After removing the chute, I watched as my friends landed. After Keesha landed, she started running over to the deck, yelling, "That was effin' awesome indeed."

After completing our jump, we gathered on the observation deck and drank champagne. Mission accomplished.

THE TRANSATLANTIC CRUISE

As I reflect on the great times, I will share a few moments and memories. In 2007, my wife, and I joined her sister, Ellena, and her husband, Chris, her brother Melvin, and his wife, Veronica, on a Celebrity transatlantic cruise. It began on May 1, 2007, on the Caribbean Island of San Juan, PR, and docked fourteen days later in Civitavecchia, Italy. After leaving San Juan, we sailed to Antigua and Barbuda, an independent nation formerly the Commonwealth of Great Britain. From there, we sailed across the Atlantic to Agadir, Morocco, along the Atlantic coast in North Africa. There, we rode camels for the first time and toured bustling local markets, where you could purchase different spices. They sold everything from pottery, jewelry, oils, clothing, leather goods, food, and various gifts. Ellen enjoyed the visit and eventually bought some spices. The spices were confiscated at the airport in Rome, Italy, about eleven days later.

Next, we prepared to sail to Casablanca, but there was allegedly "unrest" happening there, so Celebrity diverted us to Ibiza, Spain. To get there, we left the Atlantic Ocean and entered the Strait of Gibraltar, the gateway to the Mediterranean Sea. As we entered the passage, to the north was Spain, part of Europe, and to the south was Morocco, part of Africa. While traveling through the Strait, we were escorted by military warships, with helicopters buzzing off in the distance. It was quite an experience to see Europe on the Port side (red) and Africa on the starboard side (green). I learned a little about boating. If you are traveling upstream or into a harbor, you should sail such that the red buoys are on your right and the green buoys to your left.

Red and green lights also assist in boat navigation in harbor areas.

Upon arriving in Ibiza, we decided to take a taxi and tour some of the primary sites. Given the brief time of our stay, we selected the medieval castle. Fortunately, we arrived just in time for the Medieval Festival in May held each year. We enjoyed the markets, crafts, food, drink, musicians, shows, jugglers, and other diverse types of entertainment, such as magicians. We heard talk about the nightlife and clubs in Ibiza, but our cruise ship set sail to Barcelona late that afternoon. The next day, we arrived in Spain's northeastern coastal city of Barcelona. We were all in awe of the beautiful scenery as we stood on the upper deck while approaching the harbor to dock. As Spain's second most populated city, we were prepared to take the tours. After stepping on the ground in Barcelona, we would not be disappointed. The architecture is the first thing you notice as we traveled through the city on a tour bus. While we could not stop at each site, the tour guide pointed out the work by their most famous architect and designer, Antonio Gaudi. His best-known works include the Sagrada Familia, Palau Guell, Casa Calvet, Colonia Guell, Finca Guell, and more. We were utterly in awe when the driver stopped the bus as we approached the Sagrada Familia. The official name is The Basilica i Temple Expiatori del las Sagrada Familia. Groundbreaking on the Basilica was in 1882 and was expected to be completed in 2026. Due to COVID-19 delays, it may not be completed now until 2040. Gaudi's original design included eighteen spires, Twelve Apostles, four Evangelists, the Virgin Mary, and the tallest spire, Jesus Christ, making it the tallest church building in the world. That tour was the experience of a lifetime.

When traveling to Barcelona, you must visit one of the best markets in the world–Las Ramblas. The market was near the ancient harbor where our ship docked. We walked a short distance from the pier to the market area, which had pedestrian traffic. There were shops, restaurants, flower stalls, souvenir shops, tapas bars, ice cream parlors, and outdoor restaurants serving various food, fresh fruit, and vegetables. After a beautiful day in Barcelona, we set sail for our other destinations, Nice, France, and Monaco.

TRAVEL AND SKIING

In 2006, I traveled with the Southern Snow Seekers to St Moritz, Switzerland, for three days of skiing and to Paris, France. The group included about 180 people from all over the United States, many of whom did not ski. Two non-skiers who stood out are a former Georgia Bureau of Investigations Assistant Director, Moses Ector, and his wife. We departed Atlanta, Georgia, and landed in Zurich, the largest city in north-central Switzerland, with a metropolitan area population of approximately 1.9 million. We departed Zurich on a 55-passenger bus while experiencing some of the most picturesque scenery, including rivers, valleys, and snow-capped mountains. At some point on the route, we stopped for a restroom break and snacks, to stretch our legs and experience the fresh Swiss air. The skiing there was fantastic. The bright sun gave the landscape the appearance of a winter wonderland. Like most ski resorts, there were plenty of trails to choose from. Typically, I would review the ski slope map and plot my course daily to ski all the intermediate and some black diamond slopes. I recall the beer garden restaurant near the base of a gondola ski lift. We sat outside the beer garden, ate lunch, and drank beer while soaking up warmth from the bright sun. Near the beer garden was a spherical-shaped glass bar, a place to keep warm and enjoy food and beverages when the weather outside was not so welcoming.

Several club members attended the local casino to try their luck. I am not a gambler, so I entered the casino, purchased a beverage, and became a people watcher. The next day, I visited a local restaurant in downtown St. Moritz to eat and enjoy cheese fondue with several friends, including Brenda, Alfreda, Marilyn, Regina, Precious, and others. Each time I visit a new country, I aim to try their most famous or well-known food. While sitting at our table sipping wine, the fondue arrived in a brown bowl. It was made from melted Swiss cheese and served in a communal pot after cooking over a stove. We dipped bread into the cheese using long-stemmed forks. It was tasty, but not my cup of tea.

After skiing three days in St Moritz, we returned to Zurich to board a train for Paris, France. We gathered our luggage and placed it in a storage area early in the morning before boarding a bus, as our luggage would travel separately by trucks. Later that day, we arrived in Paris and exited the Gare De Nord train station near the Terminus Hotel, where we would spend the next two days. After settling in our hotel, we learned that the 180 passengers' luggage would not arrive in Paris until the next day. I was unprepared for that news since I did not carry a bag on the train. As a result, I had to go shopping for necessities such as toothpaste, toothbrush, underwear, and a change of clothing. In the meantime, we walked around after being in the same clothing for more than twelve hours. The groups formed into smaller groups to see the city on our own. My group decided to catch a bus to the Louvre Museum to view the masterpieces we had learned about in school, such as Michelangelo and the Mona Lisa. I was surprised at the small size of the Mona Lisa because I was expecting a painting covering an entire wall. My group, including Brenda Hightower, toured the Louvre and walked towards the expensive stores on Avenue des Champs Elysees, such as Swatch, Cartier, and Luis Vuitton. The ladies decided to browse the stores, but I soon realized I could not afford anything. I just walked inside Louis Vuitton, witnessed the heavy security presence, and then walked outside to watch people while waiting for the ladies. It only took a little time because I was sure they could not afford the merchandise. We walked in the area with high-end stores, cafes, and offices. The avenue runs downhill from the Arc De Triomphe to the Louvre, with trees lined on both sides of the avenue with an occasional stature for accent. After walking to the Arc, we could see the Eiffel Tower in the distance, so we decided to walk to the world-famous landmark. While navigating unknown streets, we saw a street market selling fresh fruits and vegetables and other items such as scarves, hats, belts, small carvings, key chains, leather goods, and more. Naturally, we noticed the beautiful scenery en route and enjoyed every moment. It was a pleasant stroll through the streets of Paris with no guide and no map. As we moved closer to the Eiffel Tower, we came upon a river running parallel to the direction of travel towards the Tower. When we reached the Pont d Lena Bridge, we crossed over the bridge, and the Eiffel Tower was in front of us. I have seen the photo many times, but on this day, I stood at the Eiffel Tower base in Paris, France, a long way from Juliette, Georgia.

    I returned to Italy during the 1990s while on a ski trip to Innsbruck, Austria, with the Southern Snow Seekers Ski

(SSS) Club. We skied at Stubai Glacier and Axamer Lizum for about three days. On the third day, I decided to take a day off and drive to Aviano and Venice, Italy. It became an adventure I will never forget. Before I planned the drive, I met one of the skiers, a medical doctor from Miami. I suggested we drive to Venice since he had not visited there before, and he said yes. I rented a car, and we hit the road. Our route took us through the mountains of Northern Italy through Cortina. After stopping for lunch and beverages, we continued to Aviano, where I gave him a tour, including outside the apartment where I once lived. After the tour, including downtown Aviano, we drove to Venice. When we arrived, it was very foggy and dark. Not realizing we could not drive into the city; we came upon a street that led to a vehicle ferry boat. As panic set in, we decided it was best to turn around and drive back to Austria.

When we first entered Italy from Austria, we noticed the sign indicating we passed through the Brenner Pass route. While looking for a Brenner Pass sign during the return trip, I drove and drove to a point where we did not see the sign. After driving about thirteen kilometers, we decided we did not want to go to the former Yugoslavia, so we changed direction and came upon Passo del Brennero (Brenner Pass).

Oops, that is when I realized I should have learned to read more Italian. After driving through the Passo, we encountered a traffic jam on the Autostrada (Italian expressway). There were no emergency lanes and no streetlights. The only visible lights were from people outside their cars smoking cigarettes or a dome light. We were stuck in traffic for about two to three hours. Once traffic started moving again, we continued through the mountains towards Innsbruck. Unfortunately, the snow began to fall heavily, but we continued. If nothing else went wrong, we would make it back in time to get some sleep, but, as luck would have it, that was not the case. We traveled a few miles before encountering a roadblock. A bright sign ahead of us required each car to have chains to proceed. "Oh, hell no, we are in a rental car with no chains; what now?" We waited for a while until, finally, the snowplows cleared the roads so chainless tires could proceed. We arrived back in Innsbruck between four and five that morning and caught the bus to Munich airport around 6:00 a.m.

In 2000, after I became a Chief Master Sergeant (CMS) in the Air National Guard (ANG). The promotion afforded me the privilege to lodge in the Chief's Suite at Aviano. While there, I visited Paola and hung out in Pordenone for two days before traveling to ski at Cortina, Italy with the Detroit Jim Dandy Ski Club. While in Italy, one of my goals was to return to Piancavallo and conquer the mountain that kicked my butt in 1978. It was such a success! The mountain now seemed like a small hill.

I left Aviano and turned my rental car towards Cortina Ski Resort, Cortina d'Ampezzo, a town and commune in the heart of the southern (Dolomitic) Alps in the Veneto region, Northern Italy. Situated in an alpine valley, Cortina is a summer and winter sports resort known for its skiing trails, scenery, accommodations, shops, and après-ski scene, as well as for its jet set and Italian aristocratic crowd.

As I left the city of Pordenone, I saw vineyards on both sides of the highway for several kilometers. After I started driving winding roads through the Alpine Valley, more cedar and evergreen trees began to appear, growing tall and healthy towards the beautiful blue sky. I drove several kilometers, and the scenery changed to small towns or villages, each with different personalities and layouts.

Cortina's local economy thrives on tourism, particularly during winter when the town's population increases fivefold. Cortina hosted the Winter Olympics in 1956 and other world winter sports events. It will host the Winter Olympics for a second time when it co-hosts the 2026 Winter Olympics with Milan.

Before arriving in Cortina, I had yet to arrange lodging. It was the adventurous person in me acting out. Upon arrival, I drove to the town center, which was also the location of the main ski lift. Fortunately, I found a parking spot close to a hotel. As in most small communities and towns in Europe, parking is limited. With both fingers crossed, I walked into the hotel and asked for several days' accommodation. I was overjoyed when the desk clerk told me I was lucky; only one room was available on the first floor. After moving my vehicle to an official hotel parking lot, I settled into my small room. It was cozy but not impressive. The key was attached to a three-inch wooden carving, and each time I left the hotel, I had to leave the key at the desk. I was there to ski and didn't concern myself with luxury. However, the bed was a twin size, which provided the minimum comfort needed for my ski adventure. After settling in my room, I checked out the hotel and walked around town looking for people of color from Jim Dandy Ski Club. There were many shops, restaurants, and bars to choose from as I walked along the cobblestone pedestrian lanes in the downtown center. I stopped and introduced myself once I saw some Black folks at a beer/pizza restaurant. They invited me to join them, so I sat down and enjoyed a conversation and a local beer. After about 30 minutes, I visited ski shops looking for skis to use for the next two days. As luck was still going my way, a ski rental shop was a short distance away between my hotel and the main ski lift. A beautiful sunny day was becoming overcast with clouds, but it was still pleasant weather for a skier.

    During the next two days, I waited in line to hit the slopes as soon as possible. Again, the day began displaying beautiful sunlit groomed slopes with no trees nearby. Later in the afternoon, the clouds rolled in to slightly change the ambiance. The skiing was fantastic. As I met Jim Dandy skiers on the slopes, I would join them for a few runs. However, when skiing with people with various levels of experience, sometimes you must move on and enjoy traversing the slopes alone.

    On the second day, I decided to take a bus to another mountain, a short distance away, after hearing other skiers mention the excellent skiing there. I boarded the bus around mid-morning and arrived a few minutes later. The scenery in the Dolomites was breathtaking. The mountains appeared red, with very jagged formations stretching upward from the surrounding valley covered with snow. As we traveled to the ski area, I noticed most homes and businesses were painted white with brown wood trim, shutters, and doors. It was a common theme in the area.

Once I arrived at the ski area, I enjoyed my day. However, I should have hired a ski tour guide as an afterthought. When you hire a ski tour guide, you will spend most of your day above 2000 meters, enjoying the beautiful views of the Dolomites. They arrange for a pickup at your hotel in the morning and take you to one of several connected ski areas. You will ski along stunning slopes and scenery and see four different valleys. You will be treated to lunch on a panoramic terrace at a restaurant offering delicious local food and beautiful views. These tours are only offered to intermediate skiers, and the guide will choose slopes depending on the skier's comfort level and experience. The central ski slopes include Tofane, Torri-Cagazuoi, Falzarego, and Lagazuoi.

At the end of my day, I was ready to return to Cortina with no guide and no command of the Italian language. However, I needed to remember which bus I rode on. Now, I started to feel a little uneasy. The clouds started rolling in, and I got more concerned. Now was the time to use all my communication skills, whatever I could think of, or try to find an English-speaking person. I engaged several people, and everyone said, "non capisco," which means I do not understand. Next, I recalled showing one-person pictures I had taken earlier of downtown Cortina, including my hotel. Finally, I broke through and was directed to the right bus to return to my twin hotel bed, "Casa Mia."

The resort town was everything I expected. The closest airports to Cortina are Venice, Treviso, and Verona. Also, Milan Bergamo and Bologna are convenient. When traveling by car, make sure your accommodation has adequate parking. You will enjoy the ride there. You can easily reach Cortina by taking Highway A27 from Venice and driving along Strada 51 to Cortina. It takes approximately two and one-half hours from Venice airport during normal traffic conditions.

In 1981, a James Bond movie, *For Your Eyes Only*, was filmed at Cortina. I am a massive fan of the Bond series, and Roger Moore was one of my favorite actors in the Bond role. I had experienced the Cortina scenery first-hand and considered my visit one of the most amazing places I have ever visited. If you watch the movie, you will also feel in awe of the mountains surrounding the town of Cortina. As a skier, it is the most picturesque ski resort and village I have ever enjoyed skiing for a few days.

CHAPTER 11

TAKING CARE OF FAMILY

The mantle of family leadership sometimes falls on your shoulders, whether you seek it or not. When other family members are unable or unwilling to navigate certain family situations, a profound sense of duty, a weighty responsibility, compels you to step in. While the bond of blood is undeniably strong, there are moments when you might wish to embrace the clarity of water. Due to a myriad of family issues, some stemming from vices such as alcohol and drug abuse, as well as disabilities and differences in cultural exposure, envy, and in some cases, jealousy, I found myself shouldering this responsibility early in my life. Yet, as the years passed, I found no other family members stepping up to aid those in need.

Around 1994, my grandaunt Dorothy Jones moved to Davis Street in Atlanta from Miami, Florida. She joined her half-sister Laura, who had been living on Davis Street in an apartment across the street from Mary Ward, half-sister of Mattie Mae Freeman, my great-grandmother. Laura had previously resided in the Herndon Homes Public Housing on Kennedy Street for many years during the 1970s and later moved to Sylvan Road in Southwest Atlanta in 1979. In August 1974, I stayed with her for a few weeks in Herndon Homes as I prepared to leave Atlanta for Air Force basic training. After leaving active duty, I stayed with her briefly before moving to Stone Hogan Connector.

I do not recall all the details, but I learned my aunt Laura was present when her son was shot in 1972. His wife divorced him, and his mother began her lifelong responsibility of taking care of him. Before the shooting, my cousin, her son, was an amateur photographer in Atlanta. A few of his works included photographs of Andrew Young with his wife during her pregnancy while he campaigned for Congress.

My cousin's ex-wife resides in Metro Atlanta and raised their only child after the divorce. When their son turned eighteen, he attended the University of West Georgia. I sent $75 monthly to assist with his needs, ensuring he knew it was from his father. Our communication was limited to instances when the money did not arrive on time. This was typical behavior for a college student enjoying life. He would call and inquire about the money. I never missed a payment, but there were times when it might have been delayed due to my own life and issues.

In 1994, while living on Davis Street, Anthony tampered with the natural gas line to the building, which caused all the residents to have to evacuate. His mother was also experiencing some mental disability issues. Soon after that, the state placed her in temporary custody for evaluation, and my cousin moved into an apartment with Aunt Dorothy on Gray Street. Another aunt, Carrie Gilmore, lived about fifty yards away on Gray Street.

When Laura became ill, I stepped in to become her son's caretaker and continue to hold that responsibility today. Around 1995, my uncle, Johnny, moved into an apartment upstairs from my cousin Anthony and Aunt Dorothy. Johnny worked for Randall Brothers Company, which was located a short distance from his apartment on North Avenue in the shadow of the Coca-Cola Company Headquarters and Georgia Tech University.

The area began transforming as Atlanta geared up for the 1996 Olympic Games. The Olympic Aquarium at Georgia Tech was set to be constructed nearby, along with athlete housing across from Bobby Dodd Stadium, adjacent to the Varsity and Interstate-75/85. The history of Kennedy, Davis, and Gray Streets was on the brink of a profound change. As a child, I would visit the family who lived there and would play football with the kids on the grass fields inside Herndon Homes. Every Thanksgiving, the older guys would play the Turkey Bowl, a spirited football game with no protective gear. In a community of that size, police visits for fights, drugs, and domestic disputes were common. I bore witness to all of these during my annual visits to the ATL.

Around two thousand, as growth and change continued, Aunt Dorothy accepted a down payment from the city to relocate. I encouraged her to purchase a home. I assumed the role of her agent with power of attorney and signed her up to buy a home. The house was on North Avenue in the Northwest section of Atlanta, near Baker Road and Westlake. My uncle was given the same option and purchased a home in the West End area for about the same price. He bought the house and lived in it for a brief time. He had not learned how to manage the responsibility associated with home ownership. Within a year, he lost his home.

For the next fifteen years, I paid the house notes for Aunt Dorothy. Upon purchasing the home, I suggested she get a will since she had no kids. She agreed and made me the heir to the house. She lived there until she died in 2006, one year after her sister, my grandmother, Mary Boozer, passed. Their younger sister, Laura, lived from 1937 to 2013, and her sister, Carrie Gilmore, the third oldest, lived from 1932 to 2019.

After Dorothy died in 2006, I continued to serve as a caregiver for Anthony. At times, it became difficult to take care of his needs. During the same time, I was taking care of my own family with two girls, a wife, and a dog. After Aunt Dorothy passed, Anthony became involved in drugs and frequently walked the streets to collect aluminum cans to sell for crack cocaine. He would disappear for days and return to his house filthy. My uncle once said they had to throw away his clothes because they could stand in the corner without help. He became a burden, but no one else could help him. While using drugs, along with his other challenges, he was arrested on several occasions and spent a few days in jail or Grady Hospital, where there was some help. However, he would always return to North Avenue (Westlake area), which he shared with my uncle, Johnny, who did not know how to address his problems. Johnny was no help, except he could cook, mow the lawn, and maintain the property. The emotional toll of seeing Anthony struggle with his mental health and addiction, and feeling helpless to provide the support he needed, was often overwhelming.

Before Laura's death, she would visit periodically, but one day, she convinced the caretakers in her home that she had a place to live with family. They allowed her to leave the facility and move into the house with her son and my uncle. It did not work out very well. Her mental issues became worse. The details are just too embarrassing for me to mention. However, I recall one day, I was driving on North Avenue and headed to their house when I saw her walking in the heavy rain. I knew her hygiene was not the best, but I had no choice but to give her a ride. Before stopping, I reached into the back seat, grabbed the sun visor, and placed it on the passenger seat. She got in my GMC Sport Utility Vehicle (SUV) soaking wet. I could smell the strong odor of urine, but I understood she had a disability and was not fully functioning as an average adult. After we reached the house, I placed the sun visor in the trash.

When she visited the house, I did not know Anthony, my cousin, had access to her bank account. To support his habit, he completely drained her bank account. When she died in 2013, she had returned to a live-in facility and died a pauper. My role as a family leader was to step up and help where needed. I paid for her cremation as I had done for Aunt Dorothy in 2006. Her advice and assistance to me will always be remembered. In return, I have taken on the responsibility of ensuring her son's well-being for as long as I am alive. Laura taught me the importance of making eye contact when speaking and the significance of a firm handshake. Her lessons have become a part of me, shaping my understanding of empathy and care for others.

After 1996, there was a crack epidemic in northwest Atlanta. The house directly across the street was the scene of the murder of a young man suspected of selling drugs. Within a year or two, an Atlanta Police Officer's car struck and killed his young brother after he ran into the street to retrieve a ball. The house to the right became vacant after a burglary and vandalism on more than one occasion. It remained vacant for over two years before a tree fell, causing irreparable damage. Around 2018, the City of Atlanta forced the property owner to remove the remains, leaving a vacant, overgrown lot that still exists today. The house on the left side was damaged by thieves who stole copper, doors, windows, and anything they could sell. The word on the street indicated it was "Jack, the crack addict." The house had been boarded up for about three years before an

Asian couple bought, renovated, and sold it for $269,000. Now, a young Hispanic couple from Central America lives there.

The neighborhood was on a downward spiral. Then, around 2018 or 2019, gentrification began, resulting in home renovations. Middle-class younger families began moving into the area, including the West End, like what happened in other neighborhoods across town in East Lake, Grant Park, Memorial Drive, and Cabbagetown. In 2022, I filed Aunt Dorothy's last will since she had left her assets to me. During the past few years, my cousin and my uncle, Johnny Boozer, lived in the house and put in significant effort to maintain it despite my cousin's intermittent jail stays. Johnny did a respectable job maintaining the lawn and performing minor maintenance as needed, but all good things must end. I finally realized I could no longer handle the responsibility, and I asked Anthony's son to take on the responsibility, but he declined. Following my divorce, I decided to move sixty miles south of Atlanta. It was a time of change, and it was best for my cousin to live in a more comfortable and supportive environment, such as an assisted living home.

From 2021 to 2023, I constantly received phone calls and solicitation notices in the mail inquiring about the sale of the property. However, I only made up my mind to sell once I learned Anthony was experiencing more medical problems with urination. He continued to smoke cigarettes, resulting in breathing issues. He still had wits about himself, enough to understand how to use public transportation for travel and what was happening, especially how to spend money. Periodically, I would visit the house and another cousin's home nearby.

In July 2022, I received notice from Ms. Hutton, my cousin's caretaker, informing me she took Anthony to Grady

Hospital for an appointment. The hospital was supposed to let her know when he was ready for release and pickup. That did not happen, so Anthony left the hospital and disappeared into the streets of Atlanta. He remained missing for about seven days before arriving at our Cousin Greg Gilmore's house in northwest Atlanta around 4:30 p.m. one afternoon. Greg contacted me and informed me that Anthony had lived on the street for a few days in the Sylvan Road area, Southwest Atlanta, near East Point. He also said my cousin smelled awful and had not bathed in days. Greg immediately demanded that my cousin take a bath while he searched for clean clothing. Once my cousin was clean and dressed, his caretaker, Ms. Hutton, sent Grady EMS to Greg's residence.

The caretaker had taken Anthony to Emory Midtown for a checkup. While there, it appeared to her that Emory did not care about addressing his needs. She believed Emory just wanted him released. She said two or three days later, the hospital released him without notifying anyone in the family. Once again, he was roaming the streets of Atlanta. As of July 10, 2023, he was still missing. I drove to Atlanta on the 7th and 9th and searched areas where I thought he might be wandering, but I did not see him. In the meantime, his son was visiting his mother in Atlanta. His son is retired from the Army and is an Assistant Principal at a school in another state. My cousin's grandchildren are college graduates from Spelman and Morehouse. Anthony's son assisted in the search by reporting the incident to the Atlanta Police Department. A week later, Anthony showed up at Cousin Gregory's house again. This time, I arranged for a different assisted living home in Decatur to care for him. I also purchased a new wardrobe for him after he had visited the streets of Metro Atlanta. Today, Anthony, who is now 73 years old, resides in a personal care home where his needs are addressed and managed. He is a recovering addict with some disabilities who has not used illegal drugs in many years. In 2003, my grandmother, Mary Boozer, lived with her daughter in a mobile home in Juliette on Bowdoin Road. It burned to the ground. After the fire destroyed their home, they needed a place to live. Ellen and I purchased a house on three acres in Juliette from relatives, including the grandsons of Laura and John Jackson. After the Jacksons passed, their daughter Ruby McDowell became the owner. She passed it on to her surviving sons, Johnny Sam and Wesley McDowell, who lived in East Point and College Park. My grandmother moved into our Juliette house in 2003 and lived there until she died in 2005.

CHAPTER 12

RETIREMENT AND RETURN TO JULIETTE BEFORE COVID-19 HITS

After moving back to Juliette in 2019, I visited the cemetery at Saint Paul AME and noticed Mother Nature had reclaimed most of the burial grounds to the point where most graves could not be seen. I immediately sprang into action to free my ancestors from the jungle. I began cutting trees, brush, vines, tall grass, and other growth that hid my people. Eventually, I hired a company to clean the cemetery using a Bobcat brush cutter. After the brush removal, I used a lawn mower and weed eater to maintain the grounds. As I complete this book in 2024, I continue to cut grass and maintain the grounds of the church founded by one of my ancestors, William Ishee.

In February 2020, I had been divorced for about 72 days and was on vacation in the Dominican Republic. During my flight on March 2, 2020, I learned about a COVID-related death in the United States on March 1, 2020. Later, I would learn there was a suspected COVID-related death in the States on February 6, 2020, three weeks before the reported death in Washington State. I flew back home, returned to Juliette, and took precautions to avoid contact with others. Life was about to change for everyone.

Our generation's Black Plague would change our world for years. My second granddaughter, Bri, was born on April 4, 2020, during the pandemic. On June 27, 2020, Pat, Krystal's biological mother, hosted a seventies party for her 50th birthday at her home in Gwinnett County, Georgia. About forty people were present, but I recall seeing only one person wearing a mask. On August 1, 2020, I attended a memorial service for

Alfred Dixon, former Fulton County ADA, former College Park City Judge, and former Atlanta and East Point police officer. Everyone wore a mask as required. When I started working at East Point in 1982, Al's wife, Karen Dixon, was an Identification Crime Scene Technician. Years later, they divorced while Al and I worked at the Fulton County District Attorney's Office, where we worked as a team, Investigator, and prosecutor, assigned to the courtroom of Superior Court Judge Thelma Wyatt Cummings Moore. Assistant DA Sam Lengen was also assigned there.

When I arrived in the City of College Park Convention Center parking lot, I immediately noticed people exiting their cars and placing Covid masks on their faces. As I entered the building, a person greeted us at the door with hand sanitizer. It was my first visit to the facility, and unfortunately, for an occasion that I would have preferred not to have happened. Al was a good friend and a great person to work with. We would meet for lunch at a nice restaurant on Main Street in College Park. I remember his infectious laughter and his unwavering dedication to his work as a part-time judge in College Park. Al's memorial service was a unique and touching experience. As I walked through the second set of Convention Center doors, I saw several tables to my left, each adorned with a piece of Al's history. It was a beautiful tribute, a testament to Al's work in the community. The service was a rollercoaster of emotions, from the sadness of his absence to the joy of remembering his life. It left me thinking that this is the kind of memorial service I would want: a celebration of life and the connections we make during our journey.

In October 2020, I traveled to Puerto Plata, Dominican Republic, to visit my friends who had recently rented homes there. The Dominican government had taken strict measures to ensure safety. They established a curfew and shut down all businesses after 7:00 p.m. They would arrest you if you were caught on the street not wearing a mask. I witnessed people loaded on the back of a pickup truck and hauled off to jail. When you entered any business or restaurant, they immediately checked your temperature and ensured you maintained the required spacing. We needed COVID tests to enter and exit the country at a cost of about forty US dollars.

On March 8, 2021, I received my first Johnson and Johnson COVID-19 vaccine at Walmart in Forsyth. The next shot was a Pfizer booster. On April 4, 2021, I attended my granddaughter's first birthday party at a park in Dacula, Gwinnett County, Georgia. Despite the challenges, the joy of the occasion was palpable. Family members and friends attended. Surprisingly, very few people wore masks during the event, and more than fifty attended.

BIG SKY MONTANA, THE FORTY-NINTH STATE

In March 2021, after I received a vaccination, I went snow skiing at Big Sky, Montana, and visited the Montana State University Dinosaur Museum in Bozeman. The airport required masks at the rental car counter as did all restaurants and bars, except when seated at a table away from others. Masks were also needed in the hotel and at the ski resort while in lines, including the lift line and around other people, in taxis, Uber, and Lyft Rides. The college also required masks during the tour of the Dinosaur Museum at Montana State University.

While our airplane was approaching Bozeman, I saw the beautiful snow-covered mountains. The airport sits in the valley, with mountains rising 360 degrees around it. The decor included Western and Native American themes. There were statues of bears and buffalo. The terminal's decor also included natural wood and stone, and the works of art all over the airport depicted the character and nature of Southwest Montana.

I visited the Museum of the Rockies on the campus of Montana State University. It is a world-class museum with one of the largest collections of fossils, including a full-size T-rex skeleton. I was impressed that they had collected all the fossils in Montana. The University reported that in 1990, the Museum of the Rockies' paleontology crew excavated the fossils. They used a mold created directly from the bones to cast the skeleton in bronze, making it the world's first life-size bronze T-rex.

Bozeman is a small city with a metropolitan population of about 100,000. Yet, despite its ongoing population growth, Bozeman still has the lowest crime rate of the seven most populated cities in Montana. There were excellent restaurants for breakfast, lunch, and dinner downtown. While I was there, sitting outside on a patio on a sunny day was not uncommon, according to the Kimpton Armory Hotel website. In 1941, prolific Bozeman architect Fred Fielding Wilson designed the hotel that houses the Bozeman National Guard. I visited the rooftop bar called Sky Shed, a glass-enclosed gathering place with a fire pit if needed. The view included the mountain ranges and the Montana night sky. In the basement or lower level is another bar that hosts live music. Do not expect long nights for partying—this hotel shuts down its bars at 11:00 pm on Friday and Saturday and 10:00 pm on Sunday through Thursday. The food and beverages were excellent. Although I was one of the few people of color in town, I felt amazingly comfortable in that environment.

I was treated with dignity and respect, as it should be all over America.

On day two of my visit to Bozeman, I drove to ski at Big Sky Ski Resort, a community with two large ski resorts: Big Sky Resort and Moonlight Basin. In October 2013, these resorts merged. Big Sky Resort manages both and is an alpine ski and golf resort. They describe their adventures as follows: The combined terrain of the two resorts allows them to market themselves as the "Biggest Ski Area in America," with over 5,800 acres of terrain. A limited number of ski lift tickets were available daily and could only be purchased online.

The Spanish Peaks Mountain Club is an exclusive ski and golf resort with three chairlifts and thirteen ski runs connecting it to Big Sky Resort at the base of Big Sky's Southern Comfort lift. Big Sky Resort also owns Spanish Peaks in collaboration with the Yellowstone Club. Lone Mountain Ranch is a Nordic ski and summer resort located to the south and adjacent to Big Sky Resort.

The "canyon" area of Big Sky lies in Gallatin Canyon, along the Gallatin River, a favorite for whitewater rafters and kayakers. The Gallatin River, named after Albert Gallatin, the Secretary of the Treasury during the Lewis and Clark Expedition, is a Blue-Ribbon trout stream that attracts fly-fishers worldwide.

JULIETTE TAILGATE REUNION

During Memorial Day weekend, May 28, 2021, I hosted a Tailgate Family Reunion at my house in Juliette. I had worked tirelessly for months to prepare by cleaning the property and cutting the grass. I felt a sense of pride as I sat in my reclining lawn chair sipping on a margarita, thinking that I once lived in a mobile home across the street when I was 17-18 years old, and now I own these three acres of land. Moving forward, I will be an inspiration to others.

Planning this event was risky since it was after many Americans had received the vaccine shot, but COVID-19 was still spreading. The event was held outdoors out of caution, and we encouraged everyone to wear a mask. In preparation, I purchased about one hundred masks for a fun day. Juliette residents did not attend as well as I had hoped, but it was attended well by several relatives from out of town, including Chattanooga, Tennessee, and North Carolina. I had planned it as a tailgate-type event so everyone could cook food and share if desired. My friend and high school classmate, Tom Zellner, drove his Class A recreational vehicle (RV) from McDonough, GA, and parked it near my thirty-two-foot RV travel trailer. It added something new to the event, as there were no Black RV owners in Juliette's history. The only exception is my friend Charles McDew. Seeing my sister, her husband, Aunt Jean, her grandchildren, friends, and other relatives was great.

In June 2021, my granddaughter, Cami, visited us for a few days. Joan and I took her to Robins AFB Aircraft Museum of Aviation. Masks were required. The Robins Museum of Aviation is one of the largest aviation museums in the United States. It is located just outside Warner Robins, Georgia, near Robins Air Force Base. The Museum includes four exhibit buildings and more than eighty-five historic aircraft, amongst other exhibits, on its 51 acres. The museum is also the home of the Georgia Aviation Hall of Fame, and admission is accessible to half a million visitors annually. Large aircraft on display outside the building included the B-1 and B-52 Bombers.

After my divorce, I sought every opportunity to spend time with my granddaughter since she lived seventy miles north of me in Tucker, Georgia. Spending quality time with her was necessary for me, and she would also receive educational experiences and exposure to aviation and the military. Many kids have never had this experience. I just wanted to be a part of my granddaughter's life by exposing her to different experiences.

RACCOON OR BUZZARD?

On October 14, 2023, I attended the annual cookout at one of the Redding family homes. Terri Redding Wilson hosted the event on their beautiful, well-maintained acreage. As you enter Terri's yard, her son, Ray Wilson's home, is to the left of her driveway. Complete with a concrete basketball court halfway between Terri and Ray's house. Ray graduated from Mercer University with a degree in Engineering. He is a Rapper, homeboy, music lover, and family person. He appears very loving and dedicated to his family.

When my wife and I arrived, it was around 2:00 p.m. To my surprise, no more than four or five family members were busy at work. Luckily, Ray had set up a television outside under a tent, near the barbecue grill where he and his cousin were busy cooking chicken, sausage, hamburgers, and hot dogs; we stood there for a while watching the game as Georgia was beating Vanderbilt by a score of 24-7. After small talk, we sat under the tents when other people started to arrive.

The children played in a space bubble approximately fifty feet from the shaded tents. Periodically, we would hear the children scream as the plastic balloon started to lose its air. Someone mistakenly unplugged the generator from its source.

However, someone quickly reinflated it within seconds, and the kids resumed jumping. Minutes later, one of the Redding clan blessed the food. Before the food line started, I spoke with Greg Redding about his special dish. Greg said he had prepared a raccoon. I may have eaten raccoon when I was about ten, but I don't remember eating it. Life was tough; we never ate steaks; ham and chicken were premium meat and other parts of the hog. At this point, I was thinking two different thoughts. First, I thought about my wife, who was blessed with a Doctorate Degree in Educational Leadership and serves as Executive Director of a non-profit organization. Here, she is attending her first annual Redding outdoor event. How is this going to work? As she walked towards the buffet line, I wondered if she would eat raccoons. I said, "Greg prepared a raccoon." Do you want to see it?" I asked. She politely and lady-like got up from her chair, and we walked towards the food table. I removed the aluminum foil from the pan, and to my surprise, I saw beef cooked with sweet potatoes, carrots, zucchini, and green peppers. One of the young Redding men on the grill said, "Try it; I like it." He whispered. My wife grabbed a fork in a lady-like way, reached into the container, and pulled out a piece of meat that resembled beef. She slowly placed it in her mouth and chewed as I recorded the event.

The second thought was from a story still circulating Juliette today. Of course, it involved members of the Redding clan, Ernest, and James, working on their plan. After they found a dead buzzard near the roadway or killed one with a gun, they boiled it and then fried it to resemble chicken. Allegedly, they decided to play a trick on one of their cousins, who lived only hundreds of yards away. After frying the buzzard, they invited their cousin over to share it. After he took a few bites, he liked it and continued eating. I am sure they got a massive laugh that day, but I never asked Randy if the story was true. Their plan was well executed, and the hilarity of the situation was not lost on anyone. Was this a raccoon, or was Gregg carrying on the Redding tradition with something else? As my wife enjoyed tasting wildlife from Juliette, I decided to eat a small piece of raccoon to connect back to my roots.

    I attended the annual event in 2022 and 2024 at the same location. After consuming a couple of beverages in 2022, I started feeling like a young man again. It was a beautiful sunny day in October. Randy Jones, a childhood friend born with one arm, was on the basketball court shooting baskets at age 68 or 69. I could not resist the temptation. So, I strolled out to the court and grabbed some rebounds as Randy made baskets. It is an on-court rule to continue feeding the ball to the person hitting the baskets continuously with no misses. Randy was doing his thing. Next, I started guarding one of the young members of the Redding clan. He hit a few baskets and missed. It was my chance to show some skills and my opportunity to show the young folks that I was the new sixty-six. I could do more than a 66-year-old person could do in 1970. I dribbled to the left, then to the right, spun around, and shot a fade away from the western corner of the court. At that point, I continued to fade until I contacted the concrete, and as I watched, the ball hit nothing but the net. I jumped up slowly from the ground, dusted myself off, and took the ball out with a new possession after my score. Once again, I dribbled to place myself in a position to shoot the fade away. Finally, it happened again. I dribbled left and then right, spun around, and shot a fade away. Again, I continued to fade into the concrete. I sacrificed my body to make that shot twice, and it worked. Well, the spectators did not find it amusing. Ray Wilson walked over to me and said, "Unc" (Uncle), I think you should take a break from basketball today; I don't have enough homeowner's insurance to cover you." On that same day, I decided I would not drink an alcoholic beverage before another basketball game. After almost two years, I played basketball once on a cruise ship at midnight.

PORDENONE, ITALY: THE RETURN

We had planned a trip to Italy in March 2024 with my cousin Julie McCrae and her family from my Ledbetter lineage. We departed Atlanta Hartsfield Jackson Airport and landed in Paris, France, the next day, around 10:30 a.m. After waiting two hours and another hour's delay, we ascended into the sky and landed in Venice, Italy, around 3:00 p.m. After exiting the baggage claim, we saw several people waiting for their loved ones and friends. To exit the terminal and enter the baggage claim area, there were two doors to choose from, one on the right and the other on the left. We went to the right side, anxiously scanning the crowd, looking for my friends Paola and Charles. "If I don't see them over here, I'll look on the other side," I told Joan. As I walked over and checked the crowd, I saw them standing there, waiting for us to exit. I sneaked up behind them and tapped Paola on the shoulder. "There he is," shouted Charles.

After introducing Joan, Charles hugged her, kissed her on both cheeks and said, "This is how Italians greet." The joy of reuniting with close friends after many years is always a heartwarming experience. While I had seen Paola several times since 1978, it was the first time I saw Charles in person since my last football game in November 1978. He was aging well. After leaving the Air Force, he married an Italian woman and remained in the Pordenone metropolitan area.

As we exited the airport, I noticed some friendships last forever. Charles and Paola bantered back and forth like a sister and brother. After loading luggage into Paola's car, "we hit the road" and headed towards Pordenone. Joan and I sat in the back seat. As Paola drove, both of us were pressing our brakes. She exceeded the speed limit and drove too closely to other vehicles, having to brake sharply at the last moment. After a few miles, I removed my eyes from the road before me and focused on the many vineyards around us. It appeared as if grapes were the number one product in this region.

Meanwhile, Charles was attempting to give direction and guidance to Paola. He turned to me and said, "She is Italian, just like my wife; sometimes, they just will not listen." I jokingly said, "Yes, I remember." Paola said, "You guys have lost some of your brain cells." As we entered the town of Sacile, Paola almost missed her exit but managed to quickly and safely change lanes to exit the freeway. Joan and I continued using the backseat brakes.

The first stop on my return to Italy was the apartment building I once shared with Air Force friend James "J.C." Riley, a brother from Saginaw, Michigan. This was where I slept on a waterbed with no heater for one night during winter in Northern Italy—my mistake for allowing JC to trick me. I would walk next door to an underground supermarket. We decorated our apartment with my wicker furniture and Flokati rugs. Today, forty-six years later, I still possess my Flokati rug.

We arrived at the Hotel Santini around 5:00 p.m. After more bantering, Charles and Paola returned to their homes and left us in the hotel parking lot. We were disappointed upon arrival because the restaurant would not open until 6:00 p.m. Next, we took a short walk to get something to eat. At 5:55 p.m., we returned to the Al Lido Restaurant, Via S. Giuliano 55, Pordenone, Italy. The food and service were terrific. My first order was Grappa, which is an alcoholic beverage: a fragrant, grape-based pomace brandy of Italian origin that contains 35-60 percent alcohol by volume. After pressing the grapes, it is made by distilling the skins, pulp, seeds, and stems left over from winemaking. Military friends introduced Grappa to me at age twenty-one.

Joan ordered seafood spaghetti. "How is it?" I asked. "This is delicious." She expressed it while smiling. I said, "Thanks to Paola for the excellent choices, the restaurant, and the hotel." Reflecting as we raised our glasses filled with delicious Moscato, from the days at Juliette through Forsyth until now, it has been quite a ride as we have traveled to parts unknown. May life bless us with good health, food, and friends.

After dinner, Joan and I walked to Pordenone Centro. It was around 7:30 p.m. on a Saturday. We left the restaurant, crossed the street, followed a pedestrian walkway, and crossed a river to another walkway leading to cobblestone streets and old buildings. Several restaurants and bars were on both sides of the streets as we walked for about a quarter of a mile. Tired after a long day of travel, we stopped and started our walk back to the hotel. Along the way, we stopped at a bar restaurant named Caffe Municipio, established in 1870. It has a large area for outdoor seating. I walked to the bar inside and noticed a group of Italian men standing next to the bar as the bartender prepared eight drinks, all appearing the same. I asked what it was, and he said, "Americano." "I'd like one," I said. After completing the order of eight, he mixed my Americano. I tried to remember the mixture to no avail, but it was a unique experience.

As we sat outside, me drinking an Americano and Joan a Prosecco, we watched the people. The outside temperature was around 52 degrees. Most people were wearing coats or light jackets. We wore sweaters. It felt nice in the open air. All around us were old buildings, churches, and towers. At 8:00 p.m., the tower church bell began ringing loudly. I am reminded that structures in Europe will remain forever. Centro is a gathering place—a safe place to eat, drink, have fun, and socialize. I love European outdoor restaurants, bars, and cafes.

On the next day, we arranged to meet with Paola, Jessica, and her husband for dinner in Centro Pordenone. It was wonderful to see them again after several years. Dinner was fantastic as we discussed our past in Aviano. Jessica has become quite a young woman and business owner like her brother. She and her husband own two Daycare centers in Pordenone. After dinner, we hugged and said farewell until the next time. Lamont could not attend the dinner, but we met with him and his daughter the next day. He was in Pordenone conducting business. He started a company that supplied and delivered inks to tattoo parlors. We also met two of his employees, Black Americans, who left the Air Force and decided to live in Italy. One kid was from South Carolina, and the other was from Alabama. They emphasized they did not plan to return to the States soon.

Following a couple of days in Pordenone, we returned to Venice for two days, followed by two days in Florence and Tuscany, then off to Rome, Pompeii, Sorrento, and our trip ended on the Isle of Capri. Our journey began with a heartwarming reunion at Venice Airport. Paola and Charles, our gracious hosts, greeted us, and we were overjoyed to meet our family, Julie and Louis McRae, Betty, Katherine, Derrick, and others in our tour group. The group, consisting of approximately thirty-three people, including our tour guide, Tamara, added a sense of camaraderie to our adventure. After a short stroll to the boat dock, we boarded two separate Venezia Water Taxis for a scenic ride through Venice Lagoon to Lido di Venezia.

The island, the only one where vehicles are allowed, was a unique sight, with ferries carrying cars and trucks operating daily. Our water taxi docked across the street from our hotel, Villa Mabapa. After settling into our room, Joan and I ventured down the street to the lively outdoor restaurants, ice cream shops, retail shops, and bars. The street was alive, with several people basking in the beauty of the sunny day, adding a touch of magic to our first day in Venice. We traveled by ferry to Venice the next day and began our tour. We rode the gondola in the Grand Canal with Julie and Louis, visited St Mark's Basilica, strolled through the Piazza San Marco, and did a walking tour of Venice within five blocks from the Basilica.

In Tuscany, we visited the Centro, which has cobblestone streets high on a hill with a beautiful view overlooking the valley of vineyards below. The air was filled with the sweet scent of ripening grapes, and church bells echoed through the streets. It was a well-visited area that included shops and restaurants. The ice cream shops caught my eye as we toured the retail district. We finally decided to stop for some delicious gelato. My favorite was, and still is, Pistachio. It was the most delicious. We walked up a hill to the remains of a castle or fort. It was the highest point in the area, with 360-degree views of the valley below. The sun was setting, casting a warm golden glow over the landscape. Fortunately, Joan and I had seen the movie 'Under the Tuscan Sun' at least twice. We were not disappointed.

Next, we traveled by motorcoach to Florence. Again, the scenery was breathtaking all along the route. The coach driver stopped in front of our hotel and stood outside to protect us from the cars passing as we exited on the narrow, busy one-way street. There was also continuous pedestrian traffic as well. The hotel was ideally within walking distance of all the attractions and markets. EF Tours chose an excellent location. After exiting the hotel entrance onto Via Nazionale, we turned left on Via Dell'ariento. That is where the street market begins and continues for about 100 yards. I have never seen so many leather goods for sale on one street. There were wallets, purses, belts, various leather bags, shoes, boots, vests and more. Bargaining is acceptable. Directly behind our hotel, The Hotel Corona d'Italia, is the Marcato (Centrale Market). When I first entered the market, I was immediately impressed by the fresh fruits, vegetables, oils, and meats. Vendors served various foods and products, such as pistachio cream, extra virgin olive oil, and balsamic vinegar. This market was like the one I had visited in Barcelona, Spain. They served delicious fresh pasta and, without a doubt, the world-famous Florentine steak at the food court upstairs. Once you strolled past the street market, you found yourself near Basilica di San Lorenzo. A short walk from there led you to Piazza di San Giovanni, Cathedral Santa Maria del Fiore, Piazza della Signoria, and the iconic Ponte

Vecchio Bridge that spans the Arno River. The bridge is a treasure trove of jewelry, with numerous vendors displaying their exquisite pieces.

After our enriching walking tour, Joan and I relaxed at an outdoor restaurant in one of the Piazzas, ready to savor the scenery and indulge in some people-watching. The lively atmosphere, with a mix of students and other tourists, added a touch of excitement to our dining experience.

We departed Florence on a motorcoach for Rome and arrived at the Golden Tulip Piram Hotel. While there for three nights, we visited the Colosseum, the Pantheon, and the religious and public buildings of papal Rome, the Vatican. On a guided tour, we soaked up some 2,000-year-old history in imperial Rome while viewing the Arch of Constantine, Arch of Titus, Circus Maximus (a chariot racing stadium), museums, and other locations. We ate dinner and lunch at restaurants within a five-block radius of our hotel. The food was delicious, and the atmosphere was vibrant. Numerous shops were available within a short distance from the Tulip to Via Nazionale. The Metro and Rome Train Terminal are only two blocks from the Golden Tulip Hotel. We also visited St Paul's Basilica and the Catacombs, where early Christians were buried in chambers underground. Roman Emperor Constantine the Great and houses St Paul's tomb founded St Paul's Basilica.

En route to the Sorrento Peninsula, we stopped at Pompeii for a guided walking tour of what was once a flourishing resort city for ancient Rome's elite. The personal connection to Mount Vesuvius's eruption in 79 A.D. and the subsequent burial of the town in a blanket of volcanic ash, killing 2,000 people, was profound. Our guide led us through the excavated ruins of theaters, villas, temples, brothels, and baths and showed us the mummified remains of the people of Pompeii. We walked along the cobblestone roads, feeling the footsteps of the Romans who once traveled them.

Our last stops on the Amalfi Coast included Sorrento and the Isle of Capri. Our lodging was at the Grand Hotel Cesare Augusto in Sorrento. Upon arriving at the hotel, I first noticed the lemon trees in the courtyard. We had noticed many lemon trees in yards on the road to Sorrento, but to see and touch them in the hotel garden was a unique experience. We would see more lemons and oranges hanging from trees along the streets of Sorrento. We walked down one of two brick pedestrian walkways with shops and restaurants on both sides of the street. Once we reached our destination, the Parrucchiano La Favorita Ristorante, the outside appearance in no way gave a clue of what we would experience inside. The unique dining experience that awaited us inside this unassuming facade intrigued and excited us.

Upon entering the door from the street level, after twenty feet, we walked up steps to a second level, then more steps up to the third level, where we saw a spacious restaurant enclosed by glass with a high glass ceiling. There are courtyards outside on the left and right sides of the restaurant. On the left side, a canopy of orange and lemon trees completely blocked our view of the sky with low-hanging fruit in an area of 900 square feet (83.6 meters) from the exit door. On the right side, a series of walkways allowed us to walk in the garden under a canopy of lemon and orange trees with low-hanging fruit. At night, both areas are lit with lights to highlight the experience. The restaurant offers a stunning view of the garden. Both sides connect in the back, adding to the unique dining experience surrounded by hanging oranges and lemons on three sides. There were also several benches for seating if you wanted to sit in the garden with a beverage or just to enjoy the ambiance.

From Sorrento, we traveled by ferry to the Isle of Capri, a beloved resort. We boarded a private boat for a tour around the island and saw the beautiful rock formations and caves along the shoreline. One rock with a natural arch allows boats to travel through it. Many yachts around the island are seen in the water—a vacation home for the rich and sometimes famous. The harbor features colorful buildings and boats. We rode a tram to the top of the island and visited the Gardens of Augustus. The tranquility and beauty of these gardens, seen from one of the higher points on the island, left us with a deep appreciation for the natural beauty of Capri.

PART FOUR

Meeting People, Loving Smooth Jazz, And A New Beginning

Smooth Jazz Cruise with Jonathan Butler and Larry Bragg

John Edwards, Spinners, Peachtree City Amphitheater

CHAPTER 13

UNEXPECTED ENCOUNTERS

It happens more often than we realize, meeting people unexpectedly and in unlikely places worldwide. In earlier chapters, I mentioned a chance meeting with one of my former junior high school teachers at Royal Air Force Base, Lakenheath, England, seven years after school. Walking towards my dormitory near the football field, I heard someone yell my name. "Percy Freeman." I turned and looked behind me. I saw Mr. Simmons, now a Captain. He left his teaching job at Hubbard Elementary and High School and joined the Air Force. What a pleasant surprise. We exchanged numbers and maintained limited contact for the few months left during my assignment there. I recall that his sister, Diane Simmons, visited him at Lakenheath while I was there.

I met Ronald Ogletree at Tyndall, AFB, Florida, four years after seeing him in high school. Ronald was one of Robert Ogletree's brothers. Robert was one of my high school classmates. Sadly, both Ronnie and Robert are now deceased. I also met another high school classmate at Tyndall. After Melvin Shannon arrived at Tyndall, he and I shared an apartment off-base in Parker. We enjoyed living off base, where we faced fewer restrictions. It was more like living in the local economy while working eight-hour day jobs on base. We got along well. One day, I confronted him about cleaning the kitchen after using dishes. He did not take it well, so we argued, but it never turned into violent behavior. It was more like wrestling and a test of strength.

In 1989, while attending the National Brotherhood of Skiers Summit in Steamboat Springs, CO, I walked from the gondola to the bus stop to return to my condominium after a beautiful day of skiing. The sun had lowered behind the mountains, and fresh powder snow was on the ground. The next day would be even better. When I approached the bus stop, I saw a person who resembled one of the Whispers. As I moved closer, I asked, "Are you one of the twins who sings with the Whispers?" He said, "Yes, I am." I am trying to remember if it was Scotty or Walter. I asked, "Do you mind if I take a picture?" He said, "Yes, I do." Next, he asked me to give him my camera. This was odd. I had not taken an unauthorized picture without his permission. Again, he said, "Hand me your camera, please." I handed him the camera, and he passed it to the female standing with him at the bus stop. "Please take a picture of me and this gentleman?" He asked. "You got me, brother. That was good," I said. After she took the picture, I said, "Thank you so much for what you do; I love your music." The remainder of our conversation centered around snow skiing, the role of the NBS, and all the Black people in Steamboat Springs.

In 1991, I attended the National Brotherhood of Skiers Summit in Park City, Utah. My condominium was within thirty yards of the main gondola. The skiing was fantastic, and I was enjoying myself as usual. It was an excellent Summit. I recall the late Cameron Kelsey and other skiers from Atlanta staying in the same condominium building. It was very convenient to the slopes and shopping areas. Public transportation was readily available. As I walked to the elevator for our daily NBS happy hour, I saw Sinbad, the actor/comedian, standing there. I stepped inside and said, "What's up, Sinbad?" He said, "It's all good, my brother." "Keep up the good work; you bring laughter to many who need it." He smiled and said, "Thanks again, my brother." When the elevator touched the ground floor, He said, "Catch you, brothers, later; enjoy yourselves."

While on vacation in the United States Virgin Islands, we drove up to the Mountain Top Duty-Free Store deck to enjoy the fantastic view of Magen's Bay and the Atlantic Ocean. At the same time, one can enjoy the famous frozen banana daiquiris. On two separate occasions, I met people from Georgia I did not expect to see in Saint Thomas. As I stood on the deck gazing at the beautiful scenery, a guy walked over and stood beside me. I said, "This is a beautiful island." To which he replied, "It sure is." "Where are you from?" I asked. "Georgia." "Me too. Where in Georgia are you?" "Atlanta." "I am from the Stone Mountain area," I replied. "I also live in Stone Mountain," he said. "I live in Water's Edge subdivision near North Deshon Road." That is where I live, on Water's Edge Drive. My house is on the lake with a circular driveway," he said. "Man, I know exactly where you live and your neighbors. "Your neighbor on the right has a swimming pool and is a retired Chef." Wow, I thought it was a shocker that we would meet for the first time in Saint Thomas after living in the same neighborhood for years.

Two years earlier, while standing on the same deck at Mountain Top, I saw a military officer from the 116th Bomb Wing. I yelled his name, "Leo." He responded and walked over. We shook hands and hugged. It was Leo, a former enlisted munitions technician who became an officer and dentist in the Unit. He was in Saint Thomas on vacation with his family.

Sometime around 2002, I was traveling out of Hartsfield Jackson Airport. It was a stormy day in the ATL with many flight delays. As a result, there were several gate changes.

I was traveling from Atlanta to Louisville, Kentucky, to investigate Louisville Air Traffic Control Tower personnel. After about a two-hour delay and three gate changes, I sat near the gate, patiently waiting to board our aircraft. I struck up a conversation with a guy sitting next to me. "This weather has been severe today; I hope to make it to Louisville for dinner." "Yeah, it happens, but we can do nothing except wait," he said. To continue the conversation, I said, "Your haircut gives the appearance you served in the military." "Yes, I did; I served in the United States Army," he replied. I proudly said, "I served in the United States Air Force." "Where did you serve?" I asked. He stated that he served in Italy with the 509th Airborne.

I mentioned that I served at Aviano and played football for two years with the Eagles. At that point, we had yet to introduce ourselves. He looked at me with a question on his face and said, "You are Percy Freeman, aren't you." I acknowledged that I was indeed Percy Freeman. "I loved Italy and playing football there. It was a wonderful experience. I cannot believe you and I are sitting here in the Airport after not seeing each other for over 20 years." "I always say, if people don't talk with one another, they will never know their commonalities."

Edward Williams, III, and I grew up in Juliette, Georgia, attended the same high school, and played on the same football teams from ninth through twelfth grades. While traveling for work, I flew to Milwaukee, Wisconsin, before taking a flight to Atlanta. While sitting at the gate, I saw Ed seated in the waiting area. I had not seen him since my high school graduation in 1974. Once again, more than twenty years after high school, we ran into each other in Milwaukee for a flight to Atlanta. We talked during the entire flight.

While living near Stone Mountain Park, I occasionally walked up and down the mountain to exercise and enjoy the beautiful scenery. Once you reach the top of the hill and look towards the western sky, the picturesque skyline of the Atlanta Metropolitan area stands out. Every Saturday morning, the trails are full of citizens with the same interest—exercise and walking the trails. One Saturday morning, I decided to walk the trail a little later during the day, around 10:30 a.m. That decision allowed me another chance encounter. After reaching the top of the mountain, sitting on the "Rock," and enjoying the view, I decided it was time to head down the trail and go on a five-mile run around the mountain. After walking for about three hundred yards, I saw two gentlemen walking up the trail. One of them looked familiar, so I stopped and started a conversation. I asked, "You sure look very familiar to me. Did you serve in law enforcement or the military?" The younger gentleman said, "My dad and I served in the US Air Force." I said, "You look like a guy who attended basic training with me in 1974." He said, "Man, I was in basic training in 1974." I asked, "Are you, Causey?" "Man, this is unbelievable," he said. Amos Causey and I attended the Air Force Basic Military Training Center at Lackland AFB in August 1974. Here we are walking on a mountain trail in 2012. Later, we met for lunch on at least two occasions in Tucker, Georgia.

In 2012, as I reached out to former members of the 3703 Basic Military Training Squadron (BMTS), I located W. Mungro in Pennsylvania and M. Evans in Las Vegas. Mungro suggested we get together for a reunion. It took a lot of work for everyone to agree on a location and time. Mungro suggested we take a trip to the Carnival in Rio De Janeiro. It seemed expensive for me, so I said maybe. After Melvin and Causey bailed out, the other guys agreed to take the trip. Mungro offered me a United Airlines "Buddy Pass." I accepted. He arranged for us to fly out of Newark International Airport on Superbowl Sunday, February 3, 2013, the Baltimore Ravens versus the San Francisco 49ers. When I arrived, we met and hugged after not seeing each other for 39 years. The game started at 6:30 EST. We sat in the United Club Lounge, watching the game as Alicia Keys sang the National Anthem, enjoying the complimentary food and beverages. It was an exciting time. We could not have reunited better after not seeing each other since August-September 1974. As the game continued, we began boarding our United Airlines aircraft around 9:20 p.m. and departed by 10:00 p.m. After boarding the plane, I immediately found my way to the first-class section. It was my first time sitting in a first-class section with my private resting area, which included a reclining seat that became a bed. In front of me was my monitor. Damn, this was living life. Since I had consumed alcoholic beverages in the United Club, I decided on just one more for a nightcap.

The flight attendant handed me a warm cloth to wash my face and hands the following day. I was thoroughly impressed with the first-class service. I did not know what the folks in the back were eating, but my breakfast was tasty. Mungro, seated across from me, told me once again that we were flying to Sao Paulo rather than directly to Rio. We would take a bus to Rio for about seven hours. The bus trip allowed me to see parts of the country I would not have seen had we taken a direct flight. We took a taxi to the bus station and purchased tickets for the day's trip. We arrived in Sao Paulo around 8:30 a.m. and departed the bus station around 11:00 a.m. After boarding the bus, I noticed something hugely different. The bus

had doors like those installed on commercial aircraft after September 11, 2001. Mungro explained that Brazil has a history of "bus hijackings." As we traveled towards Rio, I also noticed off-duty police and security officers
traveling on the buses to their homes free of charge. It made sense to me—free protection for the bus companies. As I traveled on the Brazilian highway, the scenery reminded me of places in Spain, France, Italy, and, unbelievably, parts of Georgia in the USA. Now, after my trip to South Africa in 2017, I can honestly say some scenes in Brazil resembled the rolling hills and countryside of South Africa.

After arriving in Rio de Janeiro around 7:00 p.m. and traveling through the city to reach our destination, Copacabana, and Atlantica Beach, passing through the streets of Rio, we saw the decorations and floats in warehouses for the massive parade on Fat Tuesday. We settled into our condominium on Avenue Atlantica. The living room had a partial view of the beach and ocean. Our lodging was about three to four blocks from the famous Copacabana Hotel. We discussed our plans to visit the beach, Sugarloaf Mountain (Cable car), Christ the Redeemer Statue (Corcovado), Ipanema Beach, Rodrigo de Freitas Lagoon, the Copacabana Palace, and places to eat good Brazilian food. The other guys were settled in their respective rooms as they had taken a direct flight to Rio. Now it was time to party and enjoy the pre-Carnival activities.

On the first evening, we strolled from the condominium down the street to a restaurant bar, The Colony, now the Dolce Vita. The eating area was a covered patio across the street from the beach. Most days, this was our meeting location for breakfast and sometimes lunch and dinner. However, we dined at various locations within two hundred yards of the condominium. The abundance of choices always left us excited for the next culinary adventure. The next day, we ventured to the beach. One of the best spots was across the street from the Copacabana Hotel. The beach side of Avenue Atlantica boasts a comprehensive, beautifully designed walking and jogging trail. The white sandy beach, one of the widest I have seen, stretches about two and a half miles, and the water is mostly calm. The Avenue is lined with skyscraper hotels, condominiums, restaurants, nightclubs, bars, apartments, and houses, creating a vibrant and diverse atmosphere. The beaches can be bustling, especially during weekends, but the lively energy is infectious. Vendors walk up and down the beach selling swimwear, mostly thong bikinis, adding to the colorful scene.

  We gathered under our umbrellas and enjoyed the ocean breeze, people-watching, and an occasional swim in the ocean. The people were friendly, including tourists from all over the world. It was a very relaxing atmosphere with no fear of crime or issues. The next day, we took a taxi to Mount Corcovado to see the 98-foot-tall statue of Christ the Redeemer overlooking Rio. To reach the peak, we purchased tickets to ride the cog railway to the top, near 2300 feet. The journey to the top took about twenty minutes through the Atlantic Forest of Tijuca. It was best to sit on the right side of the train for the upward journey.

  Each city has its own Carnival Street parties. We were there to witness and participate in the Blocos Parade through the streets of Copacabana. The band played Samba music as they rode atop an open bus or truck with a platform built on top. The partygoers followed and danced in the streets each time the bus stopped. As they say in Copacabana, "Dress lightly and dance right." The street became a dance floor as the people moved in rhythm and grace while following the bus. We had no problem getting on the dance floor as we danced in the crowd. The hospitable spirit moved us into action. It was an unforgettable and unique experience. The streets were vibrant with joy, laughter, and happiness, creating a festive atmosphere that included people of all ages having fun with no reservations. This scene would be the same theme repeated in Ipanema and other cities in the country, a testament to the rich cultural heritage of Brazil.

We planned to depart Brazil on Saturday, but no spaces were available for buddy passes. Mungro and I moved to the Copa Hotel and caught a flight on Sunday. The other guys left on Saturday. If we only had time and money to stay until Tuesday, that would have made the reunion even better. It was a great reunion and my first time traveling south beyond Columbia. The joy of the reunion and the shared memories made us feel nostalgic, wishing we could extend our stay and relive those days again.

On another occasion, I traveled to Philadelphia, PA, for work at the Air Traffic Control tower. While there, I arranged to meet with Mungro and Eric 8Since I enjoyed it so much, I scheduled a reunion with Darrell Holland, quarterback/receiver for the Camp Darby Rangers. It was great seeing Darrell again after many years. While The South is still open, Warm Daddy's closed after the pandemic. Sunday Brunch with live jazz and soul food was delicious and entertaining. Their sweet cornbread, cooked in a skillet, was so good you could eat it as a dessert.

MEETING GENE SIMMONS

The FAA assigned me to conduct an internal employee investigation near the airport in Orlando, Florida, in 2017. I had been there several times for investigations and usually secured lodging near our office building near Semoran Boulevard. I always drove a rental car while there, but I only traveled a little bit away from my hotel since there were choices of restaurants within a mile radius.

After leaving my hotel parking lot, I decided to check out the new businesses in the shopping center across from the Hampton Inn. While driving through the parking lot, I noticed a restaurant named Rock and Brews. From the outside, the planned design included a roll-up door for the bartender to serve beverages on both the inside and outside patio. I was there when the weather allowed service at both locations—a beautiful evening in Orlando. Since I was alone, I did not want to occupy a table, so I sat at the center of the bar because the large screen flat TV was directly in front of me. I ordered a beverage and food and started watching a music video of KISS performing in a previously recorded live concert. I looked to my left and saw several people gathered around a guy who looked like he was wearing an Elvis Presley wig. I watched people take photographs and shake hands with him. I asked the bartender, "Who is that guy?" "You're watching him on TV right now; he is the leader of KISS," he replied. "What is his name?" I asked. He said, "Gene Simmons." I immediately looked in Gene Simmons' direction, and as he looked at me I waved, gave him a thumbs up, then turned around to eat and drink. A few seconds later, I felt a guy place his arms around my neck and rub the top of my head. He said, "How are you, buddy? Are you enjoying yourself here?" Acting as if I knew who he was the entire time, I said, "I'm great, enjoying the food, and it's great to meet you, sir." He laughed and said they had made the right choice in selecting that location. He also said they had several restaurants nationwide but none in Georgia. "Damn." I said, "I guess I must return to Florida for the good food here." He laughed again, saying, "Enjoy yourself; I see some folks over there waiting for me." After eating, I saw a couple of young girls looking toward Gene Simmons. "One young lady said, "Wow, my mom would love it if I could get a picture of him." Minutes before, there I was. I did not know the guy, but now I am about to give advice. "Excuse me," I said, "His limo driver is standing outside next to that black limousine. Let's go stand outside, and when he exits, you can ask him for a picture." We walked outside, and within five minutes, Gene exited the restaurant. "Mr. Simmons, my mother would love it if I could get a picture with you; she loves your band." "Sure, little lady, come over here," he said. Her girlfriend smiled when she took the photo. At that point, I asked for the camera to take their picture so her friend could share the moment in a photo with Gene Simmons.

In October 2020, ten months after my divorce, Joan and I traveled to Albuquerque, New Mexico. COVID protocol was in effect. New Mexico required masks everywhere we visited. Coincidentally, we were sitting at a restaurant in Old Town Albuquerque when I noticed
Black couple was there. I could not see their faces, but as they were getting ready to leave, I heard the male say, "Percy, is that you?" Surprisingly, I saw my former Stone Mountain neighbors, Isaac, and Jamilah. I was unsure if they knew I had divorced, so I quickly explained so they would not feel uneasy. We spoke momentarily as they were preparing to leave for the airport. Again, I thought, of all the people and places in the world, I would be sitting at a restaurant eating lunch in New Mexico and bump into my neighbor from a few months ago.

On a previous trip to the US Virgin Islands, I recognized a guy walking toward my gate at Atlanta Hartsfield Jackson International Airport. It was Bruce S. Harvey, a high-profile Atlanta Criminal Defense Attorney. I had seen him in Fulton County courtrooms for years. You all know the guy with the long ponytail and a slight bald spot on the back of his head.

Bruce had always impressed me as a smooth operator in the courtroom. After a brief meeting, we exchanged numbers. Bruce was in the Virgin Islands for work, and I was on vacation. After a few days, I invited Bruce and his wife to a cookout at my sister-in-law's house. Her home, located on the island's upper part, has a fantastic view of the Caribbean from French Town to the Airport.

Later in the afternoon, around 6:00 p.m., Bruce and Paige Harvey arrived. We had opened the gate in anticipation of their arrival. I introduced them to my family, and we sat in the front yard, surrounded by a hill that rises from flat to about thirty-five feet at its highest point, next to the island road leading to Mountain Top Restaurant. Chris maintained a beautiful yard adorned with local plants. Iguanas were resting on tree branches all around the fenced yard. The menu included a low country boil and Percy's three-bean, two-pea salad, which had become my signature dish at tailgates, office parties, and unique events.

Before eating, Ellena gave the Harveys a tour of their home. "Wow, check out this view," Paige uttered. We briefly discussed my work at Fulton County DA, the Court System and life on the islands. After dinner and a few beverages, the Harveys departed in their Jeep. Months later, they invited us to their Art Museum and Studio apartment near Luckie and Cone Streets. I said, "Wow, check out this view of downtown." "Bruce, this is an awesome pad," I said.

As we sat and prepared to eat, I noticed how every item was selected and purchased specifically for placement. All the art was meticulously arranged to match the decor in the room. Life as a lawyer is a good life. Paige gave a tour of her Art studio. She is an exceptionally talented painter, mostly with oils on canvas. As you looked around the studio, you could see completed works of art, close-to-finished works of art, or masterpieces in progress.

MEETING HERMAN CAIN

Herman Cain was a Morehouse graduate, businessperson, and member of the Republican Party, who was also active in the Tea Party and co-chair of Black Voices for Trump. Unfortunately, it was his support of Donald J Trump and refusal to wear a mask during the COVID-19 pandemic that resulted in his unexpected death on July 30, 2020, at age 74. He was seen on television with no mask during a Trump rally in Tulsa, Oklahoma.

On September 15, 2012, I attended the funeral of Rosa Annette McDowell at Willie A. Watkins West End Chapel. She was the wife of Johnny Sam McDowell, Sr., my cousin with roots in Juliette, Georgia, from whom I had purchased the Juliette house on Hilltop Street in 2003. As I walked into the Chapel, I noticed Herman Cain sitting with a female, whom I assumed was his wife. Immediately, I began thinking about his comments on his radio talk show and his support for the Republican Party. After a few minutes, I introduced myself and learned why he was there. I got up and walked to him, four rows behind me. As I approached, he stood. We shook hands, and I asked, "How are you, Mr. Cain? "Fine, thank you." How do you know Mrs. McDowell?" I asked. "Oh, I am Johnny Sam Jr.'s wife's godfather. Yeah, I am Wanda's godfather," he replied. "Good to meet you, sir," I said. Now, this was some real news to me. When my friend George and I spoke regularly, we sometimes discussed Herman Cain's comments on a radio talk show in metropolitan Atlanta. We saw him as someone who was not in touch with injustice and ongoing discriminatory practices, including the creation of backward laws. I immediately sensed he was all about business.

Earlier, I mentioned Laura Dillard Jackson. Johnny Sam McDowell, Sr is Laura Jackson's grandson. Laura Jackson is also the last person my mother visited before she was burned in the house fire. On February 2, 1960, my mother went to her grand Aunt Laura Jackson's house to write a letter for her.

CHAPTER 14

INTRODUCTION TO SMOOTH JAZZ

Life has taught me that people always come together to enjoy good music and sporting events, whether it is high school, college, or professional, or a concert in a stadium, arena, or park, no matter what their nationality, race, political views, gender, age, or sexual orientation, these events allow for more diversity and interaction among different people than church attendance. It is widely believed that Sunday morning church or worship services are the most racially divided group gatherings in our nation. I love people who love smooth Jazz.

In 2009, I attended the Seabreeze Jazz Festival and continued attending for several years until 2021. The Seabreeze Jazz Festival does not compare to the Smooth Jazz Cruise. I attended at least nine Seabreeze festivals from 2009 to 2021. There, I met Boney James and Nick Colionne in person after their performances. The three or four-day festival occurs outside a theater with a grassy field facing the Gulf of Mexico. The entry line is usually long and uncomfortable as the sun bores down on the concertgoers waiting to enter the venue. The weather, a mix of sunshine and occasional rain, was always a factor, but it never dampened the spirits of the jazz enthusiasts. The concerts typically start early in the day and end between 8:30 and 9:00 p.m. Often, a blanket is needed to keep warm after the sun sets.

The Smooth Jazz cruise was a unique experience filled with anticipation and excitement. I could feel a difference in spirit among the passengers, a shared sense of thrill and anticipation. Before I boarded the ship, and upon arrival at the Miami Airport, I received good vibes when I bumped into former FAA co-workers John, Air Traffic, Director of Operations, and Shaun, Director of Air Traffic Organization, Eastern Service Area, and their wives, in the baggage claim area. They were also going on the Smooth Jazz Cruise, and the shared excitement was palpable. It was a moment of shared anticipation, a prelude to the unique experience that awaited us on the Smooth Jazz Cruise.

During the years I attended Seabreeze, I would often meet people I knew from Metro Atlanta or someone I met during my journey in life. In 2008, I located an acquaintance, friend, and opponent from Aviano, Italy. Carlos played football as a defensive end for the Red Machine 1977-78. After finding him, we planned to meet at Seabreeze. I had just heard of it when Carlos informed me he had attended for several years. Thanks to Carlos for enhancing my jazz experiences. He had rented a nice condominium on the eighth floor overlooking the Gulf of Mexico. I was immediately impressed with his selection. Our shared history in Italy and our mutual love for jazz made our reunion at Seabreeze even more special.

On the other hand, I had secured lodging at the Origins at Seahaven. It is a beautiful building across the street from Sharky's Beachfront Restaurant, a casual eatery, serving seafood and cocktails, whose backyard is a white sandy beach, complete with competition volleyball games, wave runners, parasailing, and eye candy. The menu includes Caribbean nachos, snow crab legs, and a variety of fish tacos. The view of the Gulf from the Tiki bar is fantastic. Live entertainment and events are available all year round. The parrot heads (followers of Jimmy Buffett) usually reserve a section at Sharky's, including a DJ on the beach, and have a grand time enjoying life. Their gathering in Panama City Beach usually coincides with the Seabreeze Jazz Festival in April.

The condominium was on the east side of the building. I did not have a direct view of the ocean to the south. However, I was delighted to be there for the festival and to see my friend Carlos, whom I had not seen since 1978. We talked about our days playing football and the great times we enjoyed in Italy. While in Italy, Carlos started dating a beautiful young blonde from England named Jane. I knew her from when they dated and from when she worked at the Jolly Roger bar in downtown Aviano. During our meeting, I learned Carlos and Jane were married before leaving Italy, traveled while still serving in the Air Force, and later settled in the Florida Peninsula near Eglin Air Force Base. They had two children and several grandchildren. In 2011, Carlos attended Seabreeze with another companion, so I assumed he and Jane had divorced. I recall we met at the theater, and he brought a Boston Butt and Lynchburg Lemonade. It was a beautiful sunny day as we sat in the open field under the Florida sun, enjoying the reunion, tasty food, music, and beverages. His female companion seemed genuinely lovely, and we all enjoyed the concert, sipping, eating, laughing, and listening to the beautiful sounds while reclining in our folding chairs.

A few years later, I visited Pensacola, Florida airport, and the Air Traffic Control Tower to conduct an internal investigation. While there, I attempted to meet with Carlos and Jane for dinner. Although I had assumed they were divorced, I knew they were still friends, and I had seen photographs of Carlos with his family, including his grandchildren. After Jane recommended a restaurant for dinner, I was excited to see my friends again. When I called Jane to confirm the dinner meeting, she told me that Carlos could not attend and that he did not want her to meet with me alone. Jane said Carlos was sick and he had a drinking problem. "He is a little jealous, and we are still married," she said. I was in total shock. I should not have made assumptions; at the same time, these were friends. Later, I contacted Carlos by phone. "Did you know Jane had a crush on you?" He asked. "No," I said. "It must have been from my days playing football in Italy 1977-78," I said. "Carlos, it happened over thirty years ago; why didn't you tell me you guys were still married?" I asked. "We just went through some things," he said.

Each time I planned to attend Seabreeze, I would reach out to Carlos. The last time I called, he shared some unexpected news. He had retired from his job at Eglin and was moving back to his home in Texas. However, about a year later, he informed me that he had returned to Florida. His family assumed he had plenty of money and constantly asked for financial help. This situation had made it impossible for him to stay in Texas.

In 2019, I contacted Jane after I could not reach out to Carlos, which is when I learned he had passed. It was a sad day for me; I did not notice any indications he was experiencing medical problems. Around me, he was upbeat and just wanted to have fun and enjoy life. At that point, I started to reflect on memories of our friendship. I recall one moment when Carlos showed me a picture of his grandson. I said to him, "Man, if you are walking down the street with this kid, the police will stop you and assume you kidnapped him." He laughed and said, "I never thought about that before, but I see what you're saying." Carlos had a very dark complexion; he married a white woman from England. They had two sons whose DNA comprised 50% of each parent. Both sons have noticeably light complexions and married white women. The grandson's appearance is Caucasian, with blond hair and blue eyes. God works in mysterious ways.

In 2024, U.S. News reported that a white female, Mary MacCarthy, and her racially mixed 10-year-old daughter were traveling to Denver from Los Angeles on Southwest Airlines when they were briefly detained in Denver, Colorado, "based on a racist assumption about a mixed-race family." She has since filed a lawsuit. The incident happened in October 2021 when a flight attendant reported to the police she suspected the woman of human trafficking. After an investigation by Denver Police, the case was closed as "unfounded". The incident reminded me of my late friend Carlos and his blue-eyed, blonde-haired grandson.

On the 4th of July 2023, Joan and I attended a cookout at the house on the shore of Lake Tobesofkee in Bibb County, Georgia. While there, I met Lt Colonel Odom, Retired, Air Force Reserve, also 116th Fighter Wing Alumni. The hosts are college friends with Jazz Trumpeter Lin Roundtree who performed on the back deck of their home. That same year, according to Billboard, Roundtree released 21 singles that appeared on the National Billboard Top 25 Smooth Jazz Chart.

The food, music, and live entertainment was great, and the attendees had a wonderful time. The evening ended with fireworks over the lake.

THE 2024 SMOOTH JAZZ CRUISE

The first day aboard the Celebrity Summit, January 25, 2024, included scheduled shows such as Marcus Anderson in the Sky Lounge, Norman Brown in the Cosmopolitan Restaurant, and Mindi Abair in the Celebrity Theatre.

The second day featured Jonathan Butler's Gospel Show, Larry Braggs performing in the Cosmopolitan Restaurant, Grace Kelly in the Rendezvous Lounge, Eric Marienthal in the Cosmopolitan Restaurant, Boney James in the Celebrity Theatre, Marqueal Jordan in the Sky Lounge, Cigars Under the Stars with Rick Braun, and DW3 and The Music of Motown in the Celebrity Theatre.

On Monday, day three, Marcus Miller presented the History of Jazz; Boney James performed in the Rendezvous Lounge; Brian Culbertson in the Celebrity Theatre; Ms. Monet in the Sky Lounge; and Peter White in the Cosmopolitan Restaurant. We experienced this type of schedule each day during the seven-day cruise.

On the last day, January 31, performances were all over the ship. Highlights included Grace Kelly, Mindi Abair, Brian Culbertson, Norman Brown, and Jeffrey Osborne. There were two performances in the Celebrity Theatre each day, and due to the maximum capacity for attendees, they limited the shows to one thousand passengers. As a result, the ship listed the shows as Blue or Red. The bands that played at the shows were considered either blue or red. We attended the second show each day with the Red Band. Moreover, the dinner schedules were also coded red or blue. The red passengers would attend the early shows and eat dinner later. The final show, a Jam Session, was a spectacular event. The Red Band featured Gerey Johnson, Lamar Jones, Omari Williams, and Collin Clauson, and the other band performed when needed and featured Nate Phillips,

Kevin Turner, Jay Williams, and Arlington Jones. The percussionists included Richie Gajate Garcia and Munyungo Jackson.

Artists included Marcus Miller, Boney James, Brian Culbertson, Jonathan Butler, Candy Dulfer, Peter White, Norman Brown, Richard Elliot, Mindi Abair, Rick Baun and Vincent Ingala. Featured Performers included Grace Kelly, Patches Stewart, Marqueal Jordan, Ivan Peroti, Larry Braggs, Marcus Anderson, Miss Monet, and Dr. Funk. The Music Director was Eric Marienthal, and the Special Guest was Jeffrey Osborne. The primary reason this cruise is the best cruise of my life is because of the entertainment. Joan and I love Jazz and have seen most of the same artists on the cruise perform at the Seabreeze Jazz Festival.

On Friday, January 26, Rick Braun hosted Cigars under the Stars on the 10th floor, Sunset Bar in the ship's rear. When I arrived, I saw Rick sitting alone at a table with his trumpet, wearing a green Philadelphia Eagles Kelce Jersey. I sat at the table beside him as he lit his cigar. Minutes later, he started playing the horn. At that moment, I thought, here I was, sitting next to Rick Braun, smoking a cigar, listening to him perform live. Wow, this is a long way from Juliette, Georgia. Awesome! We briefly spoke about the wonderful time everyone was having before other passengers joined in the conversation with the same excitement as me. Another great memory I will cherish forever!

On another night after Jonathan Butler's concert, he joined us for a cigar and beverages at the Sunset Bar on the 10th floor at the ship's rear. Larry Braggs accompanied him. Jonathan walked over, saw me smoking a cigar, and asked me for a lighter. "Sure, here you go," I said. I asked him to join me just before Larry arrived. He walked to the bar, purchased a beverage, and returned to our table. Another guy named Jade, who knew Jonathan from one of his Safari tours in South Africa, had joined me before Jonathan's arrival. I introduced myself as Percy Freeman from Georgia. "Nice to meet you, Percy; how are you enjoying the cruise so far?" "It is my best cruise," I said. Jonathan then ordered a beverage for Larry Braggs and offered one to everyone.

I declined since I was sipping Black Rum to enhance my cigar flavor. Larry did not have a cigar, so I opened my portable humidor case and asked him to select one. He reached over and selected a cigar I had purchased from a cigar shop in Stockbridge, Georgia. He asked, "Percy, where do you get your cigars from?" I proudly said, "I purchased twenty-five cigars for One hundred twenty-five dollars in Stockbridge, Georgia, and I purchased other cigars from a guy who produces cigars in the Dominican Republic. He took my lighter from the table and lit it up. "Not bad, "he said. As we sat at the table, I started the conversation by telling everyone I had visited South Africa in 2017 and had a wonderful time. That is when Jonathan shared with us that he operated a tour group in South Africa, including a safari, in which he participated in the tour with about twenty people max. He then turned to Larry and suggested he take the tour. Larry said he did not want to deal with those wild animals in Africa. I saw it as my opening; I said, "I'm glad I didn't see any black mambas while I was there, but I did see signs on the windows warning you not to leave your windows open because of baboons. I told them we visited the Cape of Good Hope and were warned not to feed the baboons. After we exited the tour bus near the lighthouse near the cape, we saw a baboon walking around the roof of the visitor building. Minutes later, we saw the same baboon eating a Sub-sandwich. The bus driver said the baboon had taken it from one of the tourists who had arrived on another bus. As we left the area from the lighthouse, we spotted a congress of baboons crossing the highway.

At that point, Larry and Jonathan jokingly laughed about the YouTube videos of lions climbing inside and on top of safari vehicles, rhinos and elephants going berserk and chasing safari vehicles, and a Rhino farting on the hyenas. The conversation about the dangers in Africa continued as a joke for the next two hours. It was a night of laughter and fun. At around 2:00 am, I said goodnight to everyone, "Watch out for those black mambas," I said, then left and returned to my cabin.

Sailing on a ship and listening to some of my favorite jazz artists in a small venue was a pleasure. It was even more of a pleasure to shake their hands and converse with them. Two of my favorite guitarists on board were Peter White and Norman Brown. I was satisfied. My wife is more of a reader than I am, and she was the first person to inform me that Peter White co-wrote the hit *Time Passages* by Al Stewart in 1978 after she googled his bio. In 1978, I lived in Italy and loved the song the first time I heard it. I had no idea Peter White was involved in its creation. In fact, before the cruise, I had started working on a book about my life and decided to name it *Time Passages*. When I played the song for my wife and told her it reminded me of Italy, she immediately associated it with reminding me of my ex-Italian girlfriend. I liked the music. I started listening to jazz in Italy where I began my Bob James collection.

One of my favorite Peter White songs is *Bright*. It is not easy to describe the feeling of meeting one of your favorite artists face-to-face and engaging them in conversation. I was just in awe of the talent standing before me. What an incredible experience, one that is etched in my mind forever. Another favorite song by Peter White, a remake from the Spinners back in the 1970s, is *Could it be I'm Falling in Love*. These songs, these moments, they are like bookmarks in the story of my life, each one bringing back a flood of memories and emotions.

Norman Brown is another favorite artist of mine. When he plays "That's the Way Love Goes," you feel relaxed and at ease—raw talent. When I started dating Joan, I played jazz music during our first date to impress and introduce her to the new Percy. To my surprise, she was also a lover of Jazz. This shared love for jazz brought us together and has been a constant in our relationship. Norman Brown and Peter White are now part of our jazz playlist, a collection of all the artists who sailed with us for the 20th Anniversary Smooth Jazz Cruise.

CHAPTER 15

FIFTY YEARS LATER

During the school year of 1972-73, I saw a beautiful girl walking down the hallway at Mary Persons High School. She was tall and slim, with long legs. She had a "Pecan tan complexion" and wore an Afro and glasses. I would watch her daily as we passed in the hallway, admiring her from a distance. It took all the courage I could muster to approach her, but our initial contact was filled with smiles and laughter when I did. From that day on, we would meet daily in the hallway, our interest in each other growing with each passing moment. Meanwhile, I was playing varsity football for Mary Persons High School, and in 1971, I lettered my sophomore year. As high school students do, I allowed her to wear my letterman's jacket, proudly showing the world, she was my girl.

We continued to see each other and meet at school and school grounds; it was not until late 1973, after purchasing a car, which provided transportation for me to visit her home. Her parents, Willie Ferguson, Sr., and Evelyn Tanner Ferguson lived in a brick house on Willis-Wilder Drive in Forsyth. We initially met in the hallway at school, but later, her parents approved of me visiting their home. We would sit on the couch in the living room facing Willis Wilder Drive, talk, kiss, and hug for at least two hours. We met three to four times monthly and began to fall in love. Although I was in love, I never felt like I belonged with Joan. I felt inferior due to my home environment. At age 17, I could not do much to change my situation. After the summer of 1972, I left home and lived with my aunt. That stay only lasted briefly, as I contemplated my options, which resulted in a brief sever of our relationship. The breakup in 1973 was a challenging time for me. Afterward, during the fall of that year, the Slaughter family offered me the opportunity to live with them. I did not realize until later the tremendous sacrifice they made by allowing me to live in their home with three of their children. I will forever be indebted to their kindness and hospitality.

My self-esteem improved after moving to the Slaughter's home and settling in at my new residence. Edgar, Henry, and Kenneth were all intelligent boys. It was an improvement on my previous residence. We played football and basketball together, along with Bobby and Clarence Johnson, who lived across Georgia Highway 87.

Joan and I started dating again during my junior year in high school, and our love for each other grew. I recall the romantic letters she often wrote to me that helped me survive. I knew she loved me like no one had ever loved me before. During my senior year, I played football at Mary Persons during the fall of 1973. After my Aunt Jean divorced Charlie and purchased a mobile home, I moved in with her. The former mobile home was on property owned by her great-aunt and uncle, Laura and John Jackson, and next door to her former mother-in-law, Gladys Brown. I continued living with her in the trailer until graduation from high school. It was the first time I had my room, like living in an RV. Unfortunately, I did not attend the high school prom during my junior or senior years. I could not afford a high school ring. I was still living in poverty, trying to maintain my vehicle with all the cash on hand. Life continued to be a struggle for me. However, Joan never gave up on me and expressed her dreams of us living together as a family. She continued to love me, but I always thought she would excel in life somewhere; on the other hand, I did not know what cards were in my future. Joan was a bright student who dreamed of becoming a child psychologist, and she often shared her aspirations with me.

After graduating high school, I moved to Atlanta, Georgia, and went to the Air Force Recruiting Office on West Peachtree Street. I passed the test and waited for someone to contact me. When I received orders to report for a physical, I was excited. I do not recall if I communicated it to Joan, but we were still in love, and she continued to wear my letterman's jacket beginning in the fall of 1974 into the winter of 1975. I departed Atlanta for San Antonio, Texas, on August 18, 1974. While there, Joan and I constantly wrote letters back and forth. As anyone in military training knows, your eyes are brighter, and you stick out your chest when you receive a letter from home. Joan is the only person who wrote letters to me, and each one was a balm to my soul, a reminder of the love and support waiting for me back home.

In October 1974, I departed Lackland Air Force Base for Denver, Colorado. At that point, I felt my life had changed, and I would not continue my relationship with Joan. Although I sent many pictures and letters to her, we had been apart for a while. Before going to Denver, I visited home in Juliette, Georgia. I am trying to remember the details; she was a senior in high school. I returned home to Juliette in March 1975 before her graduation and before reporting for my first Air Force assignment at Tyndall Air Force Base Florida.

In June 1975, determined to solidify our relationship, Joan came to Panama City Beach, Florida, to visit me. We did not meet because I was twenty-five miles away on the other side of town without transportation. She was highly disappointed, and so was I. Reflecting on how much she loved me, I should have done things differently. However, if that had happened, our lives would have been different. As a new Airman, my salary was less than $500 monthly. In later years, we would run into each other at least three more times before July 2019, when I attended the funeral for her husband, Marcus Whitehead. Marcus and I had once played football on the Junior varsity (B-team) during the 1970 season at Mary Persons High School, Forsyth, Georgia.

After joining the East Point Police Department in 1982, I periodically attended training at the Georgia Public Safety Training Center in Forsyth, GA. One day, after walking out to the south side parking lot, I saw Joan walking towards her car. I was shocked to see her. At the time, we both had married, and our lives had changed forever. Well, in a small town, the world travels fast. She knew I was married and later told me someone said I was married to an "exotic" woman from the Islands. When we looked directly into each other's eyes, we both knew that our feelings still existed, but there was nothing we could do; our paths had changed because of our marriages to someone else. We hugged and drove away.

The next time I saw Joan was a few years later. Each time I attended training at the academy in Forsyth, I would ride through the neighborhoods to see the changes and run into old friends. Driving on Willis Wilder Drive, I saw my former roommate and high school friend, Larry Bowden, jogging. He got in my SUV, and we continued to ride. As we approached Willie Ferguson's home, I saw Joan standing in the driveway of a house next door. It turns out she lived there. Again, I was pleased to see her, so we pulled into the driveway. I rolled down the window, and immediately, I could smell the sweat from Larry's workout drifting past my nose toward Joan. Immediately, I thought, I hope she does not believe the smell is coming from me. The conversation was brief, and Larry and I departed. I smiled, knowing the girl I once loved appeared to be doing well. However, I did not expect her to return to Forsyth after attending Clark College.

Years later, I learned Joan had divorced and was married again to Marcus Whitehead. Periodically, when I came to Forsyth, I would see Marcus someplace around the city. As far as I knew, Joan and I were happily married, but not to each other.

Around 2003, after I purchased property in Juliette, the former home of John and Laura Jackson, my aunt, who had been living there at close to no cost, moved out. I visited Juliette for a couple of days to check on my house. While there, I contacted Joan at the Bibb County School System. I just wanted to meet with her for lunch or after work for happy hour. She reluctantly agreed. I was busy working in Juliette that day and completely forgot about the meeting. Since my house was vacant for several months, my hot water tank was last used a while ago, creating stale water. When I first turned on the water to take a shower, the water smelled like rotten eggs or sulfur. I allowed it to run continuously for a while, but the sulfur smell would not go away. It was one of the moments when you just say "damn." I thought I would never be late and could not be late today. I rushed to shower and smelled like sulfur or stale water when I finished. Damn, what am I going to do now? I thought. I will load up with cologne. Polo Blue would do nicely.

After getting dressed, I drove directly south on Georgia Highway 87 to Riverside Drive to a restaurant where Joan was waiting. We sat at a table and ordered food and beverages. I did not know it then, but she revealed she was nervous about meeting me. I was thinking something different. The discomfort was palpable, and I couldn't shake the feeling that she might smell the sulfur on me. It was the second time I became concerned about what Joan smelled when I was near. We had a beverage and dinner and departed in our separate ways. I would not see or speak with her again until I attended a family reunion at Indian Springs State Park.

After years of family history research, I compiled a book that included the history of the Freeman family. My aunt told me all the Freemans in Monroe County were related. I traced one set of Freemans, Joan's side, to Samuel Freeman, born in Virginia in 1830. The only way to connect would be if Jack Freeman and Sam were brothers. That was the belief, but it was never a proven fact. For years, we assumed they were brothers and held family reunions together. I attended when Joan's family reunited at the park to get more information about the family tree. It was nice to see Joan and Marcus there. But I sensed Marcus was unhappy with my presence; he knew Joan and I had dated in high school. Joan would later tell me after Marcus' death when I showed up at the reunion, Marcus said to her, "Cousin, my ass." Then, years later, an Ancestry DNA test revealed a shocking truth: I was not related through the Freeman lineage. She is from the Sam Freeman lineage, and I am from the Jack Freeman lineage. They are not brothers.

In June 2019, after the divorce was filed, I moved from Stone Mountain to Juliette, Georgia. Since my house was not ready to move in, I purchased a 2019 recreation vehicle (RV) travel trailer and parked it at my home in Juliette. In July, Marcus Whitehead, who had been sick for years, passed away. Out of respect for him and Joan, I attended the funeral in Forsyth. Out of respect, I only contacted her during the Labor Day weekend in September 2019. I invited her to my RV for dinner in October to discuss how our lives had gone on separate paths. Now, here we were, back in Forsyth and Juliette, Georgia.

I cooked Lobster and steak for our dinner. We enjoyed white wine and listened to jazz music. That is when we learned what we have in common, especially the love of smooth Jazz. We dined and enjoyed the evening before she drove back to her home in Forsyth. I wanted her to know I would be there if she needed me. After that night, I started traveling as I had planned before retirement. Now, I was free to come and go as I pleased. We finalized my divorce in December 2019. In January, I contacted Joan for another date. She agreed. We started dating and attended various events, but then COVID-19 struck. However, it did not stop us from getting together.

In June 2020, Joan and I traveled to Savannah and Tybee Island for a vacation. Wearing masks had become the norm. We stayed at the Hampton Inn downtown. While checking in, the hotel told us there would be no room or cleaning services during our stay. If we need extra towels, we could call the front desk. As we approached the room door, we noticed a seal on the door; as a notice, the hotel cleaned the room to prevent the spread of COVID-19. After entry, we also saw a seal on the toilet seat. We were satisfied the hotel was taking the necessary precautions for us to have a safe stay that weekend. It was a warm day with overcast skies, so we decided to sit outside in one of several parks around the downtown area. We sat, ate ice cream, and noticed several people marching on one of the adjacent streets. Curiosity encouraged us to follow the group. The march ended in a park near Johnson Square City

Market. Several trees, manicured hedges, shrubs, and an Egyptian obelisk surrounded the park's center. A large crowd, including several police officers, and about ten percent of the attendees wore masks. They were there to protest the murder of George Floyd and the treatment of other African Americans by police.

In September 2020, Joan and I embarked on a thrilling journey through North Dakota, South Dakota, Minnesota, Iowa, and Nebraska. Despite the cautious atmosphere, we were filled with a sense of adventure. We donned our masks, not just because they were required, but because we knew they would keep us safe. As we kept an eye on the news, we were aware of the many deaths reported throughout the United States and around the world. However, we were determined to continue our journey, taking all the recommended precautions.

In October 2020, Joan and I set out for Albuquerque, New Mexico. The state had implemented a strict COVID protocol, but that didn't dampen our spirits. I had always dreamt of visiting and skiing at Taos, and this was the perfect opportunity. We visited Taos, fully aware that it was not ski season. I suggested we drive to the ski resort to experience it and bask in the beauty of the scenery. The following day, we headed north towards Santa Fe, New Mexico, and eventually took the winding mountainous road to Taos. To our surprise, we saw a business with a sign on the window, "Black Lives Matter". Later, during the return trip to Albuquerque, we stopped and ate lunch at a small restaurant—another day filled with inspiration and awe. On the next day, we got up early, were picked up at our hotel, and headed to the designated location for the hot air balloon ride. Upon arrival, before daylight, we sat in a van, waiting for the test. A vendor representative released several balloons to determine wind speed and direction. One of our main reasons for the trip to New Mexico was to take a hot air balloon ride. Contrary to many fears, hot air ballooning is the safest air travel, according to the Federal Aviation Administration (FAA) Accident Database. While winds may seem perfectly fine on the ground, once you reach a certain altitude, it can increase by several knots and become unsafe for balloon travel. In our case, the company canceled the ride around 7:00 a.m. The balloon company offered to reschedule the flight, but unfortunately, we departed town the next day. The weather was perfect the day after our missed hot air balloon flight. When we awoke in the morning and looked out the hotel room window, we saw several balloons with different shapes and colors. It was a beautiful scene.

From April 21-26, 2021, Joan and I attended the Seabreeze Jazz Festival in Panama City Beach, FL. We selected a small, inexpensive condominium on the Beach near the Jazz Festival venue. Each day, we walked on the beach for exercise. Two of our favorite places to eat were Sharky's Beachfront Restaurant and the Barefoot Bar and Grill. The Barefoot website notes that Barefoot is a casual street-level cafe with stunning views of the Gulf of Mexico; it serves breakfast, lunch, and dinner while offering a laid-back dining experience in an open-air setting overlooking the water. There is live music during the summer. The food and beverages at both locations were delicious.

Again, there were a limited number of people wearing masks. I assumed people felt more comfortable outside in the open air. When Jeffrey Osborn started his performance, he told us he lost a manager and a brother due to COVID-19. Usually, he would sing while walking out into the audience when he performed. This time, he said he could not do it for fear of COVID. As always, his performance was outstanding for someone over seventy. "He is only human." In 2020, the Seabreeze canceled the Jazz Festival, so all the artists expressed it was the first time they had performed in front of an audience in over a year. Out of an abundance of caution, we wore our masks when we stood near other people.

In May 2021, during Mother's Day weekend, Joan and I finally embarked on our long-awaited trip to San Juan, Puerto Rico. Originally, our travel plans were set for Joan's birthday in January, but the rapid spread of COVID-19 forced us to postpone. We found a comfortable stay at the San Juan Water Club

Beach Hotel in Carolina, Puerto Rico, just a short distance from the airport. Upon arrival, we were greeted by airport staff in full hazmat suits, diligently checking passengers for COVID-19 documents. The seriousness of the situation was further underscored when a police officer on the sidewalk sternly reminded us to wear our masks. Interestingly, there were no masked police on the beach. Several years before, I became familiar with the hotel while sitting on a restaurant patio on the same street facing the beach. On a previous trip to San Juan, while working for the FAA and enjoying food and beverage, I saw a guy and a young lady walking down the street who looked familiar. I yelled out his name, "Darryl," He responded, and it turned out to be Darryl Carver, a former Fulton County ADA. He was there on vacation, lodging at the Water Club Hotel, and I was there for work, lodging at the Embassy Suites about three to four blocks from the beach. I also knew Darryl from the Southern Snow Seekers Ski Club. We had previously traveled with the Ski Club to Paris and St. Moritz, Switzerland.

    Joan and I enjoyed walking on the beach each day and swimming in the warm water during this trip. Unfortunately, Joan was not fully prepared to deal with the consequences of not using sunscreen; she suffered from sunburn while enjoying the warmth of the sun's rays. Since I knew about activities and historical locations on the island, I arranged a schedule that included a walking tour of Old San Juan, a visit to the Old Fort, the City of Loiza, and Piñones. Loiza is located on the island's north coast and has a large Afro-Puerto Rican population. According to a taxi driver, enslaved people ran away from old San Juan and lived in Loiza. The river flows through the city and eventually flows into the ocean. The enslavers did not venture into the area because of the thick brush. They just left the enslaved people alone, and the population continued to increase over the years. The town of Loiza and the Piñones community reflect the island's Afro-Spanish culture and traditions, especially in food, music, and crafts. It is considered by many locals "the soul of the island," celebrating Puerto Rico's traditional

Afro-Caribbean community and culture. Our visit to Loiza provided us with profound cultural insights, enriching our understanding of Puerto Rico's history and heritage.

We ate dinner at the Metropol Cuban Restaurant in Isla Verde next door to the Cockfighting arena. I had eaten there several times during my work visits with the agency. Due to COVID, the Wyndham El San Juan Hotel Beach Resort Casino was closed, so we lounged around at the pool and reclined on the Wyndham Hotel beach. The resort is vast, with several swimming pools and outdoor bars. It also has a restaurant on the top floor with panoramic mountains and ocean views.

While enjoying a lovely lunch in the rooftop restaurant at the Water Club Beach Hotel when we overheard a couple and their teenage daughter talking. The male told his wife or girlfriend he did not want to pay $12 for a hamburger; she would have to pay for it. At that point, the teen daughter was eating the burger. Again, I thought his loud comment about a $12 burger was "cheap." When you go to a restaurant in a resort hotel with an ocean view in Puerto Rico, you are paying not only for a burger but also for the ambiance that includes a view of mountains, the ocean, and the surrounding skyline.

Judging people is not something I do regularly, but I notice things that need to be put in the right place or improperly done. In this case, people have become so comfortable in how they dress that they disregard any pride that may have existed in the past. Wearing hair bonnets, house slippers, and pajamas in the airport, talking loudly, using profanity while traveling, and sitting in the airport waiting area is plain "ghetto." Most people are not aware that the word "Ghetto" (gettare) originated from the name of the Jewish quarter in Venice, Italy. Venetian authorities compelled the city's Jews to live in the quarter around 1516.

As we witnessed this behavior, I jokingly told Joan, "This must be 'stimulus money weekend.'" Spirit Airlines was their choice of travel. It became evident when all the young ladies seated themselves at the Spirit boarding gate. Spirit Airlines announced an hour flight delay. Minutes later, they announced a two-hour flight delay, and that is when the young ladies started using loud profanity in the gate area. Shortly afterward, two San Juan Airport police officers positioned themselves next to the Spirit Ticket Counter. Moments later, Spirit announced a four-hour flight delay. At that point, the young ladies started to "raise hell".

In June 2021, Joan and I attended the Ledbetter Family Reunion in Amicalola Falls State Park in the north Georgia mountains. At least forty-five family members participated in the event, and no one wore a mask. It was Joan's first time meeting my family members in the Ledbetter lineage. She had no problems connecting. When asked about her experience, she said, "It was interesting." On Friday, one of my cousins hosted the annual Friday cookout at a cabin at the base of the mountain next to a creek. Usually, there are around 20-25 people present. The deck in the rear is just a few feet away from the creek, and you can hear the constant water flow rolling down the mountain. A fire pit is in the middle of the deck, perfect for a family event. We sat around talking and consuming various beverages, depending on one's choice. I always bring my most famous dish, Percy's Three-bean Salad. It is always everyone's favorite. I feel like I am family each time I attend the Ledbetter Reunion. I have felt this way from the beginning.

In July 2021, we had the pleasure of attending Joan's son's wedding near Charlotte, North Carolina. He would soon become my stepson. The wedding was a joyous event, held at a large house converted into an event center, a venue for those who could afford it. It was a unique opportunity for Joan and me to meet all my stepkids, all adults. Joan's son Jamaal and his wife, Lanika, were visiting from Germany, Jordan, and his bride, Alexis, lived in Maryland. In contrast, her daughter Marcella lived with her in Forsyth, Georgia. Joan's stepdaughter, Janese, half-sister of Jamaal and Jordan, who lived in Dallas, Georgia, was also in attendance. The wedding was a unique opportunity for Joan and me to learn more about one another and to bond with our extended family.

While I may not be one to spend a lot of money on weddings, I can't deny the beauty of this one. The bridesmaids and groomsmen looked stunning in their outfits; the caterers, disc jockeys, photographers, videographers, and other services were all top-notch. It was a beautiful celebration, even if I preferred something more straightforward and less expensive. The beauty of the event was truly a remarkable sight, and it filled the air with joy and love.

On July 25 and 26, 2021, we visited Stone Mountain Park and stayed in my RV. My granddaughter Cami stayed with us for a couple of days. We enjoyed the outdoors, walks in the park, and cooking on the grill. Several families remained in the park during that time, taking precautions to avoid staying in hotels at the risk of catching COVID-19. We shared their fears and were careful to follow all safety guidelines, ensuring a safe and enjoyable trip for everyone.

Stone Mountain Park Campground is approximately twenty miles east of Atlanta in unincorporated Stone Mountain, Georgia. The campground is nestled among 3200 acres of natural beauty. It features over 400 RV, Pop-up, Tent sites, Yurt, Safari Tent, and RV Rentals. The park also offers a variety of recreational activities and family-friendly attractions and events available seasonally. Its list of Campground Amenities includes Comfort Stations and Laundry Facilities, Grills, Picnic Tables, Fire Rings, Free Wi-Fi & Cable, Dump Stations, a General Store, Police, Fire, EMS, and a Swimming Pool. The park features fifteen miles of wooded hiking trails and offers fishing, kayaking, and paddle boarding on Stone Mountain Lake. You can enjoy paved lanes for walking, biking, and jogging or take the 1-mile hike to the top of Stone Mountain for amazing 360-degree views of Atlanta, Buckhead, Cobb, and Gwinnett Counties.

According to an article written by Dr. Beth Harris and Dr. Steven Zucker, "The Long History of Stone Mountain Park," September 30, 2021, they noted that the relief sculpture of Confederate leaders Robert E. Lee, Thomas "Stonewall"

Jackson, and Jefferson Davis at Stone Mountain Park is a potent symbol of white supremacy which has continued to define southern United States culture since before the Civil War. White supremacy also characterized the Spirit of Manifest Destiny that obscured Native presence and history in North America. The sculpture took 55 years to complete, and multiple sculptors worked on it, each with individual designs. Still today, the site reflects an ongoing conversation in Georgia and across the United States about the history, legacy, and symbolism of the Confederacy and Civil War.

From September 3-6, 2021, we traveled to Albany, New York, Vermont, New Hampshire, Maine, and Massachusetts. We arrived in Albany via Delta Airlines. As I recall, we wore our masks only in areas near other people, such as on the plane and in the airport. Some restaurants would require you to wear masks until seated at your table. As we traveled throughout the northeast, we noticed no apparent concern about COVID-19. We attended an outdoor street concert in Troy, New York, where no one wore a mask. As we traveled through Vermont and New Hampshire, we encountered two restaurants requiring us to wear masks. One of the primary reasons for the trip was to check off the state of Vermont from my bucket list. My goal was to visit all fifty states in the United States. Vermont was number 50. Mission complete. We stopped at the state line as we traveled and memorialized the moment with a photograph of the state's entry sign.

In September 2021, we attended the Monroe County African American History Museum opening. The outside event was in the open air. Still, several people wore masks out of an abundance of caution when gathering for a group photo. After our visit, I donated items to the museum, including my Air Force uniform. For the history records, I am one of the first Black Chief Master Sergeants born in Monroe County, Georgia. Harold Phillips, MPHS class of 1971, is also a retired Air Force Chief. I also donated the original layout for an article in the Stars and Stripes Newspaper on November 8, 1977. The article is titled "Eagles' Freeman Destroys Bosco, Aviano Back

Scored Seven Touchdowns." Once again, I am the only football player in the history of Monroe County, Georgia, to score seven TDs in one game playing semi-professional football. I also donated a photograph of me racing during a NASTAR snow ski racing event in British Columbia at Whistler-Blackcomb Ski Resort. Since I don't know any Blacks in Monroe County, Georgia, who snow ski, I thought the photograph would inspire others to participate in the sport. I first started skiing in Italy at age 21. I donated these items simply because they might encourage others to seek opportunities and life experiences outside Monroe County.

The Hubbard High and Elementary School Museum is in the former seventh-grade building, also one of the original buildings from Hubbard. I donated an East Point Police uniform shirt and badge in a shadow box. Again, I intended to inspire others to pursue a career in law enforcement. The profession can be gratifying when you are helping people in the community and treating them with dignity and respect, protecting and serving without regard to race, religion, or economic status. Everyone wants equal and fair justice. Again, when people visit this museum, especially children, I hope they will see other career opportunities.

On October 10, 2021, Joan and I took Cami to the Georgia National Fair in Perry, GA. We all wore masks out of caution; however, the Trump effect still worked in South Georgia. Few people were wearing masks, but many were buying Trump merchandise and wearing Trump brand clothing as a fashion and political statement. He left office on January 20, 2021, but he left an impact on the conservatives in Georgia. They were still spending money to show support for the previously defeated president.

We received a booster shot on November 1, 2021, Pfizer on April 14, 2022, and the final booster on September 15, 2022. Hallelujah, we survived. Unfortunately, I know several people, including an aunt, who was hospitalized for a week or more. One of my cousins and high school classmate, Betty

Freeman Stewart, who attended my retirement luncheon ceremony in March 2019, became a victim and died. While the world was trying to deal with everyday tragedies, we constantly heard about people stealing the previous election. People started to rally behind the idea that some people cheated Trump out of an election. Were they really that naive? Yes, they were!

From November 9-14, 2021, Joan and I attended a destination wedding in Cancun, Mexico. During the Veterans Day Holiday, we traveled to Cancun and were required to take the COVID-19 test within 72 hours before travel and to wear masks on our flights. Once we arrived in Mexico and exited the airport, the taxi required us to wear a mask. When we arrived at our resort, we were only required to wear a mask when we approached the lobby desk and entered the food court area before being seated in a restaurant. The resort staff always wore masks.

In December 2021, Joan and I went on a Princess Cruise to Princess Cay and Paradise Cove, Dominican Republic. We toured the downtown area of Puerto Plata and ate lunch at La Catalina Ranch in the mountains. The restaurant featured exotic birds, llamas, donkeys, and other animals. The food was delicious, focusing on local and Caribbean dishes, such as rice and beans, fried plantains, and fried fish, including avocado, mango, limes, and coconut dishes. Open dining areas also had a fantastic view of open farmland leading downhill towards the ocean. I had previously visited that location and thought Joan would like it. We continued to wear masks on buses and at some businesses as required. However, many places were more relaxed about mask-wearing once you were seated.

In September 2022, we departed Atlanta on Virgin Atlantic Airlines for London, England, to start our 10-day Oktoberfest cruise from Southampton to Hamburg, Germany; Sweden; Copenhagen, Denmark; Oslo, Norway; Amsterdam, the Netherlands; and Bruges, Belgium. Upon arrival at London Heathrow Airport, we boarded a bus for the Leonardo Royal Hotel, approximately five blocks from London Tower Bridge. We had arranged to meet with Kira, a London resident and

Brandon's former wife. Brandon met in daycare and attended Grambling State University with Joan's son, Jamaal. After settling in our hotel room, we met with her in the lobby and walked over to the Sushi Samba Restaurant, about three to four blocks away. After arriving, we took an elevator to the top floor. The view of London was beautiful. Although the day was partly cloudy and a little windy, the view of the Thames River and around the city was incredible. Because of the light, windy conditions, we could not eat dinner outside but were allowed to walk outside briefly for photographs. Kira was delightful company and a great ambassador for her city. We ordered special drinks and, later, delicious food from the Sushi Samba menu that celebrates the culture and cuisine of Japan, Brazil, and Peru. After great beverages, delicious food, and friendly conversation, we walked to Tower Bridge for a close-up view of the Thames and more photographs. Kira departed, and we returned to our hotel to prepare for our cruise departure the next day.

On September 27, 2022, we boarded a bus for the seaport city of Southampton. After driving through the terrible traffic, we finally ended up on the Motorway. We thoroughly enjoyed the scenery during the drive, which took about two and a half hours due to the traffic in London. I learned later that a train from London to Southampton costs about eight US dollars and takes one hour and eight minutes. Princess Cruise Lines also offers transfers from Heathrow directly to Southampton.

After boarding the Island Princess and settling in our cabin with a balcony on the starboard or left side of the ship, we discovered we had selected the best location. As we entered each port, our balcony view was perfect for photographs, providing the city's best view as we approached. It also offered a beautiful view of the city before departure. The view from our balcony was great in Rotterdam, the Netherlands; Hamburg, Germany; Oslo, Norway; and Bruges, Belgium.

In Oslo, we toured Vigeland Park. It has beautiful landscapes and well-manicured lawns. The park houses numerous sculptures created by Gustav Vigeland, a native of Norway. Its most famous sculpture is "The Angry Boy." The park includes innumerable sculptures, large and small bridges, and fountains. It is a must-see place to visit in Oslo. We walked the park for about thirty minutes on ninety percent flat grounds. There are also open, well-groomed, and manicured grass fields. Be aware that ninety-five percent of the sculptures are nude, including the "Angry Boy."

Through several years of European travel, I have found Europeans more open and receptive to art than Americans. There is too much hypocrisy in America, especially for political and religious reasons.

After arrival in Gothenburg, Sweden, on October 1, 2022, the dock could have been more impressive. It is an industrial area lined with business buildings. Directly across from the starboard side of the ship, approximately ninety yards away, is the Volvo Museum. We visited it as our last tour before returning to the boat. We planned to eat local food during our cruise to experience a part of the local culture. In Oslo, we walked along the beautiful waterfront opposite the harbor from the docked cruise ship. We located a restaurant named Rorbua at Aker Brygge. First, I ordered a locally brewed beer. After a quick view of the menu, I ordered a skewer that included whale, deer, lamb, and reindeer. After eating whale for the first time, I would describe it as beefy to chew, slightly rubbery, with a fishy taste and smell, and a dark reddish-brown color.

Another good place to visit in Oslo is the Holmenkollbakken Ski Jump, the site of the 1952 Winter Olympics. They built the current structure between 2008 and 2010. From downtown Oslo, the ride takes you up a winding road while passing beautiful homes along the way with impressive panoramic views of Oslo harbor. My Ancestry.com DNA results indicate my makeup is 1% Norwegian. As a result, I attempted to experience a little culture from a different world than my own.

In 2022, I began spending more time at Joan's house in Forsyth, Georgia. Since I like to work in the yard and do handyperson work, a lot of work needed to be completed, so I went into action. Joan had paid a company to maintain her lawn for years. Dwight and Dwaine Sanders, twin brothers from Warner Robins, Georgia, owned a lawn service. When I first saw them working in the yard, they were speeding across the yard on their twin zero-turn mowers. They completed the yard in a brief time. Joan met Dwight while working with his wife, Cheryl, at Hubbard ES, and they both worked for the Bibb County School System.

Following our 2023 marriage, we vacationed with Dwight, his wife, my daughters, and one granddaughter on a cruise to Honduras, Belize, Cozumel, and Costa Maya. Since my daughters did not attend our midnight wedding, I wanted them to meet my new wife. It turned out to be a great decision. We enjoyed the beaches and participated in activities together on the ship. The best time was when we all met for dinner each day. Unfortunately, I did not spend time with Dwight's twin brother, Dwaine "Peedy" Sanders. He was buried on May 29, 2024, after a sudden death. He had worked for forty-two years at the Bibb Distributing Company for Anheuser-Busch.

Maintaining the yard was a way to occupy my time each day. Suddenly, retirement sounded like a word I was not familiar with. I cut brush and trees, cleared land, and expanded the yard. I paid to have dirt hauled in to fill holes left by the builders to bury trees. Years after the trees are covered with dirt, they rot, creating a prominent bowl appearance. Next, I hired experienced friends to develop a sidewalk for the front of the house. I went to work in the backyard. We had previously invited friends over for a backyard cookout and sat in lawn chairs in the backyard. The back porch was small, but ideas were running through my mind. We were not married, but I began making improvements at Joan's home for us to spend time enjoying life. I painted walls, replaced bathroom faucets, painted garage handrails, pressure-washed the house, stained cabinets, replaced light fixtures, and more. Each improvement was a labor of love, a way to make our home more comfortable and beautiful. In the meantime, Joan diligently worked on completing her dissertation for her doctorate. Along with the work I completed at Joan's house, I also worked on my house in Juliette, Georgia, and maintained the lawn at Saint Paul AME Church.

As I spent more time at Joan's house, I began to feel more comfortable. One day, she asked, "What are we doing?" "Please explain," I said. "What are we going to do with our lives?" She asked. I knew what she was hinting at, so I asked, "What do you want to do?" "Are you saying you want to marry me?" I jokingly said, "I will marry you when you become a doctor." In December 2022, Joan received her Doctorate Degree in Educational Leadership, a significant achievement that filled us both with immense pride. It was a joyous moment when I proposed to her, and she said yes.

Before December, we started preparing for our January 1st wedding with great anticipation. We decided to get married on the new concrete patio. We purchased two large white tents that fit perfectly in the patio space. Joan's best friend from college, Vicky Burns, decorated the tent and the inside of our home with great care and attention to detail. We rented chairs and a wedding arch for the ceremony. My friend from high school, Edgar Slaughter, Jr., agreed to perform the ceremony. We invited about fifty guests. Since the weather was cool but not too cold, I built a temporary wall between the tents and the porch. Another of my home construction projects included building a bar from pallets on the back porch and a deck extending from the concrete patio. We placed propane heaters inside the tent if needed. However, there was enough body heat to keep everyone warm. We hired one of Joan's Delta Sigma Theta Sorors to serve as bartender, who kept the drinks flowing throughout the evening. Ironically, January 1 is Joan's son Jordan's birthday.

On the highly anticipated New Year's Eve, December 31, 2022, our family, and friends began to gather as we eagerly watched the University of Georgia versus Alabama game for the National Championship.

Our family room was abuzz with guests glued to the television. We had originally planned to exchange our vows one second after midnight, but our plans took an unexpected turn when the game between Georgia and Alabama continued. At the stroke of midnight, the Mistress of Ceremonies, Joan's cousin Adelia, made her entrance and announced the move to the tent. The room was filled with looks of disbelief, including my own. I found myself thinking of Venus and Mars. I politely declared, "We won't begin until this game concludes; there's only a few minutes left." The room erupted in cheers and applause.

Immediately after the game, everyone walked to the tent and prepared for our entrance. It was a magical moment, a lasting memory, a joyous moment. After Slaughter pronounced us Husband and Wife, I thought about how long it took to marry my first love—50 years to prepare for this union. As we kissed like newlyweds, I heard Joan's cousin Derrick Wilder yell, "Get a hotel room." Immediately following the wedding, after midnight on New Year's Day, guests started to leave. January 1 is Jordan's birthday. He started his celebration immediately after our wedding and began pumping up the music from his generation. Guests from our generation quickly exited the building. It was New Year's Day, and now I am married to my high school sweetheart.

JOAN'S FULL CIRCLE

During my 10th grade year, I was approached by this boy, Percy Freeman, in the hallway at school. He was soft-spoken but spoke intelligently. I had never encountered him before, even though we had attended the same segregated school through our 7th and 8th-grade years at Hubbard Elementary and High School.

We met at the same time each day at school and eventually became friends. We talked on the phone each night, and after a while, he was one of the two boys in Forsyth, Georgia, permitted to come and sit on my mother's couch. Ironically, I married them both. Percy was an athlete. He played football. I was a cheerleader for the basketball team. There was this connection between us that at the youthful age of 16, I cannot explain, but I was certain that he was the one for me. During my 11th-grade year, he gave me his letterman's jacket (#42) to wear, and it was official. We were a couple. We talked at school and on the phone at night. And on some Wednesday nights, he visited when I was allowed to receive company. Only once did we go out on a date in his Plymouth Fury that had no reverse. It was to a movie—I cannot remember which one, but it was around my 17th birthday. We loved each other by now, and I was convinced we would spend the rest of our lives together.

Percy graduated in May 1974 and made plans to go to the Air Force. By the time my Senior year began, he was an airman at Lackland AFB in San Antonio, Texas, and I wrote to him almost every day, sharing my dreams for our future together. I would give anything to read one of those letters today. I wore #42 throughout my Senior year as I waited to graduate, looking forward to going to college to prepare for our future together.

A couple of weeks after graduation in 1975, my friend Melba, a teacher at Mary Persons, invited me to the beach with her and her kids in Panama City. By this time, Percy was at Tyndall AFB in Panama City, so I was excitedly looking forward to seeing him while I was there. I was 18. I graduated. I was grown. I was going to see the man I was going to spend the rest of my life with. But I was disappointed. Things did not come together as planned, so I came back home feeling sad, dejected, and rejected, but driven to move on because life goes on.

I would move into the dorm at Clark College in August and begin my life again. The weeks prior to moving into the dorm, I moved in with my cousin, Harriet, who lived in Atlanta at Franciscan Apartments. This was my chance to become acclimated to city life. I loved being in the city. I was surrounded by progressive, professional people who represented what I hoped to become. I loved catching the MARTA bus downtown and exploring. There was freedom in this, and I thought I would never live in the country again.

College life was good, and I loved Wonderful Wednesdays—no classes, Tuesday night parties. Lou and Jackie from MPHS were my roommates, but there were plenty of new friendships to develop at Holmes Hall: Melanie, Winnie, Penny, Diana, Kyra, Harriet, Sloan, and many others. But after one semester, I moved out of the dorm and back with my cousin, Harriet, because it was cheaper, and I would have more freedom. In hindsight, I regret the move, but Que Sera Sera.

As an off-campus student, I met Vicky one day when eating lunch at the campus hangout. We discovered we lived near each other and became instant friends, and 48 years later, we remain dear friends. She had gotten married during the Christmas holidays and had moved off campus with her husband. She introduced me to her cousin, Vanessa, who was in respiratory therapy school at Grady Hospital, and we became the three musketeers—having fun and enjoying city nightlife with all the rewards that came with it.

After two years at Clark, I decided to transfer to Georgia State University (GSU) since it was a less expensive option in the heart of downtown Atlanta. While at Clark, I learned about Greek Life and had friends who were members of Alpha Kappa Alpha Sorority, Incorporated, and Delta Sigma Theta Sorority, Incorporated. I found out Deltas had the highest GPA at GSU, so my decision was made. I applied and was accepted, and nine of us crossed the burning sands and became Deltas on May 20, 1978.

Some of my line sisters, I have not seen since, but I have bumped into Eleanor professionally and found out she and Percy Freeman had dated briefly. I maintained contact off and on with Shirley, who passed unexpectedly in the fall of 2020 after we had just celebrated our birthdays the previous January in Washington, DC; Sheila, who called me out at a Delta Conference in Florida after not having seen each other in 25 years or more; and Tyna, who I made an effort to keep in touch with over the years.

I worked briefly as a teller at Trust Company Bank, but it was too much on top of school and my nightlife. Too much fun and city nightlife resulted in my move back to the country in 1981. Before that move, in 1979, Percy Freeman contacted me, and we saw each other for the first time since the failed attempt in Panama City. It didn't go well, and I regretted not being open to rekindling that relationship for years.

My sons' dad, Caesar Harvey, followed me back to Forsyth, and we were married in November 1982. I knew immediately that I had made a mistake, but I stayed, hoping things would change. In July 1984, I received a 14-year-old bonus daughter, Janese, from Chicago when her mother decided she needed to live with her dad, who had seen her once or twice since they divorced when she was three years old. Niecy arrived in July, and Jamaal was born two months later in September.

Once Jamaal was born, from that point on, I assumed the role of mother. I was determined to be the best mother I could be and was intentional in making sure positive experiences were the childhood memories he had. I was the child who felt afraid, anxious, and physically ill if my parents had an argument or disagreement. I vowed to never expose Jamaal to that. I intended to have an only child. A child who would only absorb all the good, positive things which I could expose him to, as many things possible that there are in life to enjoy including an unquenchable thirst for learning. I wanted to instill the desire to explore all there is in the world; all that can be imagined or perceived to be possible after experiencing humane interactions with multiple people from multiple cultures, from multiple stars and stripes, from all, or at least multiple, shades of the human race, absorbing the good there is. My desire was to ensure the good outweighed the distrust that is often present recognizing that people are people, and should we choose to have humane interactions with the people we meet, we recognize and embrace our commonalities and humanity. This is how we learn. But that's in another book.

Well, life was a roller coaster moving into adulthood, and I hate roller coasters. Back in Forsyth, I applied for jobs. I worked a year or so as a timekeeper when Georgia Power's Plant Scherer was under construction until that job evolved into using computerized software. I was replaced by a computer, but I was inspired to apply to Tift College and finish my degree. As I neared being done at Tift, I made the ultimatum that shaped the next years of my life. I finished the coursework for my degree in early November 1982. The boys' father and I were married on Thanksgiving Day, 1982. I knew before the sun went down that I had made a mistake. But I tried to make it right. Until I just couldn't anymore.

I saw Mrs. Oreatha Sewell at Ingles after I completed my degree. She had been my 6th-grade teacher but was now Assistant Principal at Hubbard Elementary School. She was always a very distinguished woman that I admired. People noticed when she entered the room, any room. She had always been kind to me and was one of my many teachers from Hubbard whom I felt had my best interest at heart. So, after that conversation, I was on the substitute teacher list. Mrs. Sadie Smith had announced to me that when I was in 3rd grade that I was going to be a teacher. I fought against it after Mrs. Dillard and I butted heads when I was in 8th grade, and after I watched my classmates in the 10th or 11th grade run Ms. Logan away, back to Canada, I think, before the year's end.

Substitute teaching was no joke! My first day subbing in high school signaled I was out of my league. In the first period, two girls who were nearing delivery time entered, and in my mind, I repeated the line from Gone with the Wind, "I don't know nothin' bout birthin no baby!" The students in the other classes used other people's names instead of their own. One day, a kindergarten class convinced me that kindergarten was not a fit. Most of my time was in middle school, and I did my first extended job, maternity leave, which led me to the light and helped me find my niche. It was between October through December 1983. They were fifth graders, and I fell in love with them. Carolann, whom I knew from high school, had planned everything to the minute, guaranteeing that her children would not miss a thing in her absence. My next long-term assignment was in 4th grade, January 1984. The teacher did not leave the first lesson plan. The lesson learned was that all teachers are not created equal. I knew the type I wanted to be as I was already back at Tift, taking evening classes toward my teaching certificate. Mr. Querry, the principal of Hubbard ES, assured me I had a job when my certification was completed.

I signed my first contract in the summer of 1985. I bought my first new car, a Mazda 626, in 1986. I was a single mother of a toddler and a teenager in the late 80s, but I built the house next to my parents around 1989-1990. The boys' father reappeared, and we tried to make it right again. Jordan was born on January 1, 1992, three weeks after my daddy passed away. The "straw that broke the camel's back" in that relationship was around Christmas 1993. The divorce was final in August 1994.

Marc called from Colorado Springs in late September. He had heard I was divorced, and he was in the process of a divorce. He came through Forsyth in October 1994. We met at Shoney's. He had his young nephew, Mikey, with him. In November, he asked my mom if I could come to New Orleans with him for the Bayou Classic. I was 37 years old, so she told him that it had to be my decision. In December, Marc came to Forsyth bearing gifts—a fire truck for Jordan, Star Wars books and videos for Jamaal, and a diamond ring for me that I didn't wear until late January or February. We were married in June 1995. We bought land to build and moved into our house in October 1997. Marcella was born in November 1997. Now, as a mother of three and even more determined to ensure positive experiences and exposure for each child, I was responsible for being on earth. In 2003, Marc was working in Lafayette, Louisiana, after the dot.com industry crashed. When I was overlooked for the third or fourth administrative position I had applied for, we decided I would interview in Lafayette. I was hired the night before the interview to teach 2nd grade at Broadmoor Elementary School in Lafayette Parish while at dinner with one of Marc's colleagues who lived across the street from Broadmoor's principal. We were there for only a year—Marcella was in kindergarten at Broadmoor; Jordan completed 6th grade at Edgar Martin Middle School; Jamaal was a first-year student at Grambling State University, and he remained in Louisiana until he graduated.

Still committed to providing positive experiences and exposure to my children, I read books to and with them. If a movie was being released, the book had to be read with an Accelerated Reader test score of 80 or higher, before we went to see it. Until 2009, summer vacation was centered around our Moore Family Reunion, during which we visited cities to explore history or cultural elements or cruised. Because Jamaal was at Grambling from 2003-2007, we attended the Bayou Classic every Thanksgiving. We attended sporadically during Jordan's tour of duty at Grambling from 2010-2014. In 2016, Marcella graduated from Howard High School and attended Tuskegee State University in Alabama.

We moved back to Forsyth in July of 2004, where I thought I would go back to my 3rd-grade classroom at Hubbard or the newly built T.G. Scott Elementary School. I had applied to surrounding counties and had been contacted within 24-48 hours by two Bibb County principals. When Angie Dillon informed me she had filled the 5th-grade teacher position listed on Teach Georgia, I called the first principal, Mr. David Dillard, in Bibb who had called me. An interview was scheduled, and I was hired to teach 4th grade, but when I called to schedule a time for me to get my classroom set up, Mr. Dillard had another "opportunity" for me as an instructional lead teacher at Barden Elementary School. I served for five and a half years in this role until I was named Response to Intervention (RtI) Coordinator for the District in December 2009.

As RtI Coordinator, I attended the annual Student Support Team Association for Georgia Educators (SSTAGE) conferences that provided professional development related to Student Support Teams and RtI. By 2012 I was invited to serve on the SSTAGE Board of Directors. After 34 years of serving public schools, I retired to become the SSTAGE Executive Director in 2019.

In October 2014, Marc became critically ill with diabetic complications and was hospitalized for six months. He came home in March from the hospital with a wheelchair and a walker but was back in his office as Recruiting Manager within months. It was miraculous! Marc and I took his annual company trips to Cancun, Costa Rica, Cabo San Lucas, and Jamaica until his death in July 2019, three weeks after I retired from serving 34 years in public education and assumed the role of Executive Director for the Student Support Team Association for Georgia Educators (SSTAGE).

Life can change in the twinkling of an eye. At the age of 62, my life took an unexpected turn, and I was resigned to spending the rest of my life as a widow once the kids were back in Germany, Maryland, and Tuskegee. On August 12, Marcella left for band camp and her senior year at Tuskegee. The loss of her dad was major—she was the ultimate "Daddy's Girl"—her first and closest death experience at age 21. Despite her deep grief, she put her nose to the grindstone and finished with all A's. Then the world shut down around March 17, 2020, due to the COVID-19 Pandemic. Marcella moved back home to finish her classes, and to prepare for her Virtual Graduation from Tuskegee State University.

Around October 2019, Percy Freeman invited me to dinner at his RV in Juliette, days before the Fried Green Tomato Festival. He had called my house phone a couple of times to check on how I was doing after the funeral, and I learned he was back in town and was going through a divorce after 38 years of marriage. That to me was amazing since I had asked on the first day after I was home alone, "Ok, Lord, what's next?" I saw Percy in the churchyard as I exited Marc's funeral and headed to the limousine for the ride to the cemetery. It was the fourth time I had seen him in 40-plus years, but the same reaction I had had the other three times occurred. I almost fainted, but I was able to play it off. Before I could get to the limo, a line of people formed to greet me and to express their condolences. Percy made his way to the lengthy line, and I said to myself, "Not today! I am not strong enough for this!" He made it to me; we hugged politely, he expressed his condolences and moved on for the next person in line, but my head and heart were spinning and doing flips like the other three times we bumped into each other and the few times I was surprised on January 10th with a Happy Birthday message on my office phone as I wondered how in the world he had found me. When he called on the house phone, you could have knocked me over with a feather when his name popped up on the caller ID. Again, I said to myself, "Not today! I am not strong enough for this!" I had begun to work on my dissertation seriously, which had been on the back burner during Marc's illness. I was also focusing on completing my tenure as President of the Macon Alumnae Chapter (MAC) of Delta Sigma Theta Sorority, Incorporated. That was my focus since I was home alone and had no excuse to do otherwise. We talked, and I was shocked to learn about his divorce, which would be final in December. I had heard he was married to someone from the islands, and I assumed she was an exotic island girl with whom I could not compete. Although there was some serious chemistry the four times we were in each other's presence during our 40 years of living separate lives in separate worlds, I had chalked it up as a missed opportunity and a regret I would take to my grave. A regret that I had kicked myself about since I let him walk away from me after we saw each other one day at my apartment when he returned from active duty in the Air Force and to Atlanta back in 1979.

So, dinner at the RV in Juliette was a spark of hope. When I arrived, music from my playlist was playing. He offered me a glass of wine as he put the final additions on the meal he was preparing—steak, lobster tails, baked potatoes, and a salad. I was impressed, to say the least. It was a lovely evening, and as I drove back to Forsyth and home alone again, my head and heart were at it again.

Percy shared that he loved to travel, and since he retired, his plans were to see the world. I was impressed that he had seen much more of the world than most people I knew. Weeks passed, and I didn't hear from him; he was out enjoying himself as a single man and seeing the world. In January 2020, he asked me to go to Savannah and Tybee Island for my birthday. I had never been to Tybee before. It was a beautiful weekend, and afterward, I shared a picture with the kids. The boys were fine. Marcella was not. But they had been made aware that I was alive and living my life. Life is for the living. I had fulfilled my vows.

Of course, weeks passed as Percy traveled to see the world. Then COVID-19 brought things to a screeching halt. We spent time together in Juliette and Forsyth until Marcella came home in March, and then we mostly spent time together in Juliette. We went back to Savannah in June and experienced a Black Lives Matter rally in the park there shortly after the George Floyd murder. We traveled to Maryland in June for Jordan's proposal to Alexis. While visiting Silver Spring, we connected with my elementary and high school best friend, Lou. She and her husband, Tony, picked us up from the hotel, and we shared a fabulous dinner together.

Percy had visited most of the 50 states with just a few left to visit. I had visited more than half, but now this has become my goal, too. In September 2020, we flew to South Dakota. This weekend required that we were fully masked and followed social distancing protocols. We also visited North Dakota, Iowa, Nebraska, and Minnesota. The countryside was beautiful, and in the Dakotas, the speed limit was surprisingly 80 mph. Wind turbines were everywhere, and a truck carrying one of the blades made clear just how large the turbines were.

My last Genuent President's Club trip was to Puerto Vallarta, where Marc was honored posthumously. His sister Pam was my plus one. It was a fabulous trip to a beautiful resort, and I'll never forget it—tequila tastings, sea turtles, catamarans. Later in October, we flew to Albuquerque, New Mexico. Percy wanted to see Taos Ski Resort, so I held my breath as we traveled through the mountains. While eating lunch in Albuquerque, I heard someone say, "Percy, is that you?" It was his former neighbor and his wife who were not aware of the recent divorce. It is a small world, after all. Albuquerque is the home of the Hot Air Balloon Festival, and we were scheduled to experience it. We were picked up at 6 am, but the air and weather conditions did not allow us to experience. The next morning as we were packing for our return flight home, the sky was full of beautifully colored balloons. Next time.

Percy began the sidewalk home improvement project shortly after our return from New Mexico. Jordan has named him Project Percy. He's cleared trees, filled holes, poured a patio, built a deck, built a bar, installed Ring cameras, and replaced light fixtures and faucets. Other home improvement projects have occurred, and if I were to make a prediction, Percy would always have some project underway.

We experienced the Seabreeze Jazz Festival in April 2021–my first but Percy started the tradition in 2009. While in Panama City, Percy gave me a tour of Tyndall Air Force Base and the area where he had lived. For Mother's Day, we went to Puerto Rico. This was my most favorite trip of all time until we visited Italy. I failed to slather on the sunscreen, and a terrible sunburn was the only negative highlight of that Puerto Rican trip. I attended my first Ledbetter Family Reunion in June 2021 at Amicalola Falls State Park. One of the cousins wore his Tuskegee Airman T-shirt just for me, for us, I thought. I jokingly told the kids that my location was on and to monitor periodically.

Lou and I had dinner when I was in Silver Spring for Alexis' Bridal Shower days later. The wedding, a fabulous event, was on July 17, 2021. The next week, we took the RV to Stone Mountain Park for a few days. We had dinner one day with Vicky and Joe. Cami, Percy's granddaughter, spent a couple of nights with us.

In September 2021, Percy finished his 50 states goal. We flew into Albany, New York and found our hotel. We visited Historic Downtown Troy—a nice walking community with restaurants, breweries, and live music. We traveled the next day to Vermont—Percy's 50th state, New Hampshire, Maine, Massachusetts, and back to Albany. It was a beautiful day, and I was able to add Maine to my list of states visited. This visit included the freshest lobster dinner at Lobster Cove, which was directly across from the beach.

In mid-September, Percy drove me to College Park, where he met, and we experienced a genuinely nice brunch with two of my Line Sisters, Sheila, and Tyna. Later in the month, we went to the shooting range for the first time, where I fired my first 9mm pistol. In October, another Soror, Paquita, moved back home after retiring from Houston. Percy and I attended the retirement celebration wearing our masks still. Forever the host, I'm learning; Percy suggested we have a backyard bonfire for my family. Folks wore their Western wear, and everyone had a blast. It was a nice event. His daughters, Krystal, and Kari were invited but did not attend. We crashed the Christian's (their last name) wedding in Cancun over the Veteran's Day weekend at the Moon Palace Resort when my friend Phyllis, a travel planner, had extra slots for the destination wedding folks had backed out of because of the pandemic. When we arrived in Cancun, masked, and socially distanced, all the airport workers took our temperature and checked our immunization records. Cancun was fabulous!!! I'll never forget all the bubbles. Percy snorkeled when we were out on the catamaran.

The Delta National Convention was at the Georgia World Congress Center the following week, and I attended it during my final biennium as Chapter President. When the convention closed, Linda and I checked out of the Omni Hotel and headed home to Forsyth on the Monday before Thanksgiving. I dropped Linda off at her house and headed straight to Macon for my annual mammogram appointment. Two days later, while in the kitchen preparing our holiday dinner, I got test results from Atrium. For the next few weeks, I prepared for the lumpectomy scheduled for February after my SSTAGE conference in January. We took the planned Carnival Cruise to Amber Cove before Christmas; I spent time with the J&J moms; Percy and I attended an event at the Grand Opera House honoring my Soror, Colonel Armour-Lightner. I flew to Silver Spring to spend Christmas with my kids—all of them and their significant others—Nikk, Alexis, Jahi—and Alexis' mom, Lisa—at Deep Creek Ski Resort. A sign outside my window mentioned beware of bears, but I enjoyed playing the spelling games my kids introduced to me. We wore masks and practiced social distancing when in public. On the drive back to Silver Spring, we made a slight detour so I could check West Virginia off my list of states to visit.

My 2022 STAGE January conference was VIRTUAL. Winter GAEL (Georgia Association of Educational Leaders) was a hybrid. Percy came with me. The Women's Coalition was doing its thing, preparing for the 2022 Virtual Education Program, "Healthy Heart, Healthy Brain, Healthy Brain, "for Go RED month and the remaining activities in collaboration with Extension's Healthy Georgia Office. Our Chapter hosted an Elderly Fraud Webinar. Life went on as usual, even with the surgery, and I had Percy by my side all the way.

Ralph and Cynthia Moore joined us, and we had front-row seats for Kenny G at the City Auditorium. Bob and Molly

Harris sat behind us on March 31st. Kenny G was fabulous, and as usual, an audience member received a signature horn he gives at each of his concerts. In April, we spent a few days at Seacrest at Jenn's condominium. It was Seabreeze Jazz Festival week, and Percy's friends were in town. We went by the house they usually rent and arrived just in time for me to experience the best frog legs I've ever had. We cruised to the Bahamas in May. During the Veterans meeting, Percy shared a military Chief's coin with a fellow veteran who was heading to assist in Ukraine soon.

In June, Macon Alumnae Chapter (MAC) and the Macon-Warner Robins Chapter of Kappa Alpha Psi initiated our first CODE Red-Spring Edition, "Talk Derby to Me," with food, a cash bar, and a cigar bar. We dressed for the derby, and I was pleased to have my handsome and debonair Percy at my side. Home improvements continued with the addition of the deck in time for the family to celebrate the 4th of July at our house. Another opportunity for Percy to entertain. We took the RV to Tybee Island in August, and Cami joined us before her school year began. We then had a quick weekend in Chattanooga, where I learned about the Contempt of Court and Ed Johnson's story. We also explored the historic Pleasant Garden Cemetery, which was in desperate need of some tender, loving care.

Percy, the host with the most, prepared for the Moore Family's event during Labor Day weekend at our house. At the end of the month, we flew to London for a 10-day Western Europe cruise, pre-honeymoon, to Hamburg, Germany; Gothenburg, Sweden; Copenhagen, Denmark; Oslo, Norway; Rotterdam, Netherlands; and Brussels, Belgium. It was the whirlwind trip of my lifetime, and we enjoyed an evening with Kira, a friend of Jamaal's, who lives in London and was our personal guide when we were there. Jamaal and Nikk drove over from Kaiserslautern to meet us in Bruges, Belgium, and we enjoyed a few hours together.

Back at home, it was time for the final edits of my dissertation. In July 2022, just as I submitted my final chapter and could begin to see the light at the end of my doctoral journey, my dissertation chair, Dr. Rudo Tsemunhu, informed me she was moving from Valdosta State University to Illinois State University and that she had asked her colleague, Dr. Gwen Ruttencutter, to serve as my chair and to select my new committee. This turned out to be a great blessing. Dr. Nicole Gunn and Dr. Sara Bond served on my committee and led me to the finish line. I defended my dissertation by Zoom on December 2, 2022, my late mother's 80th birthday. I was asked to leave the Zoom for the committee to discuss my defense. After the longest 15-20 minutes of my life, Dr. Ruttencutter texted me to come back to the Zoom room, and I was greeted with the words I'll remember forever, "Congratulations, Dr. Whitehead!" Of course, there were a few edits to make before submitting my dissertation to the graduate school to be bound, but I was allowed to participate in the graduation ceremony on December 9th. Shirley and Dr. Forrest Thompson drove up to Valdosta State University from Tallahassee, Florida, to celebrate with Percy and me.

During the Labor Day weekend family gathering, I asked my kids to plan to be home on New Year's Eve for Percy's and my wedding, which was to happen around midnight. After graduation, we replaced the roof, Percy built a bar on the back porch, my cousin Damon installed a gazebo on the deck, and Vicky orchestrated the plans for decorating the house and the tent for the big event. It was a beautiful evening with close friends and family. January 1, 2023, marked a New Year and Percy's and my New Life together.

Our first trip as a married couple was to Maggie Valley Ski Resort for Percy to spend time enjoying his favorite winter sport. We stopped in Athens for my Winter GAEL (Georgia Association of Educational Leaders) Conference before returning home. We had a cruise planned for April, and Percy invited his daughters, who had not been available, to attend our wedding. I had met Krystal and her young daughter, Brielle. It would be Kari's and my first official meeting at the airport on the way to Fort Lauderdale for a 7-day Western Caribbean cruise to Cozumel, Mexico; Roatan, Honduras; Belize City, Belize; and Costa Maya, Mexico. It was a wonderful time, and Kari and I were able to begin to bond. Dwight and Cheryl Sanders also joined us on this cruise.

In May, Marcella completed her master's degree, and Kari and Cami attended the celebration along with Kari's fiancé Chad and his daughter Avery. Cami graduated from middle school, and I attended this event along with the entire original Freeman Family and served as the official photographer. For Memorial Day weekend, we participated at the USAFE Reunion in Tampa, and Percy connected with others who had played football while serving in the Armed Forces in Europe. On the way home, we spent a few days with my friends Carolyn and Chris Johnson in Lithia, Florida.

Percy was inducted into the Monroe County Sports Hall of Fame in June, and both daughters, both granddaughters and Chad, were in attendance. Cami and Kari stayed the night, but Cami remained with us until after she and my cousin's daughter, Eriona, accompanied me to my annual Summer GAEL

Conference in Jekyll Island in July. We visited the Civil Rights Museum in Montgomery in June with Cami and Eriona. Cami and Kari joined us on a trip to Chattanooga in September. We rented an Airbnb on the banks of the Tennessee River. In downtown Chattanooga, Percy and Cami recreated a picture they had taken at the same spot when Cami was much younger. During the school year, Cami and Eriona participated in the Delta Academy/Delta GEMS program and were with us once a month throughout the year.

My cousin James Henry who lives in the Caribbean, and his wife Yolaida accompanied us on a 14-day cruise to St. Kitts, Guadeloupe, Martinique, Barbados, Grenada, Trinidad and Tobago, St. Lucia, and Aruba before Christmas. The boys and my girlfriend Vicky surprised me with a Smooth Jazz Cruise for my 65th birthday in 2022 that was canceled due to COVID-19. That girl's trip became a couples' trip in January 2024, with Percy and Vicky's husband, Joe, joining us on the 20th Smooth Jazz Cruise to Aruba and Curaçao, where Percy met Peter White, who had co-written the song Percy titled this memoir after. Many of our favorite smooth jazz artists were on board. It was the most FABULOUS!!!

The trip to Italy had been on the books for about a year, thanks to one of Percy's Ledbetter relatives, Julie. We flew into Venice a couple of days before our EF Tours group and were met at the airport by Percy's friends, Paola (his former girlfriend) and Charlie (his former teammate) for a couple of days in Pordenone, Italy, before heading back to Venice to meet Julie and the EF group to tour Venice, Florence, Rome, Sorrento, and Capri. This trip is my favorite adventure with Percy to date. So much history. So much beauty.

Alaska is called the Last Frontier, and we checked it, and Oregon is off my list of 50 states in May. We flew into Portland a couple of days before the cruise, spent the night, and drove to Seattle, where we had a delicious and delightful dinner with my high school classmate and Percy's newly found cousin Kelvin and his wife Jill before cruising to Juneau, Skagway, and Victoria, BC. I fell in love with smoked salmon in Alaska, was fascinated by the Mendenhall Glaciers, and somehow survived the train ride up the Klondike without having a panic attack. No return trip is needed.

We went to Chattanooga in June to meet Marcella's boyfriend Myles' parents before she left to Teach for America in Houston. We could see Percy's newly found aunt, who lived in Chattanooga for the last time. She passed away in July. The girls and Chad came down for a Father's Day brunch, and Cami spent the week with us before Percy and I headed to Amicalola Falls State Park for the annual Ledbetter Family Reunion. Percy met more of my family at our 2024 Moore Family Reunion in Savannah for the Fourth of July weekend.

Our life together thus far has been full of adventure for me. It is the time for us to celebrate and enjoy what life we have left. Life is for the living. We are still getting to know each other even though we have known each other since we were 16 and 17. We spent 40-plus years living separate lives, experiencing separate things. I am amazed and grateful that we have been allowed to come full circle. I am grateful for this time of our lives. Grateful to spend my remaining years with the man I have loved all my life. Looking forward to making many more memories that our blended families will be able to cherish after we are long gone.

PART ONE

BOWDOIN'S RESTAURANT And SERVICE STATION
On The
Jackson Short Route at the Juliette Road

EL Williams General Merchandise Store, Circa 1956

Mary Persons High School Football Offense 1973

Joan K. Ferguson, Basketball Cheerleader, MPHS

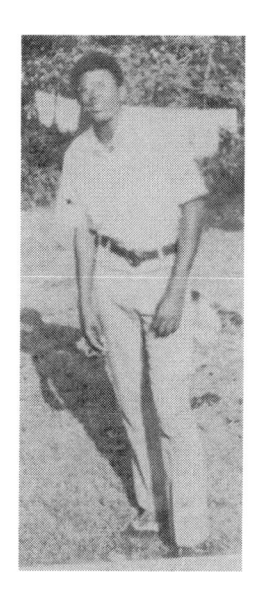

Percy Freeman, Age 16   *Johnny Boozer, Jr, Age 18*

Johnny Boozer, Sr

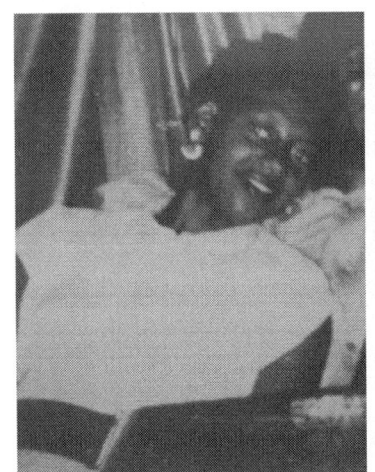

Mother, R. Louise Freeman

Graduation 1986, Saint Leo University
Grandmother, Mary Freeman Boozer

Hattie Sands and Willie Gordon
Gladesville, Georgia

Mary Freeman Boozer, Carrie Freeman Gilmore, Laura Dillard Jackson and Vinnie Dillard

PART TWO

Missile Systems Specialist Technical School, Lowry AFB, CO

Georgia Department of Defense Human Relations Team

East Point Police Patrol Division, Circa, 1983

Joint Base Andrews, departure of POTUS to Martha's Vinyard

TRACTOR TRAILER CHASE on Interstate(I) 285 and I-85 North. The wrecked car was driven by Officer Carlotta Harris.

ANG Mentoring Process Coordinator Training
24 - 26 June 2002

Aviano Red Machine/Eagles Reunion with Linebacker, Fred McPhee

Aviano Eagles versus Camp Darby Rangers. Freeman #26

TANGLED MESS: Construction workers survey damage caused by a crane that tore down a light pole and some power lines as it fell at the intersection of Central Avenue and Martin Luther King Jr. Drive during lunch hour Thursday.

Crane fall causes scare downtown

'I came within 4 feet of my death on the last day of the year'

By Gary Hendricks
Staff Writer

When Percy Freeman saw the 120-foot crane twist and crash into the middle of the intersection of Martin Luther King Jr. Drive and Central Avenue next to his car New Year's Eve, he said he knew "the good Lord was with us."

Neither Freeman, an investigator for the Fulton County district attorney, nor anyone else was hurt when the crane fell while lifting a huge concrete support during lunch hour Thursday at the Underground Atlanta parking lot project.

"I came within 4 feet of my death on the last day of the year," Freeman said. His New Year's Eve plans were to be "at home, I know that."

There were several other close calls, bystanders said. The downed crane crushed the cab of an unoccupied construction truck parked on the street.

A light pole snapped at its base when the crane hit some wires and dragged the pole down. The pole landed directly beside the driver's side of the car in which Freeman was a passenger, with fellow investigator Yvonne Fuller-Jones at the driver's wheel.

"We were turning when the screamed and I looked up to see it twisting and coming down," Freeman said as he stood a few feet from the car.

It took crews working most of the afternoon with sledgehammers and torches to dismantle the crane and clear it, the light pole and traffic signal.

CAB OF TRUCK CRUSHED: A worker points the way during the removal of a 120-foot crane from on top of a construction company truck Thursday; the vehicle was unoccupied.

The accident caused Central Avenue to be closed in the area of the Underground project and the Fulton County Courthouse.

What caused the 140-ton crane to give way was uncertain Thursday, according to H.C. Beck-TWC project manager Andrew Francolini. The crane twisted out over the street before it slammed into the street.

"It's fortunate it's New Year's and there's not very much traffic," said Holmes. Normally, the intersection is heavily traveled during noontime.

Georgia's Diversity Initiatives Capture National NGB Award; 116th Guardsman Wins Top Diversity Individual Award

Georgia's pioneering efforts in creating a highly diversified and motivated workplace won national recognition recently with presentation of the first Excellence in Diversity Award to the state. The honor came at a formal ceremony presided over by Lieutenant General Daniel James III, Chief of the Air Natio Guard who presented the award to Major General David B. Poythress.

Receiving the Individual Excellence in Diversity Award for personal initiatives and accomplishments in field of diversity was Chief Master Sgt Percy L. Freeman, Human Resources Advisor for the 116th Air Control Wing, Robins AFB.

"These national awards culminates a long journey which we began in 1997 to consciously transform the Georgia National Guard into an organization that values, respects and appreciates its people", said Col Jimmy Davis, Director of Human for the Georgia Department of Defense.

Davis chairs the 30-member Human Resources Team organized to guide the diversity process, and to advise the Adjutant General on all issues of diversity and human relations and to provide recommendations for continuing improvements.

Christopher Gardner, director of the National Guard Bureau's Joint Staff, presents the National Excellence in Diversity Award to Maj. Gen. David Poythress, Col. Jimmy Davis and Mr. Ed Chamberlain, Director of GaDOD's Directorate of Workplace Development

"Georgia is the only state that has established a joint team of this kind and should be applauded for its unique accomplishments and care for its people", said Jack Broderick, former director of the NGB-EO.

At the heart of Georgia's diversity program is the state's Diversity Strategic Plan, a benchmark document presents a systematic, carefully analyzed and documented course of action that has been emulated by stat throughout the nation, , according to Guard Bureau evaluators.

Dr. Samuel Betances, an expert in diversity and an advisor to the National Guard Bureau praised Georgi pioneering efforts in promoting diversity throughout the workplace. "Diversity does not happen by accid said Betances, "but through a conscious application of initiatives that brings about awareness, acceptance and action throughout the organization."

"CMsgt Percy Freeman has charted the course for diversity in our unit," said Co Tom Lynn, Commander of the 116th Air Control Wing who accepted the Individual Excellence in Diversity Award on behalf of Freeman. An original member of the GA DOD Human Relations Team, Freeman distinguished himse through innovative diversity initiatives including diversity training, mentoring training, development of the First Sergeant's Council, and the creation of an "I Guard America" that recognizes junior members' military and community involvement and accomplishment.

http://www2.state.ga.us/gadod/news/pages/gadoddiversityaward.html   2/11/2003

PART THREE

Dr. Ben Carson has Juliette roots in the Darden-Carson families

Anderson Redding, Investor, Juliette, GA Roots

TIME PASSAGES

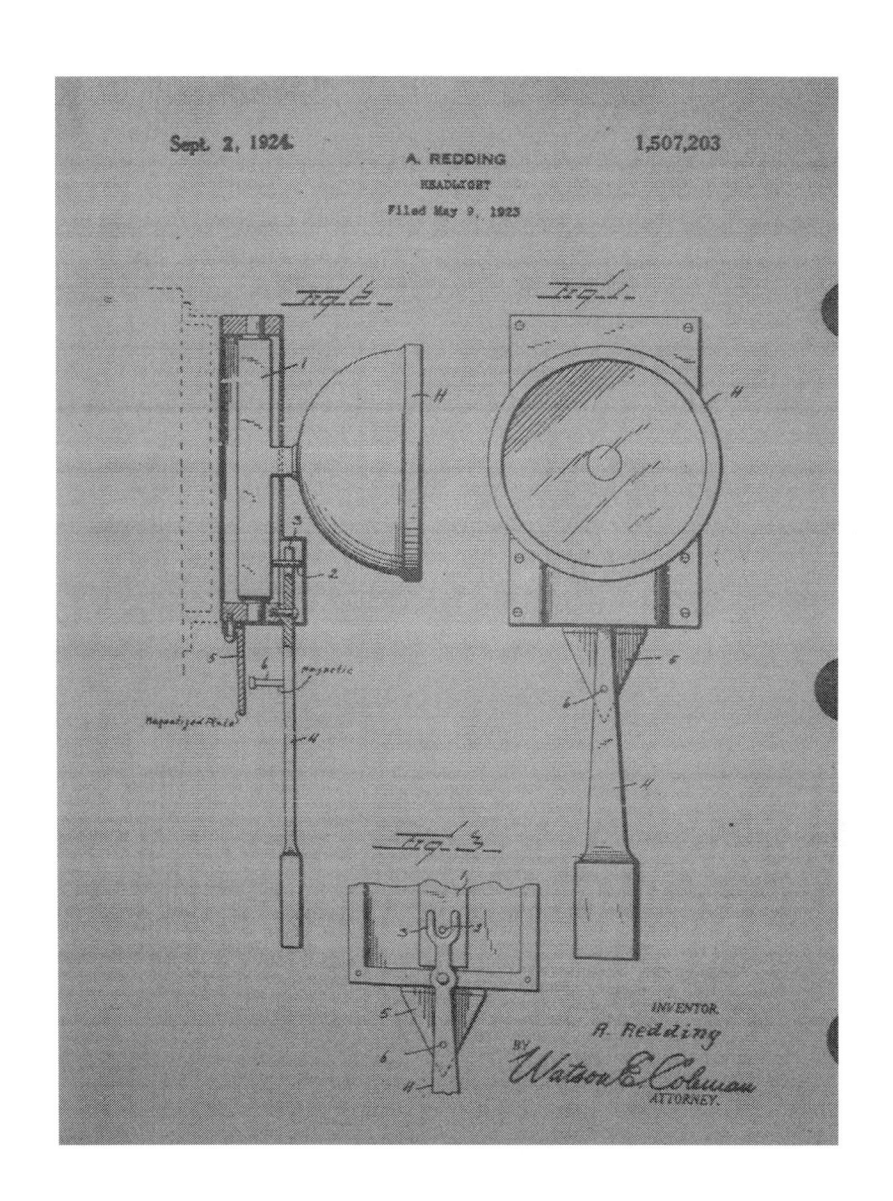

FINDING YOUR ROOTS PPT CREATED IN 2003

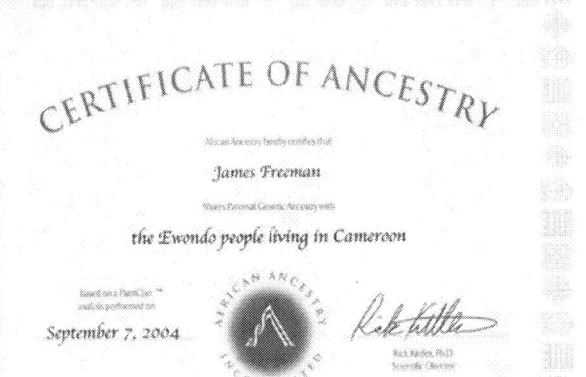

CERTIFICATE OF ANCESTRY

African Ancestry hereby certifies that

James Freeman

Shares Paternal Genetic Ancestry with

the Ewondo people living in Cameroon

Based on a PatriClan™
analysis performed on

September 7, 2004

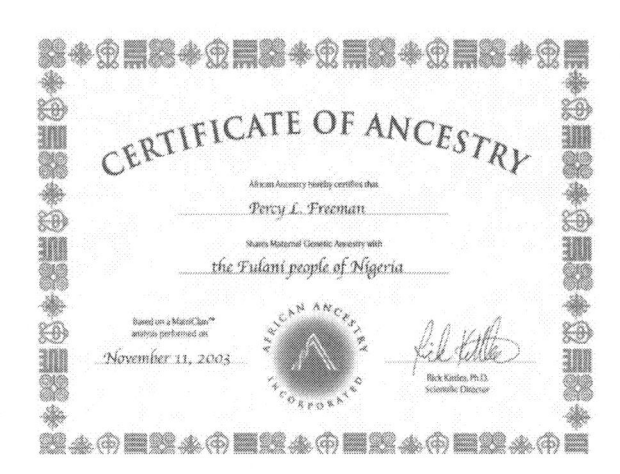

Rick Kittles, Ph.D.
Scientific Director

CERTIFICATE OF ANCESTRY

African Ancestry hereby certifies that

Percy L. Freeman

Shares Maternal Genetic Ancestry with

the Fulani people of Nigeria

Based on a MatriClan™
analysis performed on

November 11, 2003

Rick Kittles, Ph.D.
Scientific Director

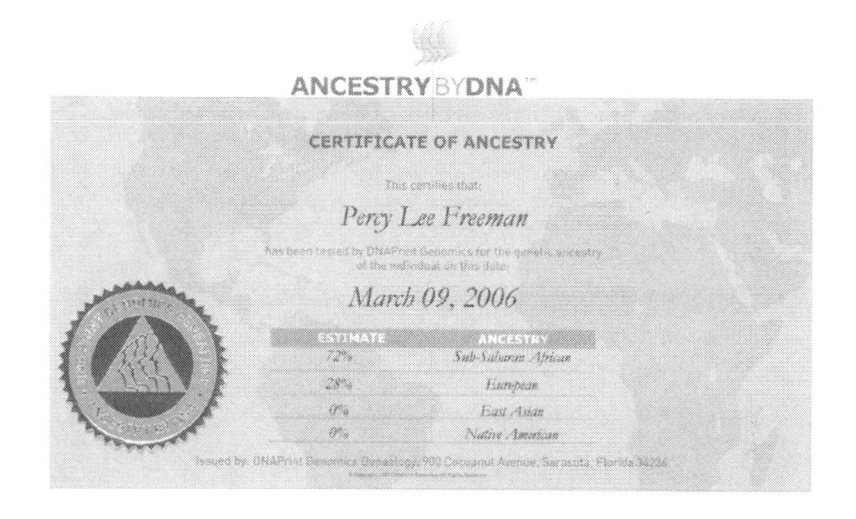

Ledbetter Men

TIME PASSAGES

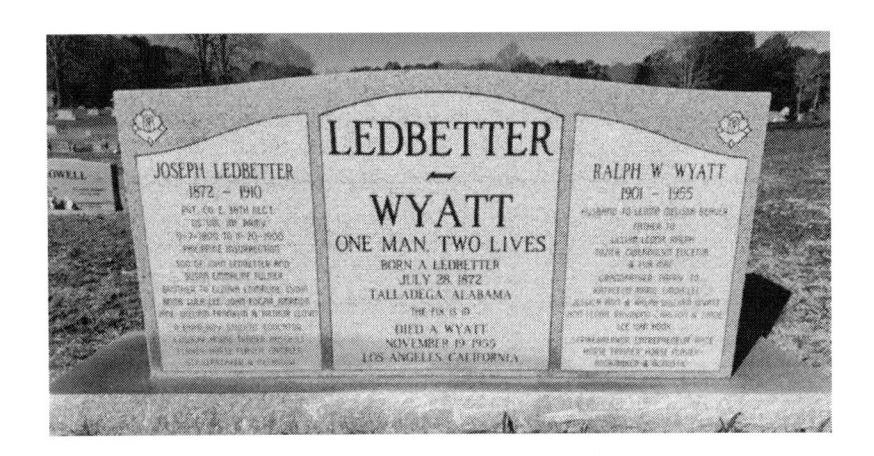

Darden, Rooks and Johnson Roots, Juliette, GA

Ledbetter Reunion

PART FOUR

Dugans Crew

W Mungro and Eric at Warmdaddy's Philadelphia, PA

Green, Boschulte, and Freeman family in Sait Croix, VI

Darrell Holland, Camp Darby Rangers, at Warmdaddy's

Boney James at Seabreeze Jazz Festival

Smooth Jazz Cruise with Rick Braun

Smooth Jazz Cruise with Richard Elliott

Smooth Jazz Cruise with Peter White

FAA Retirees on the Smooth Jazz Cruise

Brian Culbertson on Smooth Jazz Cruise

Norman Brown on the Smooth Jazz Cruise

Nick Collionne at Seabreeze Jazz Festival

TIME PASSAGES

ACKNOWLEDGEMENTS

To Erma Freeman, my daughters, and the Sprauve and Boschulte families, your presence in my life has been a profound blessing. Your unwavering support, love, and the world you've opened my eyes to have profoundly enriched my life. The impact of your connection is immeasurable, and I am forever grateful for it.

To all my former teachers, coaches, and mentors, thank you for not just giving me direction and guidance, but for shaping the very journey I'm on. Your influence has been profound, and I am deeply appreciative of it.

Thank you, Juliette's family and friends. You have been and always will be in my heart.

To Brigadier Generals (retired) Jimmy Davis and Tommy Lynn, Lieutenant General David B. Poythress and Major General Thomas F. Grabowski, MSgt Yelton, SMS Gigli, CMSs Watson Fluellen and Pete Bagley, Col William Bryan, and others, thanks for your support, mentoring, and leadership. You all helped me soar to a higher place.

To all my newly found families, including Darden, Swan, Clark, Heulett, Smith, Jones, Ledbetter, and Walton. Research and technological innovations have genuinely revealed my DNA makeup. Thanks for welcoming me with open arms.

To all my friends, including the group we call "The Dugans Crew," you have made my life richer with the countless memories we've shared at parties, cookouts, football games, and the

Seabreeze Jazz Festival. I am deeply grateful for your participation in my journey.

Thanks to all my friends in metropolitan Atlanta, Georgia, especially those I've known for over forty years: Gregory Scott, George Studgeon, Bobby Owens, and Larry Bowden. Your support has been a constant in my life, and I am deeply grateful for your friendship.

To Peter White, thank you immensely for reading and sharing my story. Meeting you during the 20th Anniversary Smooth Jazz Cruise was a joyous occasion, a memory I will always cherish.

To the Harvey, Whitehead, and Wilder families. Your love has made me feel accepted in your family, and I am deeply grateful.

To my beloved wife, Dr. Joan Whitehead-Freeman, your unwavering patience, understanding, and support for all I do are immeasurable and the cornerstone of my life. I am deeply grateful for your love and companionship.

Thanks to Joan for authoring her version of the impact of our multi-decade separation and separate journeys.

Made in the USA
Columbia, SC
20 January 2025

dc7b63a9-696c-469a-bdfd-8aecdf3b871aR01